Luxury HOME PLANS

Cover Photography By John Ehrenclou

Library of Congress No.: 93-080471

ISBN: 0-938708-54-6

Submit all Canadian plan orders to:
The Garlinghouse Company
20 Cedar Street North
Kitchener, Ontario N2H 2WB

Canadians Order only: 1-800-561-4169
Fax#: 1-519-743-1282
Customer Service#: 1-519-743-4169

DESIGN 91613

Impressive Stucco Design

Massive stucco columns combine with floor-to-ceiling glass walls to create a fascinating home you'll be proud to own. The impressive foyer affords a view of the cozy den with adjoining full bath, the fireplaced living room that flows into the dining room, and the balcony overhead that links three bedrooms and two skylit baths. Step through the center hallway to family areas at the rear of the house, where the island kitchen, glass-walled nook, and fireplaced family room with wetbar share the backyard view. Reach the upper levels on the elegant staircase that arcs over the foyer, or the U-shaped staircase off the kitchen. The enchanting master suite features a private sitting room, fabulous spa bath, and walk-in closet. There's even a bonus room over the garage.

PLAN INFO:

First Flr.	2,268 sq. ft.
Second Flr.	1,484 sq. ft.
Bonus Rm.	300 sq. ft.
Sq. Footage	3,752 sq. ft.
Foundation	Crawl space Crawl/Bsmt
Bedrooms	Three
Baths	Three

SECOND FLOOR

FIRST FLOOR

The photographed home was modified to suit individual tastes.

S0-EHX-237

Exquisite Interior Highlights Brick Masterpiece

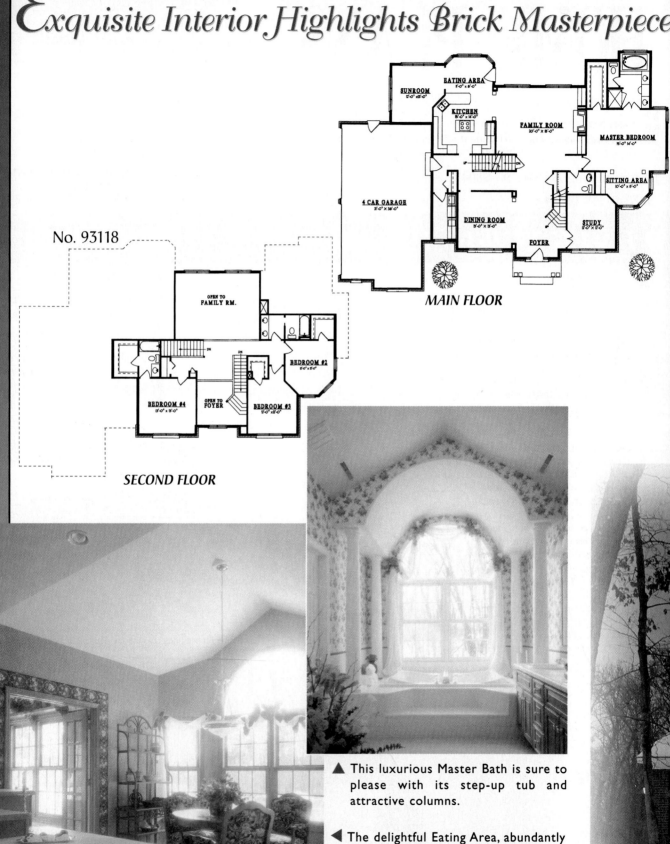

No. 93118

SUNROOM
EATING AREA
KITCHEN
FAMILY ROOM
MASTER BEDROOM
4 CAR GARAGE
SITTING AREA
DINING ROOM
STUDY
FOYER

MAIN FLOOR

OPEN TO FAMILY RM.

BEDROOM #2
BEDROOM #4
OPEN TO FOYER
BEDROOM #3

SECOND FLOOR

▲ This luxurious Master Bath is sure to please with its step-up tub and attractive columns.

◄ The delightful Eating Area, abundantly windowed and conveniently located next to the Kitchen, is a wonderful spot for informal meals or curling up with your favorite book. The formal Dining Room can be saved for special gatherings.

DESIGN 93118

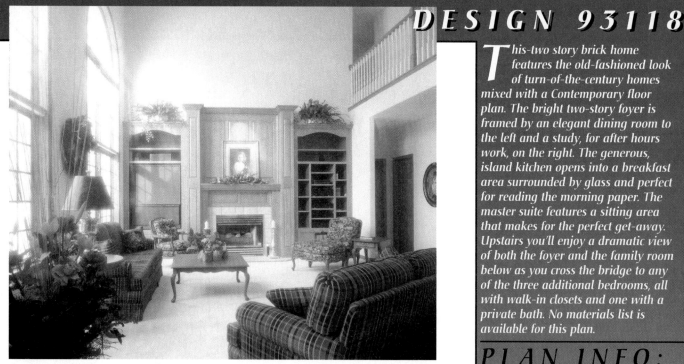

This-two story brick home features the old-fashioned look of turn-of-the-century homes mixed with a Contemporary floor plan. The bright two-story foyer is framed by an elegant dining room to the left and a study, for after hours work, on the right. The generous, island kitchen opens into a breakfast area surrounded by glass and perfect for reading the morning paper. The master suite features a sitting area that makes for the perfect get-away. Upstairs you'll enjoy a dramatic view of both the foyer and the family room below as you cross the bridge to any of the three additional bedrooms, all with walk-in closets and one with a private bath. No materials list is available for this plan.

PLAN INFO:

First Flr.	2,385 sq. ft.
Second Flr.	1,012 sq. ft.
Basement	2,385 sq. ft.
Garage	846 sq. ft.
Sq. Footage	3,397 sq. ft.
Foundation	Basement
Bedrooms	Four
Baths	(3)Full, (1)Half

▲ Enjoy the cozy Family Room with its two-story window wall and wood-burning fireplace guaranteed to warm up the coldest nights. One can gaze down upon this room from the second floor balcony which adjoins the three secondary bedrooms.

This plan is not to be built within a 25 mile radius of Cedar Rapids, IA.

Contemporary Touches Throughout
This European Classic

FIRST FLOOR

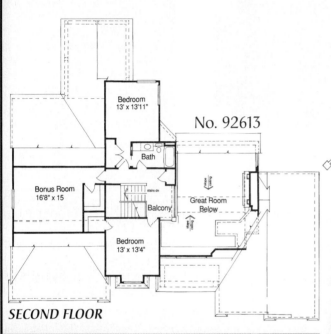

No. 92613

SECOND FLOOR

▲ Step up into the tub of this deluxe Master Suite and watch the sun set after a long day at the office.

◀ Cut out spaces and the unique architectural structural of this Great Room will spark your creative decorating skills and make for a room you'll love for many years.

DESIGN 92613

*M*ultiple gables, a box window and easy maintenance combine to create a dramatic appearance to this two-story European classic home. Excitement abounds in the Great room beginning with a wall of windows across the rear, a sloped ceiling, and an entertainment center nestled in the corner set to one side of the columned fireplace. The kitchen offers an island with a sink that looks directly through French doors onto the patio and into the oversized breakfast room. The dining room ceiling has a raised center section with molding and a furniture alcove is added for extra roominess around the table. The luxury and convenience of the first floor master bedroom suite is highlighted by his-n-her vanities, a shower and whirlpool tub. The second floor provides a private retreat for a guest suite or for a family with teenagers The rear of this home is stepped for privacy and uses windows for an infusion of light. No materials list is available for this plan.

▲ This great Kitchen, with an abundance of cabinets, easily accomodates two or more cooks when meal preparation is to be shared. Serving takes place in either the Formal Dining Room or the Breakfast area, both conveniently located.

PLAN INFO:

First Flr.	2,192 sq. ft.
Second Flr.	654 sq. ft.
Bonus Room	325 sq. ft.
Sq. Footage	2,846 sq. ft.
Foundation	Basement
Bedrooms	Three
Baths	(2)Full, (2)Half

Photography by Donna & Rob Kolb of Exposures Unlimited

Distinctive Two-Story Colonial Design

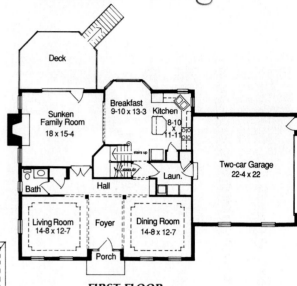

Deck

Sunken Family Room 18 x 15-4

Breakfast 9-10 x 13-3

Kitchen 8-10 x 11-11

stairs up

Two-car Garage 22-4 x 22

Bath

Hall

Laun.

Living Room 14-8 x 12-7

Foyer

Dining Room 14-8 x 12-7

Porch

FIRST FLOOR

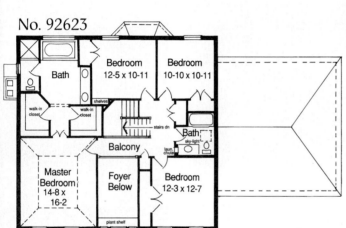

No. 92623

Bath

Bedroom 12-5 x 10-11

Bedroom 10-10 x 10-11

walk-in closet

walk-in closet

shelves

stairs dn

Bath sky-light

laun. chute

Balcony

Master Bedroom 14-8 x 16-2

Foyer Below

Bedroom 12-3 x 12-7

plant shelf

SECOND FLOOR

▲ Formal entertaining is easy in this well-lit Dining Room with a classic decorative ceiling.

◄ Not in the mood for a formal sitdown dinner? Dine in the sunny Breakfast area adjacent to the center island Kitchen and sunken, fireplaced Family Room.

DESIGN 92623

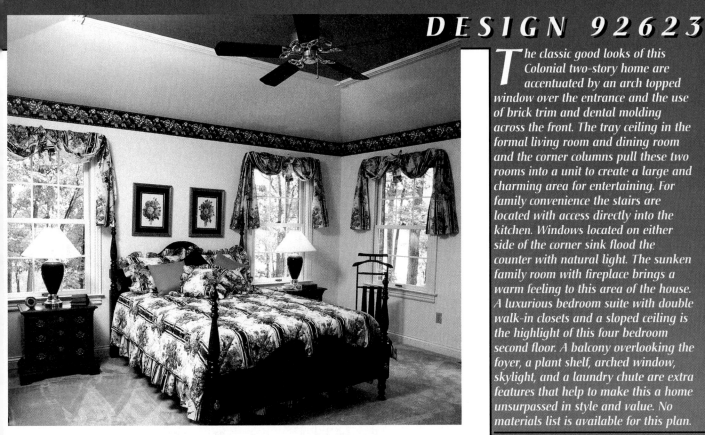

The classic good looks of this Colonial two-story home are accentuated by an arch topped window over the entrance and the use of brick trim and dental molding across the front. The tray ceiling in the formal living room and dining room and the corner columns pull these two rooms into a unit to create a large and charming area for entertaining. For family convenience the stairs are located with access directly into the kitchen. Windows located on either side of the corner sink flood the counter with natural light. The sunken family room with fireplace brings a warm feeling to this area of the house. A luxurious bedroom suite with double walk-in closets and a sloped ceiling is the highlight of this four bedroom second floor. A balcony overlooking the foyer, a plant shelf, arched window, skylight, and a laundry chute are extra features that help to make this a home unsurpassed in style and value. No materials list is available for this plan.

▲ Enjoy the good looks of this Master Bedroom complete with a decorative ceiling and just steps away from two walk-in closets and a luxurious bathroom guaranteed to pamper your every need.

PLAN INFO:

First Flr.	1,365 sq. ft.
Second Flr.	1,288 sq. ft.
Sq. Footage	2,653 sq. ft.
Foundation	Basement
Bedrooms	Four
Baths	(2)Full, (1)Half

Photography by Donna & Rob Kolb of Exposures Unlimited

Intricate Angles & Abundant Windows Help Set This Design Apart

SECOND FLOOR

No. 10666

FIRST FLOOR

▲ His-n-her separate bath areas are guaranteed to ease the morning rush while two-and-a-half other baths take care of the rest of the household.

Look down upon the two-story Living Room, containing a fireplace and a window wall, from the second floor bridge that leads to a small library alcove with two skylights. ▶

DESIGN 10666

*G*racious living is the rule in this brick masterpiece designed with an eye toward elegant entertaining. Window walls and French doors link the in-ground pool and surrounding brick patio with interior living spaces. The wetbar with wine storage provides a convenient space for a large buffet in the family room. Built-in bookcases in the living room, family room, and skylit second-floor library can house even the largest collection. Separated from living areas by halls or a bridge, every bedroom is a quiet retreat, with its own dressing room and adjoining bath.

PLAN INFO:

First Flr.	3,625 sq. ft.
Second Flr.	937 sq. ft.
Garage	636 sq. ft.
Sq. Footage	4,562 sq. ft.
Foundation	Basement
Bedrooms	Five
Baths	(4)Full, (1)Half

▲ Upon entering the foyer of this lovely brick home, with enticing angles and intricate detailing, you will notice all the elegant touches and amenities throughout the interior layout that make for luxurious living.

Georgian Drama At Its Best In This Sprawling Beauty

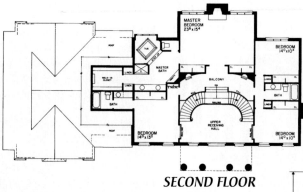

SECOND FLOOR

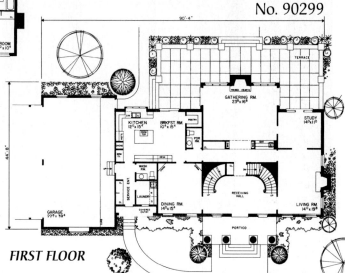

No. 90299

FIRST FLOOR

▲ Windows grace both sides of the fireplace in the Formal Living Room, and make for an eye-catching layout.

Turn your Basement into a deluxe ▶ Gameroom/Entertainment area like these Garlinghouse homeowners did. This home has everything and much, much more!

Imagine living in the graceful elegance of this sprawling, Georgian beauty. From the impressive columned facade to the two-story drama of the receiving hall, this home has style! Flanked by the formal living and dining rooms, the receiving hall leads straight back to a sun-filled, fireplaced gathering room surrounded by an outdoor terrace. The open kitchen and breakfast room combination features a cooktop island and extra-large storage pantry. Walk up the curving staircases of the receiving hall to four spacious bedrooms, each adjoining a bath. The master suite enjoys the toasty warmth of a fireplace, a garden tub, a built-in vanity and double sinks.

PLAN INFO:

First Flr.	2,529 sq. ft.
Second Flr.	1,872 sq. ft.
Sq. Footage	4,401 sq. ft.
Foundation	Basement
Bedrooms	Four
Baths	(3)Full, (2)Half

▲ A two-story Receiving Hall with a double curved staircase will definitely make a lasting first impression. To the right is the Formal Living Room with a fireplace, and to the left is the formal Dining Room that is just steps away from the Kitchen.

Photography by John Ehrenclou

DESIGN 10492

Appealing Rear & Front Elevations

Photography by John Ehrenclou

With a special television room plus a family room and an upstairs sitting room, there's plenty of opportunity for everyone in the family to enjoy personal activities and pursuits. The well-designed kitchen adjoins the formal dining room and also has its own dining nook with lots of windows for sunny family breakfasts and lunches. Both the living room and family room open onto patios for indoor/outdoor entertaining. The second floor sitting room, complete with a fireplace and warm hearth, adjoins the spacious master suite with its six-piece bath complete with Roman tub and oversized, walk-in closet. Two smaller bedrooms flank a walk-through bath to complete the second floor of this roomy, family home.

▲ An elegant addition to any neighborhood...this luxurious two-story has it all!!

The photographed home was modified to suit individual tastes.

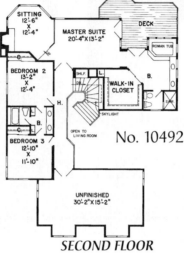

No. 10492

SECOND FLOOR

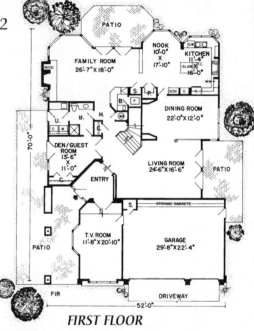

FIRST FLOOR

PLAN INFO:

First Flr.	2,409 sq. ft.
Second Flr.	2,032 sq. ft.
Garage	690 sq. ft.
Sq. Footage	4,441 sq. ft.
Foundation	Slab
Bedrooms	Three (Opt. Fourth)
Baths	Three

Energy Efficient Tudor Design

▲ A step-up whirlpool tub is sure to please, but that's only the beginning of the amenities that you'll find in this Tudor-style gem.

No. 20071

Take advantage of Southern exposure and save on energy costs in this beautiful family Tudor. Heat is stored in the floor of the sun room, adjoining the living and breakfast rooms. When the sun goes down, close the French doors and light a fire in the massive fireplace. State-of-the-art energy saving is not the only modern convenience in this house. You'll love the balcony overlooking the soaring two-story foyer and living room. In addition to providing great views, the balcony links the upstairs bedrooms. You're sure to enjoy the island kitchen, centrally located between formal and informal dining rooms. And, you'll never want to leave the luxurious master suite, with its double vanities and step-up whirlpool.

SECOND FLOOR

FIRST FLOOR

PLAN INFO:

First Flr.	2,186 sq. ft.
Second Flr.	983 sq. ft.
Basement	2,186 sq. ft.
Garage	704 sq. ft.
Sq. Footage	3,169 sq. ft.
Foundation	Basement
Bedrooms	Four
Baths	(3)Full, (1)Half

The photographed home was modified to suit individual tastes.

An EXCLUSIVE DESIGN *By Karl Kreeger*

Exciting Contemporary On One Level

*T*his classic stucco has a high hip roof and an angled three-car garage all combining to give this house elegance. Bedrooms are offered at separate locations with a den located next to the master suite. The foyer adds columns and starts the elegant high ceiling trend throughout the house. Kitchen, nook and curved family room allow for spacious entertaining and views.

▲ This contemporary Kitchen, with plenty of white cabinets, natural wood floors and ample counter space is one of our favorites!

PLAN INFO:

First Flr.	2,598 sq. ft.
Garage	828 sq. ft.
Sq. Footage	2,598 sq. ft.
Foundation	Crawl space
Bedrooms	Three
Baths	(2)Full, (1)Half

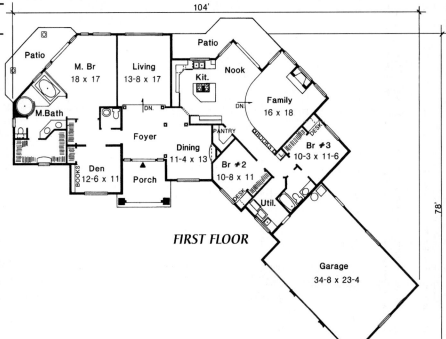

FIRST FLOOR

Photography by James Reuter Jr.

Windows Illuminate This Brick Beauty

SECOND FLOOR

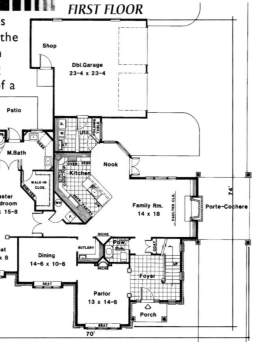

Bedroom 12-8 x 11-8

Bedroom 12-8 x 10-6

OPEN TO BELOW

Library 12-6 x 14

BALCONY

Bath

OPEN TO BELOW

*A*rched, multi-paned windows and an elegant brick design that looks much larger than its square footage indicates, are just a few of the features of this plan. The impressive foyer with columns features a sky-bridge above the family room. The parlor and dining rooms are designed to provide an elegant entertaining area. The island kitchen is enhanced by the convenience to both the breakfast nook and the formal dining room. The master suite with its privacy on the first floor has a first class bath and a retreat. Take notice of the library, which features a wood mantel fireplace and window seats. Upstairs, two large bedrooms have window seats and share another bath.

▲ What an entrance! This archway, that leads to the formal parlor and then onto the formal dining room, is to the right of a grand two-story foyer.

FIRST FLOOR

Shop

Dbl.Garage 23-4 x 23-4

Patio

Util.

M.Bath

Nook

WALK-IN CLOS.

Kitchen

Family Rm. 14 x 18

Porte-Cochere

Master Bedroom 15 x 15-8

NICHE

Pow. Rm.

Retreat 10-8 x 8

Dining 14-6 x 10-6

BUTLERY

COAT

Foyer

UP

Parlor 13 x 14-6

Porch

74'

70'

PLAN INFO:

First Flr.	2,024 sq. ft.
Second Flr.	874 sq. ft.
Garage	648 sq. ft.
Sq. Footage	2,898 sq. ft.
Foundation	Crawl space
Bedrooms	Three
Baths	(2)Full, (1)Half

Photography by James Reuter Jr.

DESIGN 92116

Brick & Stucco Facade Accentuates This Breathtaking Design

▲ A roaring fire, a step-down Living Room and a glorious architectural structure are just a few reasons why you'll love this home today and tomorrow.

Brick and stucco make for an exciting combination in this two-story design. The three-car garage entry to the rear allows for a full exterior architectural display. The grand foyer, with a lovely curved staircase, adjoins the formal step-down living and dining room. The kitchen presents a uniquely different geometric concept by allowing a full two-sided view. An additional rear staircase adds ease in reaching the second floor bedrooms, game room and master suite with it's own luxurious bath and walk-in closet.

PLAN INFO:

First Flr.	2,108 sq. ft.
Second Flr.	1,884 sq. ft.
Sq. Footage	3,992 sq. ft.
Foundation	Crawl space
Bedrooms	Three
Baths	(3)Full, (1)Half

SECOND FLOOR

Br #3 10 x 12-8

Master Bedroom

Game Rm. 22-6 x 15-6

Br #2 13-6 x 11-6

M.Bath

OPEN TO BELOW

DN.

FIRST FLOOR

No. 92116

85'-6"

59'-2"

Garage 34-6 x 24

Util. 9 x 11

PANTRY

Kitchen

Family 16-8 x 17-4

Dining 15-6 x 13

Foyer

Den 11-8 x 13-4

Porch

Living 14 x 17-4

Photography by James Reuter Jr.

*U*pdated Saltbox Design

- Flower boxes and an old-fashioned front porch add friendly charm to this updated Saltbox

- Formal Dining Room and Parlor located on each side of the Foyer offer a classic arrangement with a Contemporary approach

- Spacious family living guaranteed by the Kitchen, Breakfast area, and

Family Room joined together in an expansive open space accented by a window wall overlooking the rear deck

- Guest Suite features a full Bath with handicapped access

- Private Deck, a large walk-in closet and a luxurious Bath highlight the Master Bedroom Suite

PLAN INFO:

First Flr.	2,285 sq. ft.
Second Flr.	660 sq. ft.
Garage	565 sq. ft.
Sq. Footage	2,945 sq. ft.
Foundation	Basement
Bedrooms	Five
Baths	Three

No. 20404

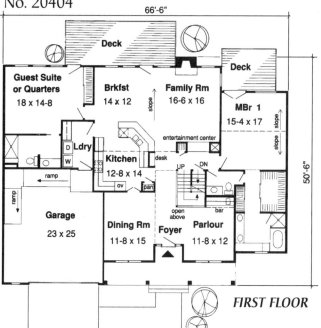

FIRST FLOOR

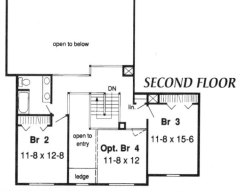

SECOND FLOOR

This Beauty Has A Uniquely Shaped Kitchen

PLAN INFO:

First Flr.	2,800 sq. ft.
Second Flr.	1,113 sq. ft.
Basement	2,800 sq. ft.
Garage	598 sq. ft.
Sq. Footage	3,913 sq. ft.
Foundation	Basement
Bedrooms	Five
Baths	4(Full), 1(Half)

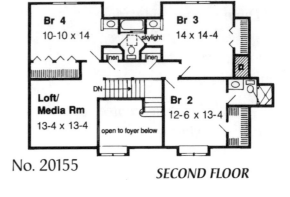

No. 20155

SECOND FLOOR

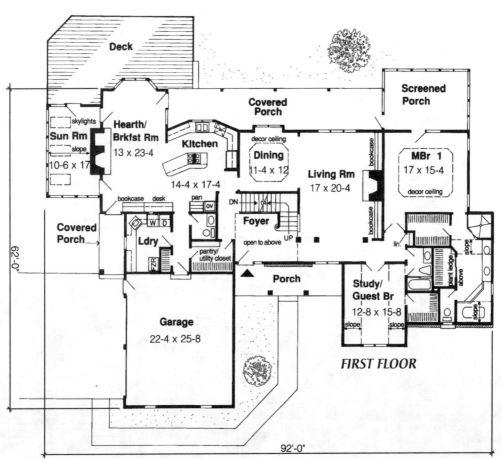

FIRST FLOOR

An
EXCLUSIVE DESIGN
By Karl Kreeger

- *Sprawling family home has an attractive fieldstone clapboard facade*

- *The open Foyer has an L-shaped Living and Dining Room arrangement wrapping around it*

- *An elegant Bath, walk-in closet and private access to a Screened Porch highlight the Master Suite*

- *Three additional bedrooms with private access to a full Bath are on the second floor*

- *Separating the informal Hearth/Breakfast Room and the skylit Sun Room is a fireplace with wood storage*

- *A gourmet Kitchen with a built-in pantry, planning desk and bookshelves and a fantastic cook top island and eating bar will thrill the cook in your family*

Accent On Curved Staircase
& Staggered Rooflines

No. 10537

PLAN INFO:

First Flr.	3,282 sq. ft.
Second Flr.	956 sq. ft.
Basement	3,235 sq. ft.
Garage	936 sq. ft.
Sq. Footage	4,238 sq. ft.
Foundation	Basement
Bedrooms	Four
Baths	4(Full), 1(Half)

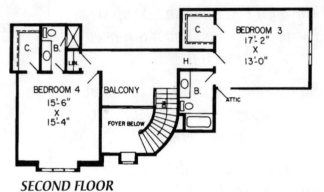

BEDROOM 3
17'-2" X 13'-0"

BEDROOM 4
15'-6" X 15'-4"

BALCONY

FOYER BELOW

ATTIC

SECOND FLOOR

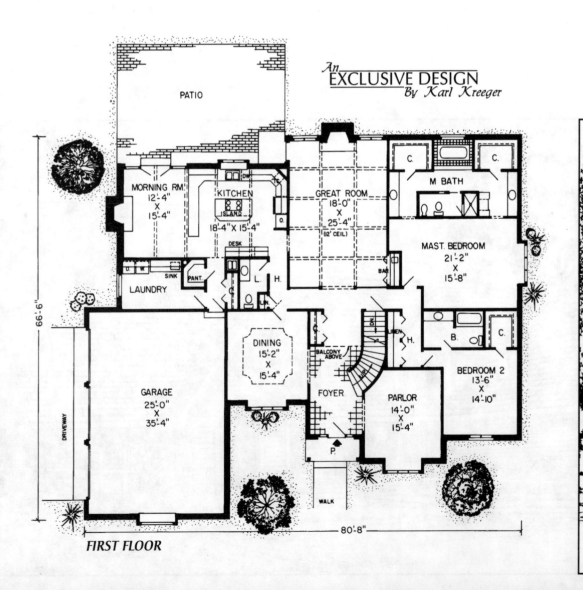

An **EXCLUSIVE DESIGN**
By Karl Kreeger

PATIO

MORNING RM.
12'-4" X 15'-4"

KITCHEN
ISLAND
18'-4" X 15'-4"

GREAT ROOM
18'-0" X 25'-4"
(12' CEIL)

M BATH

MAST. BEDROOM
21'-2" X 15'-8"

DESK

LAUNDRY

SINK
PANT.

DINING
15'-2" X 15'-4"

BALCONY ABOVE

GARAGE
25'-0" X 35'-4"

DRIVEWAY

FOYER

PARLOR
14'-0" X 15'-4"

BEDROOM 2
13'-6" X 14'-10"

WALK

66'-6"

80'-8"

FIRST FLOOR

- Overlook the impressive tiled Foyer with gracefully curving staircase from the Balcony on the second floor

- Enter the spacious Great Room featuring wood ceiling beams, bar, and welcoming fireplace

- Generous Laundry Room leads to 3-car Garage

- Expansive Kitchen includes lots of counter space, cook center island, pantry, and desk

- Formal Dining Room with interesting ceiling lies just steps away from Kitchen

- Large fireplace and entry onto patio for year round enjoyment complement unique Morning Room

- Luxurious Master Bedroom boasts his-n-her basins and roomy walk-in closets

- Three additional bedrooms each have walk-in closets and personal Baths

Spacious Stucco Has Everything You Need & More

PLAN INFO:

First Flr.	1,452 sq. ft.
Second Flr.	1,431 sq. ft.
Bonus Rm.	316 sq. ft.
Garage	3-car
Sq. Footage	2,883 sq. ft.
Foundation	Crawl space
Bedrooms	Five
Baths	3(Full), 1(Half)

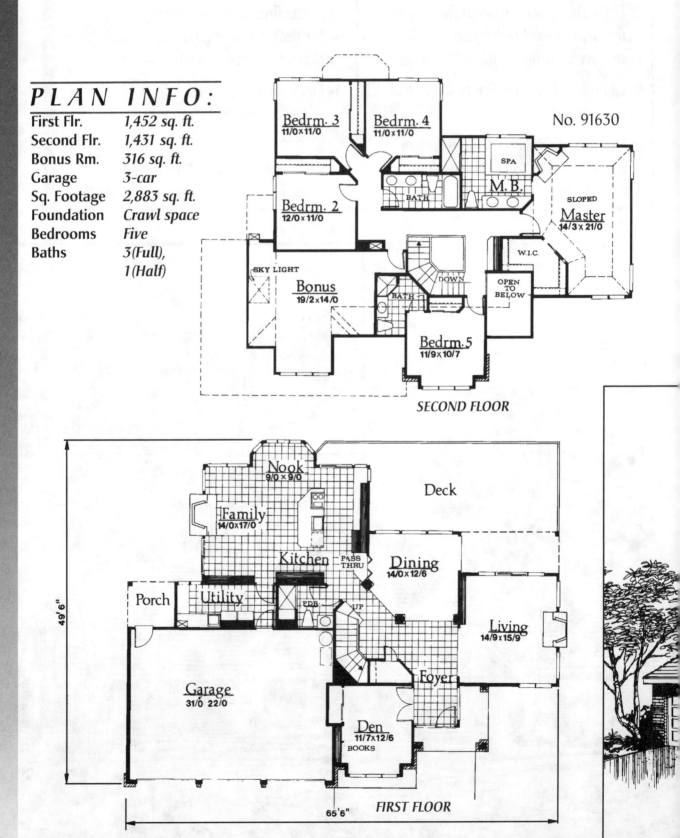

No. 91630

SECOND FLOOR

FIRST FLOOR

- Open Foyer gives sunny, airy atmosphere and leads straight through to rear of home

- Fireplaced Living Room off Foyer is studded with windows on three sides and has sliders to the deck

- Four other bedrooms are all good-sized with extra closet space and are effectively located near two equally beautiful baths

- Powder room with shower makes the book-lined Den ideal guest room

- Plush Master Bedroom shows sloped ceilings, large walk-in closet and private Bath

- Magnificent Family Room has efficiency of a fireplace, added light from desirable sliding glass doors and plenty of windows, and adds outdoor feeling to wide-open Nook and Kitchen

Skylit Spa Room Catches The Eye

PLAN INFO:

First Flr.	3,453 sq. ft.
Garage	637 sq. ft.
Sq. Footage	3,453 sq. ft.
Foundation	Crawl space
Bedrooms	Three
Baths	3(Full), 1(Half)

WIDTH 99'-3"
DEPTH 80'-0"

No. 91732

FIREPLACE

FAMILY ROOM
17⁰ x 15⁶

DECK

DECK

SPA EQUIP.

SPA ROOM

NOOK
8⁰ x 11⁴

DW

SPA

SKYLIGHTS

KITCHEN
17⁰ x 11⁴

VEG. SINK

COOKTOP

PANTRY

MIX. CNTR.

OVEN & MW

BEDROOM 2
11¹⁰ x 11⁴

WALK-IN CLOSET

BEDROOM 3
14⁸ x 11⁴

WALK-IN CLOSET

WALK-IN CLOSET

DN

MASTER SUITE
17⁰ x 22⁶

ENTRY

BRM.

FAU

WH

FIREPLACE

LIVING ROOM
18⁶ x 11¹⁰

STORAGE

DINING ROOM
14⁶ x 9¹⁰

LINEN

DRYR/WSR

UTILITY

SINK

BENCH

DN

GUEST SUITE
15⁰ x 13⁰

WALK-IN CLOSET

SKYLIGHT

LINEN

DEN / OFFICE
13⁶ x 9¹⁰

PORCH

DN

UP

TUB

SHOWER

TRASH

FIRST FLOOR

GARAGE
23⁴ x 23⁸

- *Stepping into the Entry, the glassed-in Spa Room grabs attention of all who enter*

- *Master Suite has plenty of room for sleeping area and sitting and/or exercise area*

- *Unique clover-leaf spa nestled in glass block-lined corner nook of Master Suite*

- *Other features of the Master suite include huge walk-in closet and double vanities*

- *Room serving as Office, Den, hobby room, or artist's studio conveniently situated close to Master Suite and front entry*

- *Country Kitchen with island and pantry fills one corner of large Family Room*

- *Spa Room reached from Bathroom, Nook, or through two sets of triple sliding glass doors from deck*

- *Three additional bedrooms have walk-in closets and adjoining Baths*

Master Suite Crowns Outstanding Plan

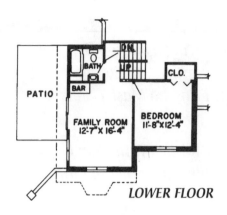

LOWER FLOOR

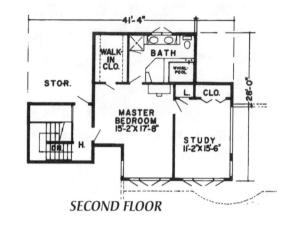

SECOND FLOOR

PLAN INFO:

First Flr.	*1,742 sq. ft.*
Second Flr.	*809 sq. ft.*
Lower Flr.	*443 sq. ft.*
Basement	*1,270 sq. ft.*
Garage	*558 sq. ft.*
Sq. Footage	*2,994 sq. ft.*
Foundation	*Basement*
Bedrooms	*Four*
Baths	*3(Full), 1(Half)*

No. 10334

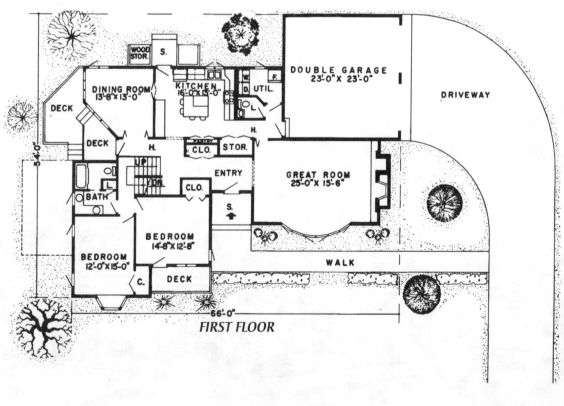

FIRST FLOOR

- ■ *Luxurious Master Suite includes private Study and walk-in closet*

- ■ *Master Bath sports double vanities, shower and whirlpool for total relaxation in privacy*

- ■ *Two additional bedrooms situated away from living areas provide ample space for children*

- ■ *Fourth Bedroom adjoins the Family Room on lower level*

- ■ *Spacious Kitchen boasts pantry and snack island*

- ■ *Family Room joins backyard patio via sliding glass doors*

- ■ *25-foot oak floors and bow window in Great Room portray magnificent appreciation of finer things in life*

- ■ *Slate floors add elegance to formal Dining area*

- ■ *Plan features numerous decks for added enjoyment of outdoor living*

- ■ *Extra storage space provided on second floor*

$\mathscr{E}$xpandable $\mathscr{F}$rench $\mathscr{P}$rovincial

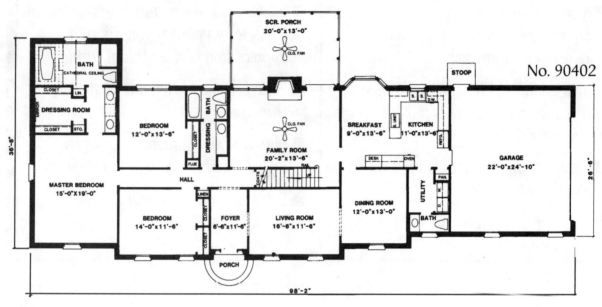

No. 90402

FIRST FLOOR

PLAN INFO:

First Flr.	*2,400 sq. ft.*
Second Flr.	*751 sq. ft.*
Sq. Footage	*3,151 sq. ft.*
Foundation	Specify *Bsmt, Slab, or Crawl space**
Bedrooms	*Five*
Baths	*3(Full), 1(Half)*

*Please specify when ordering

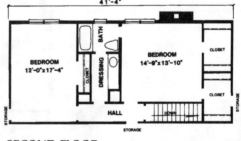

SECOND FLOOR

- *Quiet elegance is the first impression of this five bedroom design*

- *Formal Living Room and Dining Room flow into each other for ease in entertaining*

- *Casual living offered by the Family Room and adjacent screened Porch includes ceiling fans and a hearth fireplace*

- *U-shaped Kitchen provides an efficient layout with a peninsula counter and a sunny Breakfast bay*

- *Deluxe Master Suite features a Master Bath with vaulted ceiling and sky-lights, a garden tub, shower and linen closet, and a separate Dressing Room with a double vanity and a large walk-in closet*

- *Two additional bedrooms with ample closet space share a second segmented Bath*

- *Two more bedrooms, on the second floor, share a full hall Bath*

*T*hree *F*ireplaces *A*dd *E*legant *W*armth

No. 10779

PLAN INFO:

First Flr.	2,962 sq. ft.
Second Flr.	1,883 sq. ft.
Basement	2,962 sq. ft.
Garage	890 sq. ft.
Sq. Footage	4,845 sq. ft.
Foundation	Basement
Bedrooms	Four
Baths	3(Full), 1(Half)

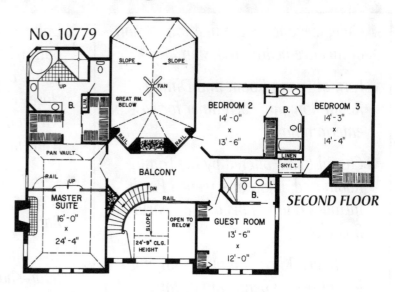

SECOND FLOOR

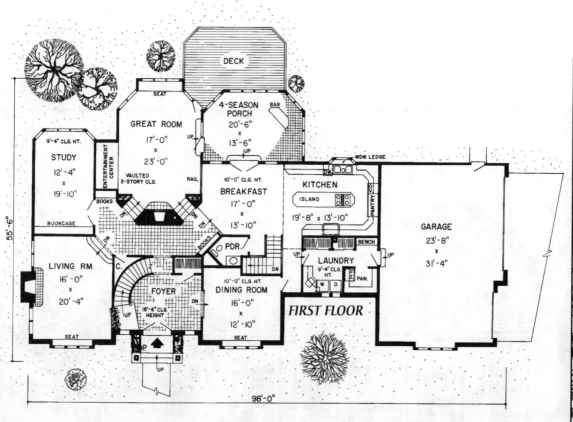

FIRST FLOOR

- *Enjoy sweeping view of the vaulted Great Room and two-story Foyer from the second floor Balcony*

- *Bi-level Master Suite features unique ceiling lines, personal fireplace, and two walk-in closets*

- *Relax in billions of bubbles designed to tantalize the senses in your raised tub in the Master Bath*

- *Each remaining Bedroom off the skylit hall adjoins a full Bath and possesses plenty of individual closet space*

- *Country Kitchen features cooktop island and greenhouse window ledge ideal for growing herbs*

- *Four-season Porch adjoins Breakfast Room and Great Room, and exits onto deck in backyard*

- *Impressive Great Room features built-in seats, fireplace, entertainment center, and vaulted two-story ceiling*

- *Retreat to the book-lined Study next to the Living Room for a quiet spot to get away from it all*

Mixture Of Stucco & Stone
Create An Elegant Facade

No. 92505

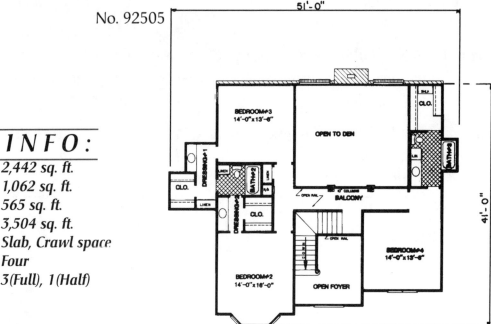

SECOND FLOOR

PLAN INFO:

First Flr.	2,442 sq. ft.
Second Flr.	1,062 sq. ft.
Garage	565 sq. ft.
Sq. Footage	3,504 sq. ft.
Foundation	Slab, Crawl space
Bedrooms	Four
Baths	3(Full), 1(Half)

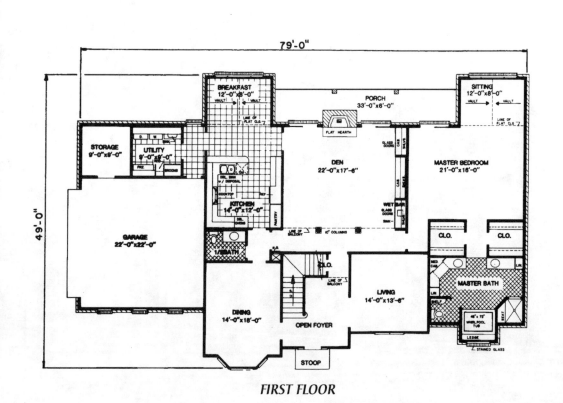

FIRST FLOOR

■ *Arched top windows, copper roof over the two-story bay, and a detailed mixture of stucco and stone create a unique and elegant home*

■ *Grand Foyer shows off a wide and open staircase, two-story ceiling and a magnificent balcony*

■ *Large two-story columns frame the entrance to the magnificent Den featuring built-in cabinets and shelves, a wetbar and a full two-story fireplace framed by glass door leading to the outdoor porch*

■ *A vaulted ceiling adds to the spacious feel of the gourmet Kitchen that includes a breakfast bar and built-in pantry*

■ *Cozy, private Sitting Area with a vaulted ceiling provides quite moments in the Master Suite*

■ *Master Bath features his-n-her walk-in closets, separate vanities and linen closets, and a whirlpool garden tub*

■ *Three large additional bedrooms, each with walk-in closets and adjacent baths, are located on the second floor*

Comfortable Living Is Easy With This Design

PLAN INFO:

First Flr.	2,267 sq. ft.
Second Flr.	705 sq. ft.
Basement	2,267 sq. ft.
Garage	793 sq. ft.
Sq. Footage	2,972 sq. ft.
Foundation	Basement
Bedrooms	Three
Baths	Three

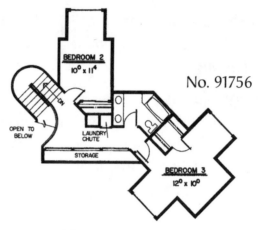

No. 91756

SECOND FLOOR

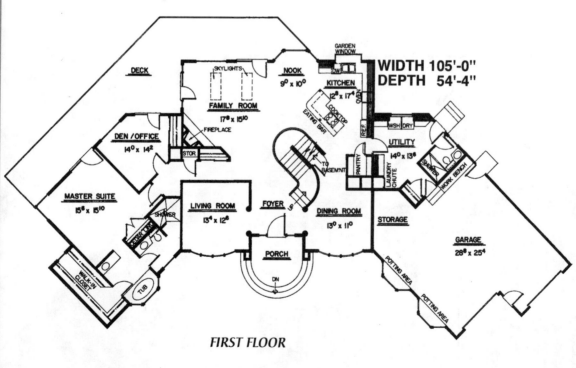

WIDTH 105'-0"
DEPTH 54'-4"

FIRST FLOOR

- *Exterior Tudor and Queen Anne styling hides a comfortable, Contemporary interior*

- *Stately, formal two-story Foyer leads smoothly into all living areas*

- *Formal Dining Room and Living Room are traditionally placed at the front of the home*

- *Gourmet Kitchen with garden window includes double sinks, a L-shaped cook top island/eating bar and a walk-in pantry*

- *Expansive Family Room is equipped with a corner fireplace and two skylights naturally illuminating the room*

- *First floor Master Suite, adjacent to Den/Office, has a enormous walk-in closet, an oversized tub tucked into its own nook with a bay window, and private access to the outdoor deck*

- *Two additional bedrooms on the second floor share a full hall Bath and enjoy the added convenience of a laundry chute*

*B*edrooms Secluded On The Second Level

PLAN INFO:

First Flr.	1,926 sq. ft.
Second Flr.	1,606 sq. ft.
Basement	1,926 sq. ft.
Garage	840 sq. ft.
Sq. Footage	3,532 sq. ft.
Foundation	Basement
Bedrooms	Four
Baths	3(Full), 1(Half)

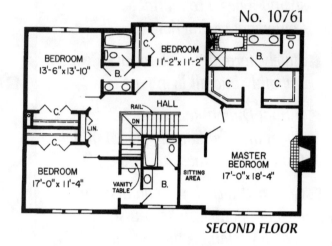

No. 10761

SECOND FLOOR

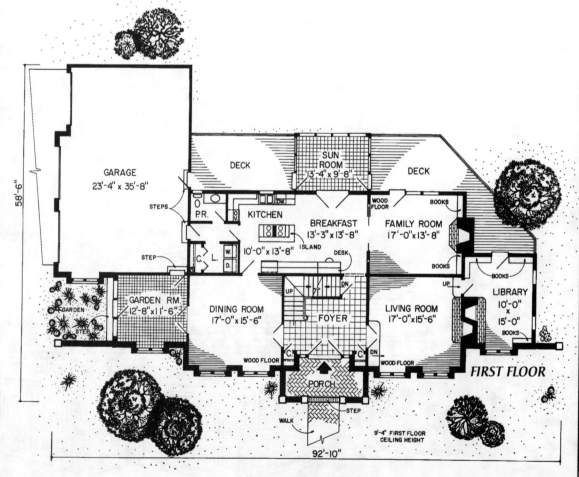

FIRST FLOOR

- Double doors open to a huge Foyer from the fireplaced, sunken Living Room

- Cozy elegance of a book-lined Library allows needed solitude for concentration

- Convenient Kitchen with rangetop island adjacent to formal Dining Room opens to the sunny Breakfast Room

- Informal areas overlooking your back-yard unite into one wide-open space

- Four bedrooms share private second floor location

- Enter from the 3-car Garage into a conveniently situated Laundry room and half-Bath

- Fireplaced Master Bedroom features his-n-her walk-in closets and double vanities

- All bedrooms include ample closet space for individual storage

- Scintillating odors filtrate house from plants and flowers in Garden Room

*A*rched Entrances In *F*oyer
*A*re Simply Captivating

No. 93039

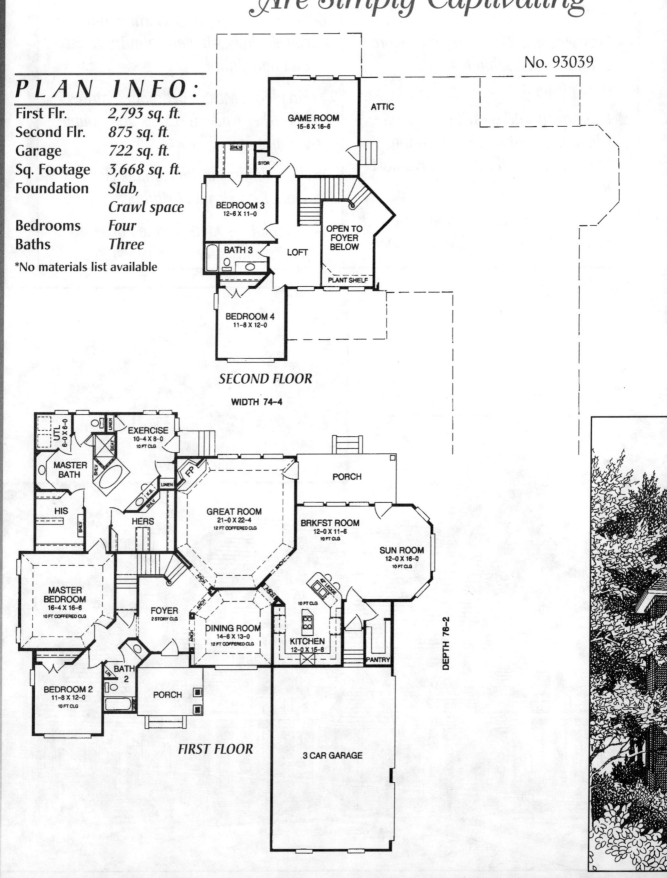

PLAN INFO:

First Flr.	2,793 sq. ft.
Second Flr.	875 sq. ft.
Garage	722 sq. ft.
Sq. Footage	3,668 sq. ft.
Foundation	Slab, Crawl space
Bedrooms	Four
Baths	Three

*No materials list available

ATTIC

GAME ROOM
15-6 X 16-6

SHLV

STOR

BEDROOM 3
12-6 X 11-0

OPEN TO FOYER BELOW

BATH 3

LOFT

PLANT SHELF

BEDROOM 4
11-8 X 12-0

SECOND FLOOR

WIDTH 74-4

UTL
6-0 X 6-0

LINEN

EXERCISE
10-4 X 8-0
10 FT CLG

MASTER BATH

SHLV

SEAT

SEAT

K.T.

LINEN

FP

PORCH

HIS

SHLV

HERS

GREAT ROOM
21-0 X 22-4
12 FT COFFERED CLG

BRKFST ROOM
12-0 X 11-6
10 FT CLG

SUN ROOM
12-0 X 16-0
10 FT CLG

ARCH

ARCH

MASTER BEDROOM
16-4 X 16-6
10 FT COFFERED CLG

FOYER
2 STORY CLG

ARCH

DINING ROOM
14-6 X 13-0
12 FT COFFERED CLG

10 FT CLG

LEDGE

KITCHEN
12-0 X 15-8

PANTRY

DEPTH 76-2

BATH 2

BEDROOM 2
11-8 X 12-0
10 FT CLG

PORCH

FIRST FLOOR

3 CAR GARAGE

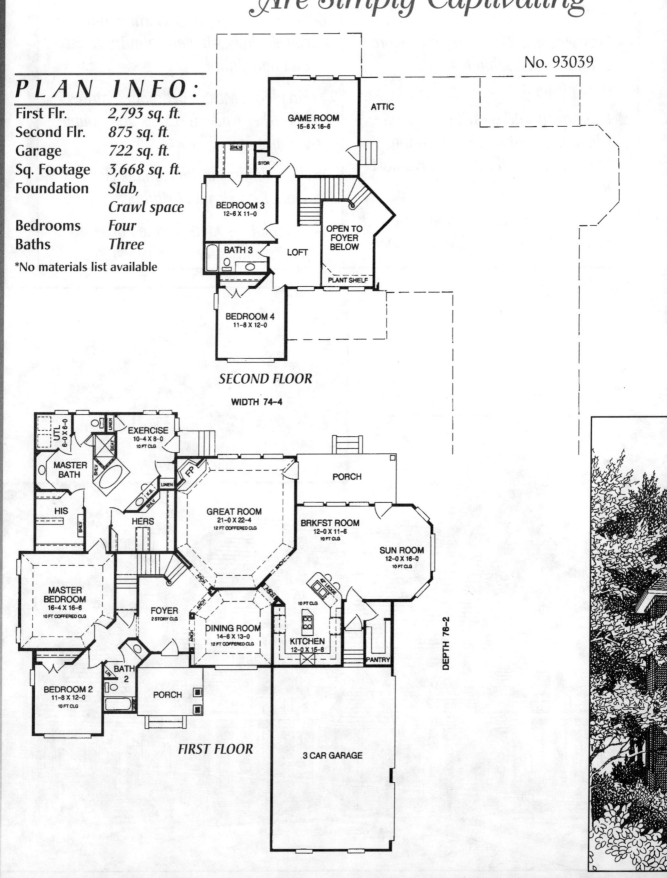

■ *Series of arched openings off the Foyer give this home a feeling of casual elegance*

■ *Decorative ceilings in the Great Room, Dining Room, and Master Bedroom add a feeling of luxury throughout*

■ *Corner fireplace enhances the warmth and coziness of the Great Room*

■ *Enormous his-n-her walk-in closets, his-n-her vanities, and a separate Exercise room in the Master Suite pamper the most discerning taste*

■ *Two upstairs bedrooms, and a Game Room share a Loft and a full Bath*

■ *Lovely Sun Room located adjacent to the Kitchen and Breakfast Room also provides access to an outdoor porch*

$\mathcal{D}$ecorative Ceiling Treatments

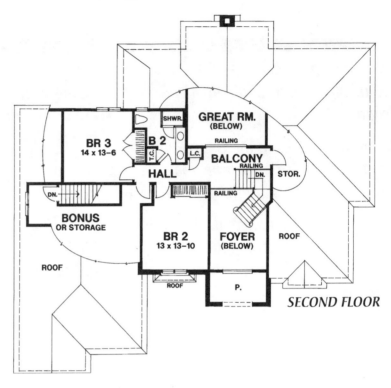

PLAN INFO:

First Flr.	2,282 sq. ft.
Second Flr.	660 sq. ft.
Basement	2,282 sq. ft.
Garage	772 sq. ft.
Sq. Footage	2,942 sq. ft.
Foundation	Basement
Bedrooms	Three
Baths	2(Full), 1(Half)

*No materials list available

SECOND FLOOR

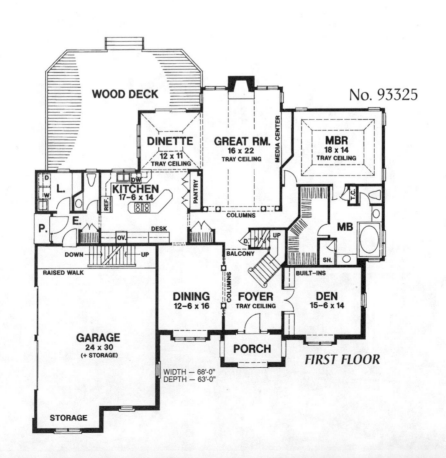

No. 93325

FIRST FLOOR

WIDTH — 68'-0"
DEPTH — 63'-0"

- *Distinctive entrance created by a covered Porch, windows surrounding the front door, a tray ceiling in the Foyer with an open staircase and balcony, columns framing entrance to the formal Dining Room and French doors leading into the Den*

- *Elegant formal Dining Room also has a decorative bumped out window*

- *More columns create a dramatic entrance into the Great Room equipped with a Media center, a huge fireplace surrounded by windows and topped with a tray ceiling*

- *Oversized Kitchen is a dream come true with a cooktop island/snack bar, built-in pantry and adjacent Dinette with tray ceiling and sliding glass doors to an outdoor deck*

- *Large Master Bedroom Suite with yet another tray ceiling offers luxurious privacy with an over-sized walk-in closet, raised corner window tub and two vanities*

- *Two second floor bedrooms share a full hall Bath, loads of storage and access to front and back stairways*

Balcony Offers Sweeping Views

No. 10778

DECK

SITTING
10'-6"
x
14'-6"

OPEN TO BELOW

PAN VAULT CLG.

MASTER SUITE
22'-6"
x
18'-0"

DESK

BR. 2
12'-8"
x
12'-0"

BATH

BALCONY

B.

VAN.

BOOKS

UP

BR. 3
13'-8"
x
12'-3"
SEAT

RAILING

OPEN TO BELOW

LIN.
DN

GUEST RM.
11'-3"
x
12'-6"
SEAT

SPA

B.

SLOPE **SLOPE**

SECOND FLOOR

PLAN INFO:

First Flr.	*1,978 sq. ft.*
Second Flr.	*1,768 sq. ft.*
Basement	*1,978 sq. ft.*
Garage	*3-car*
Sq. Footage	*3,746 sq. ft.*
Foundation	*Basement*
Bedrooms	*Four*
Baths	*3(Full), 1(Half)*

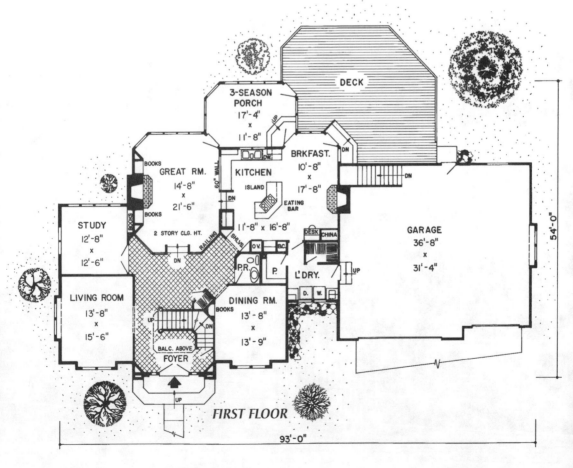

DECK

3-SEASON PORCH
17'-4"
x
11'-8"

BRKFAST.
10'-8"
x
17'-8"

GREAT RM.
14'-8"
x
21'-6"
2 STORY CLG. HT.

KITCHEN
ISLAND

EATING BAR
11'-8" x 16'-8"

GARAGE
36'-8"
x
31'-4"

BOOKS

60" WALL

DN

DN

DN

STUDY
12'-8"
x
12'-6"

DESK **CHINA**

O.V. **B.C.**

P.R. **P.**

L'DRY.

UP

D. **W.**

RAILING

SHLVS.

LIVING ROOM
13'-8"
x
15'-6"

DINING RM.
13'-8"
x
13'-9"

BOOKS

UP

DN

BALC. ABOVE
FOYER

UP

FIRST FLOOR

54'-0"

93'-0"

- *Greet arriving guests in the impressive Foyer enhanced by a two-story ceiling and attractive staircase*

- *Large Living Room adjacent to Foyer offers ample accommodations for entertaining many guests*

- *Step out from the Three-Season Porch to enjoy a breath of fresh air on the deck in backyard*

- *Master Suite on second floor provides ideal retreat with raised spa, walk-in*

- *closet, sunny Sitting Room, and private deck*

- *Overlook beauty of Great Room from Balcony connecting three additional Bedrooms*

- *Each bedroom features built-in window seats or deck and loads of closet space*

- *Kitchen opening to Breakfast Room features stove-top island, built-in shelving, eating bar, and much more!*

With All The Amenities You Need

No. 93329

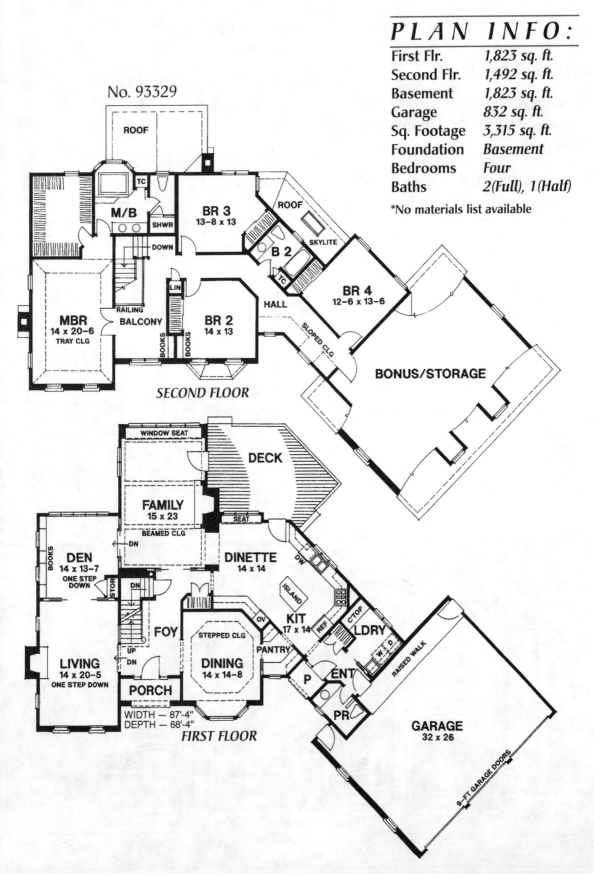

PLAN INFO:

First Flr.	1,823 sq. ft.
Second Flr.	1,492 sq. ft.
Basement	1,823 sq. ft.
Garage	832 sq. ft.
Sq. Footage	3,315 sq. ft.
Foundation	Basement
Bedrooms	Four
Baths	2(Full), 1(Half)

*No materials list available

ROOF

M/B
SHWR
DOWN
TC

BR 3
13-8 x 13

ROOF
SKYLITE

B 2
TC

BR 4
12-6 x 13-6

HALL

SLOPED CLG

MBR
14 x 20-6
TRAY CLG

RAILING
BALCONY

LIN

BR 2
14 x 13

BOOKS

BONUS/STORAGE

SECOND FLOOR

WINDOW SEAT

DECK

FAMILY
15 x 23
BEAMED CLG

SEAT

DN

DEN
14 x 13-7
ONE STEP DOWN

BOOKS

STOR

DN

DINETTE
14 x 14

DW

ISLAND

KIT
17 x 14

REF

CTOP

LDRY

W.D.

FOY

STEPPED CLG

OV

PANTRY

RAISED WALK

UP
DN

LIVING
14 x 20-5
ONE STEP DOWN

DINING
14 x 14-8

P

ENT

PORCH

PR

GARAGE
32 x 26

WIDTH — 87'-4"
DEPTH — 68'-4"

9-FT GARAGE DOORS

FIRST FLOOR

- *Arched, covered front entrance with sidelights and a fan transom window greets one and all into the Foyer and formal living areas*

- *Step down into the Formal Living Room with lots of windows and a hearth fireplace, easily expanded by opening pocket doors into the adjoining Den*

- *Bay window and stepped ceiling add elegance to the formal Dining Room*

- *Comfortable Family Room with another fireplace, beamed ceiling, a wall of glass above a long window seat, and direct access to the outdoor deck*

- *Large but efficient, gourmet Kitchen features a work island, walk-through pantry, loads of counter and cabinet space, a Dinette area with another window seat, and easy access to the Laundry area, Garage, and yards*

- *Scrumptious Master Bedroom Suite, topped with a tray ceiling, has windows on three sides, a walk-in closet large enough to be another room, and a segmented Bath with double vanity and a raised atrium tub*

- *Three additional large bedrooms have ample closet space and share a full hall Bath*

*S*tucco *Opulence*

No. 93270

SECOND FLOOR

PLAN INFO:

First Flr.	*2,329 sq. ft.*
Second Flr.	*1,259 sq. ft.*
Lower(Stairs)	*68 sq. ft.*
Basement	*1,806 sq. ft.*
Garage	*528 sq. ft.*
Sq. Footage	*3,656 sq. ft.*
Foundation	*Basement*
Bedrooms	*Four*
Baths	*3(Full), 2(Half)*

*No materials list available

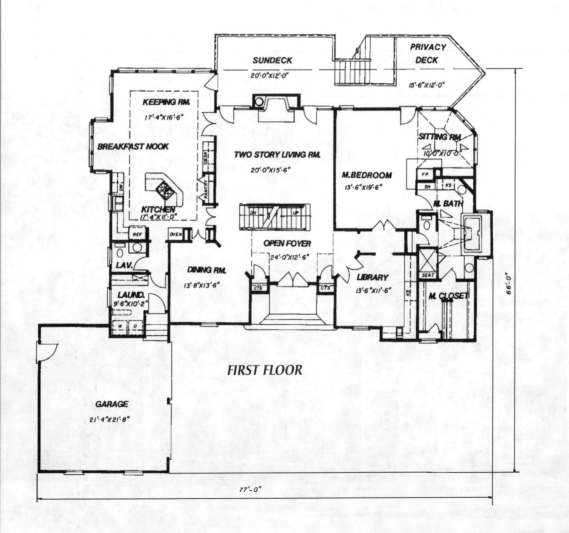

FIRST FLOOR

- Impressive double door entrance with a two-story glass Foyer leads graciously into an open Foyer centered by an elegant staircase

- Fantastic two-story Living Room includes a cozy fireplace framed by windows and doors with direct access to an outdoor Sundeck

- Expansive Kitchen is equipped with a cooktop island/snack bar, built-in pantry and desk, as well as a Breakfast Nook and Keeping Room, topped with a decorative ceiling

- Scrumptious, three-sided glass Sitting Room with direct access to a private outdoor Deck, an unusual corner fireplace, luxurious Bath with an atrium tub, and a double walk-in closet add to the appeal of the Master Bedroom Suite

- Double door entry to the Library, directly off the Foyer and across from the Master Suite, offers a quiet corner, loads of built-in shelves and a possible home office

- Three additional bedrooms on the second floor have walk-in closets and easy access to full baths and a separate Children's Den

$\mathcal{U}$ncommon Brickwork Enhances Facade

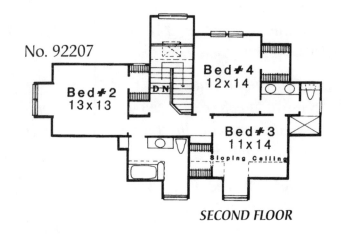

No. 92207

SECOND FLOOR

PLAN INFO:

First Flr.	*2,304 sq. ft.*
Second Flr.	*852 sq. ft.*
Garage	*3-car*
Sq. Footage	*3,156 sq. ft.*
Foundation	*Slab*
Bedrooms	*Four*
Baths	*3(Full), 1(Half)*

*No materials list available

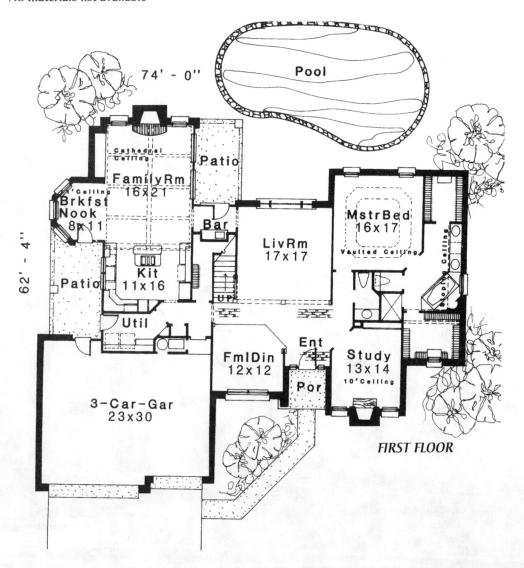

FIRST FLOOR

- Study adjacent to main Entry located in Master Suite wing to insure quiet solitude

- Vaulted Master Suite sports individual his-n-her walk-in closets and twin basin vanity

- Provocative raised tub with window overlooking side yard and sloping ceiling is focal feature of Master Bath

- Placement of wetbar just off formal Living Room conducive to simplified servicing of guests

- Living Room with sliding glass doors overlooks poolside vistas

- Spacious Kitchen with food preparation island flows directly into Family Room with exposed beams on the cathedral ceiling

- Breakfast Nook with lots of windows provides eating area for informal family meals

- Three additional bedrooms and two full baths on second floor supply plenty of room for remainder of family

Country Charm With Modern Amenities

PLAN INFO:

First Flr.	1,947 sq. ft.
Second Flr.	1,390 sq. ft.
Basement	1,947 sq. ft.
Garage	680 sq. ft.
Sq. Footage	3,337 sq. ft.
Foundation	Basement
Bedrooms	Four
Baths	2(Full), 1(Half)

*No materials list available

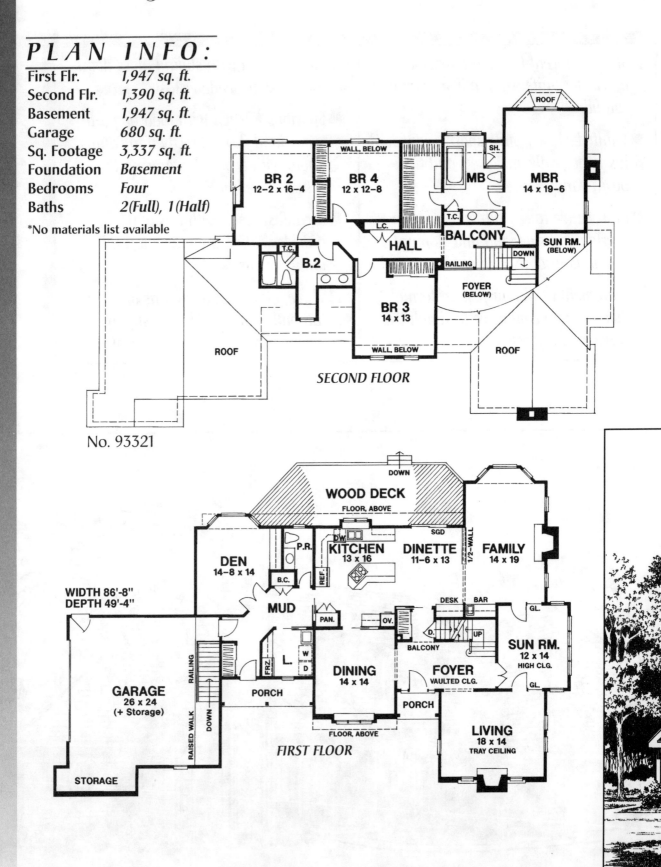

SECOND FLOOR

No. 93321

WIDTH 86'-8"
DEPTH 49'-4"

FIRST FLOOR

- *Vaulted ceiling and balcony give the Foyer an open feeling for a great first impression*

- *A tray ceiling is the crowning touch to the formal Living Room which also has a hearth fireplace framed by arched windows*

- *Well-appointed Kitchen is equipped with a cooktop island/eating bar, greenhouse window and a built-in pantry*

- *Large family room with a beamed ceiling, bay window and a cozy*

fireplace provide a wonderful atmosphere for family gatherings

- *Wonderful Sun Room connects Family Room, Foyer, and Living Room to make traffic flow easily*

- *Master Bedroom suite has a stepped ceiling, double vanity private Bath with a window tub, and a huge walk-in closet*

- *Three additional bedrooms with ample closet space share an extra large, full hall Bath*

Upper Deck Affords Roadside View

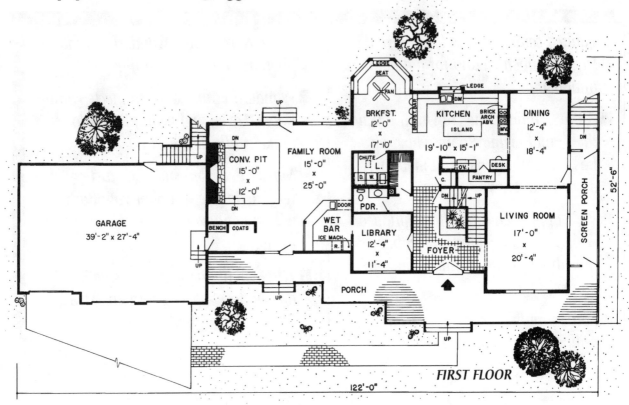

FIRST FLOOR

- BRKFST. 12'-0" x 17'-10"
- KITCHEN 19'-10" x 15'-1"
- DINING 12'-4" x 18'-4"
- FAMILY ROOM 15'-0" x 25'-0"
- CONV. PIT 15'-0" x 12'-0"
- GARAGE 39'-2" x 27'-4"
- WET BAR
- LIBRARY 12'-4" x 11'-4"
- PDR.
- FOYER
- LIVING ROOM 17'-0" x 20'-4"
- SCREEN PORCH
- PORCH
- 122'-0"
- 52'-6"

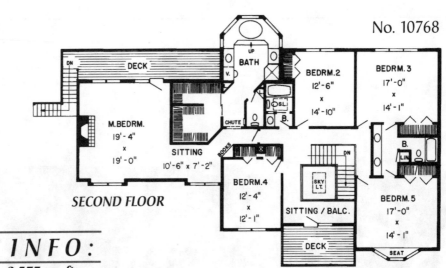

No. 10768

SECOND FLOOR

- M. BEDRM. 19'-4" x 19'-0"
- SITTING 10'-6" x 7'-2"
- DECK
- BATH
- BEDRM. 2 12'-6" x 14'-10"
- BEDRM. 3 17'-0" x 14'-1"
- BEDRM. 4 12'-4" x 12'-1"
- SITTING / BALC.
- BEDRM. 5 17'-0" x 14'-1"
- SKY LT.
- DECK

PLAN INFO:

First Flr.	2,573 sq. ft.
Second Flr.	2,390 sq. ft.
Basement	1,844 sq. ft.
Crawl Space	793 sq. ft.
Garage	1,080 sq. ft.
Sq. Footage	4,963 sq. ft.
Foundation	Basement
Bedrooms	Five
Baths	3(Full), 1(Half)

- *Dominating staircase in Foyer wraps around planter basking in light from skylight far above*

- *Flanked by the Library and Living Room, the Foyer leads back to the island Kitchen with extra amenities*

- *Kitchen centrally located to serve the formal Dining Area and Breakfast Room*

- *Warm up informal gatherings at the fireplace in the Family Room containing large wetbar*

- *Master Suite on upper floor presents formidable escape spot from remainder of home*

- *Private deck, oversized double walk-in closet, double vanities and special tub setting render Master Suite truly luxurious*

- *Three additional Bedrooms on second floor provide ample room for children*

- *Overlook staircase and planter in Foyer from Sitting Area/Balcony or enjoy roadside view from deck*

*E*xquisite *T*aste *T*hroughout *T*his *D*esign

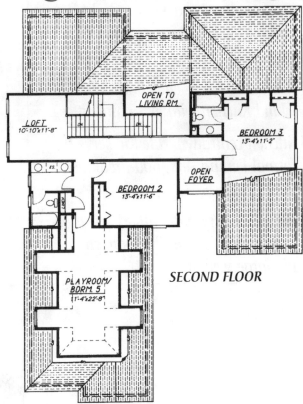

SECOND FLOOR

OPEN TO LIVING RM

LOFT
10'-10"x11'-8"

BEDROOM 3
13'-4"x11'-2"

BEDROOM 2
13'-4"x11'-6"

OPEN FOYER

PLAYROOM/
BDRM. 5
11'-4"x22'-8"

PLAN INFO:

First Flr.	*2,055 sq. ft.*
Second Flr.	*898 sq. ft.*
Basement	*1,866 sq. ft.*
Garage	*508 sq. ft.*
Sq. Footage	*2,953 sq. ft.*
Foundation	*Basement*
Bedrooms	*Four*
Baths	*4(Full), 1(Half)*

*No materials list available

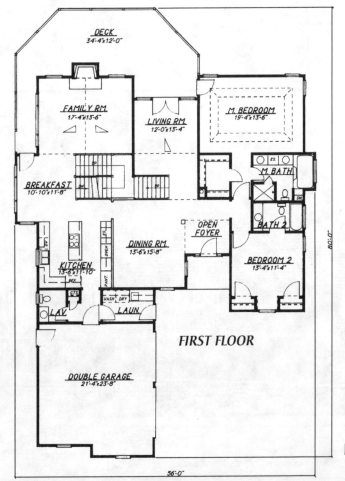

DECK
34'-4"x12'-0"

FAMILY RM
17'-4"x13'-6"

LIVING RM
12'-0"x13'-4"

M. BEDROOM
19'-4"x13'-6"

BREAKFAST
10'-10"x11'-8"

M. BATH

BATH 2

DINING RM
13'-6"x15'-8"

OPEN FOYER

KITCHEN
13'-6"x11'-10"

BEDROOM 2
13'-4"x11'-4"

LAV

LAUN.

WASH DRY

FIRST FLOOR

DOUBLE GARAGE
21'-4"x23'-8"

56'-0"

No. 93271

- Alcove two-story glass entrance greets one and all into an open floor plan that makes both living and entertaining a joy

- Formal Living Room features French doors to an outdoor deck and divided from the formal Dining Room by an open staircase and balcony

- Fabulous Kitchen, with a cook top island/snack bar, built-in pantry and desk, expands into the sunny Breakfast nook

- A cozy fireplace framed by windows and adjacent to the kitchen area

- makes the Family Room a great gathering place

- Decorative ceiling crowns the Master Bedroom Suite that includes a private Bath with a window tub and a walk-in closet

- Second Bedroom on the first floor is also equipped with a private bath, making it a perfect guest room

- Three additional bedrooms on the second floor, one large enough to be a Playroom, share a full hall Bath and a Loft

*A*ngled Garage *D*raws Eyes
*T*oward *T*his *H*ome

No. 93042

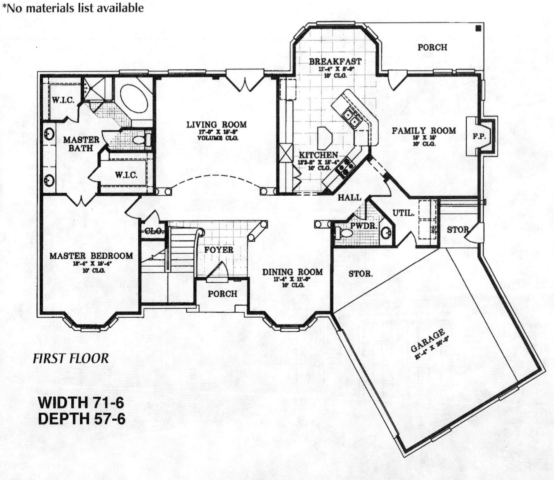

SECOND FLOOR

PLAN INFO:

First Flr.	*1,832 sq. ft.*
Second Flr.	*1,163 sq. ft.*
Garage	*591 sq. ft.*
Sq. Footage	*2,995 sq. ft.*
Foundation	*Slab, Crawl space*
Bedrooms	*Four*
Baths	*2(Full), 1(Half)*

*No materials list available

FIRST FLOOR

WIDTH 71-6
DEPTH 57-6

- *Elegance accented by twin bay windows and an angled Garage*

- *Tiled Foyer opens to a breath-taking two-story Living Room framed by columns and featuring French doors*

- *Elegant formal Dining Room also features a column entrance and one of the lovely bay windows*

- *Island dream Kitchen, with a peninsula counter and eating bar,* connects with the Breakfast Room that flows easily into the Family Room

- *Spacious Family Room that includes a cozy fireplace and access to an outdoor porch*

- *Pampering Master Suite features the other bay window, his-n-her walk-in closets and a segmented Master Bath*

- *Three bedrooms share a full double vanity hall Bath*

You Deserve This Spacious Design

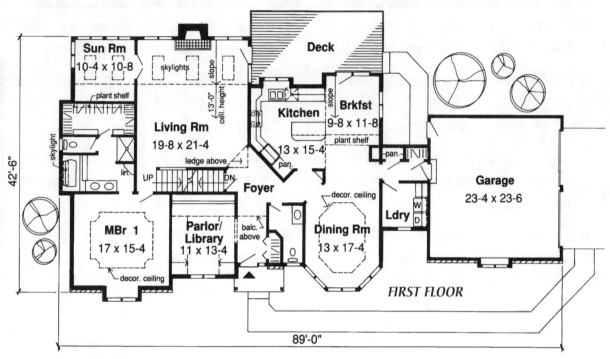

FIRST FLOOR

- Sun Rm 10-4 x 10-8
- skylights
- plant shelf
- skylight
- Living Rm 19-8 x 21-4
- ledge above
- Deck
- Kitchen 13 x 15-4
- Brkfst 9-8 x 11-8
- plant shelf
- 13'-0" ceil. height
- slope
- pan.
- UP
- DN
- Foyer
- decor. ceiling
- pan.
- Garage 23-4 x 23-6
- MBr 1 17 x 15-4
- Parlor/Library 11 x 13-4
- balc. above
- Dining Rm 13 x 17-4
- Ldry
- W D
- decor. ceiling

42'-6"

89'-0"

No. 20167

PLAN INFO:

First Flr.	*2,216 sq. ft.*
Second Flr.	*916 sq. ft.*
Basement	*2,089 sq. ft.*
Garage	*576 sq. ft.*
Sq. Footage	*3,132 sq. ft.*
Foundation	*Basement*
Bedrooms	*Four*
Baths	*2 (Full), 1 (Half)*

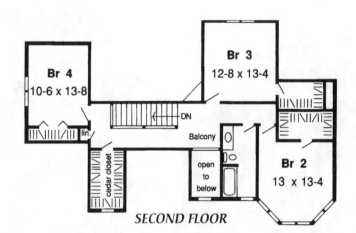

SECOND FLOOR

- Br 4 10-6 x 13-8
- lin.
- cedar closet
- DN
- Br 3 12-8 x 13-4
- Balcony
- open to below
- Br 2 13 x 13-4

An
EXCLUSIVE DESIGN
By Karl Kreeger

- *Two-story Foyer adjoins the Parlor/Library and the spectacular Living Room with skylights and a large cozy fireplace*

- *Gourmet island Kitchen, with a built-in pantry, double sink, and an over abundance of counter and storage space*

- *Just steps away from the Kitchen is the sunny Breakfast Room and elegant Dining Room with Bay windows and a decorative ceiling*

- *Stupendous Sun Room with skylights and plant shelves adds solar benefits for all seasons*

- *First floor Master Suite with decorative ceiling treatment, private Bath with skylights and a room-sized walk-in closet*

- *Three bedrooms, each with abundant closet space, share the second floor with a walk-in cedar closet and a full Bath*

Secluded Master Bedroom
Guarantees Peace & Quiet

PLAN INFO:

First Flr.	*3,252 sq. ft.*
Second Flr.	*873 sq. ft.*
Garage	*746 sq. ft.*
Sq. Footage	*4,125 sq. ft.*
Foundation	*Slab*
Bedrooms	*Four*
Baths	*Four*

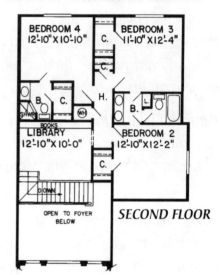

BEDROOM 4
12'-10"X10'-10"

BEDROOM 3
11'-10"X12'-4"

BEDROOM 2
12'-10"X12'-2"

LIBRARY
12'-10"X10'-0"

BOOKS

SHWR B. C. H. B. WH

C. C.

DOWN

OPEN TO FOYER BELOW

SECOND FLOOR

No. 10696

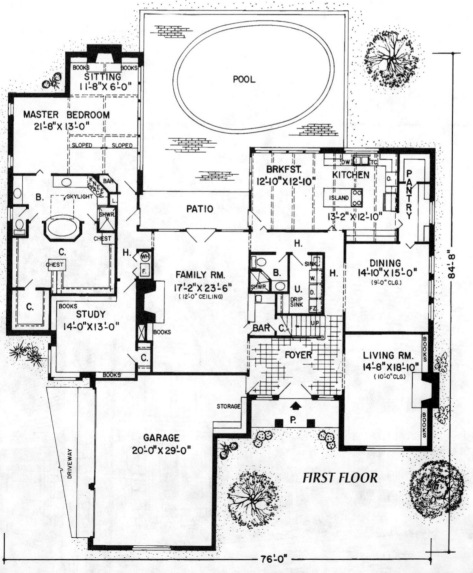

POOL

SITTING
11'-8"X 6'-0"
BOOKS   BOOKS

MASTER BEDROOM
21'-8"X 13'-0"
SLOPED   SLOPED

KNEE SPACE   BAR
B.   SKYLIGHT   L.
SHWR
CHEST
C.
CHEST
C.

BOOKS   STUDY
14'-0"X13'-0"
BOOKS
C.
BOOKS

H.   WH
F.

PATIO

BRKFST.
12'-10"X12'-10"

KITCHEN
ISLAND
13'-2"X 12'-10"

PANTRY

FAMILY RM.
17'-2"X 23'-6"
(12'-0" CEILING)

H.
B.   SINK
SHWR   W.
U.   D.
DRIP SINK   FZ.

DINING
14'-10"X15'-0"
(9'-0" CLG.)

H.

84'-8"

BAR   C.

UP

FOYER

STORAGE

P.

LIVING RM.
14'-8"X18'-10"
(10'-0" CLG.)
BOOKS
BOOKS

DRIVEWAY

GARAGE
20'-0"X 29'-0"

FIRST FLOOR

76'-0"

- *Colossal walk-in closet in Master Suite includes two built-in chests*

- *Skylight above whirlpool bath dispenses cheerful sunlight into roomy Master Bath*

- *Book-lined Study provides tranquil retreat for concentration*

- *Fully-equipped island Kitchen flows into Breakfast Room bathed with light streaming through numerous windows*

- *Immense pantry adjacent to Kitchen offers substantial shelf room*

- *Master Bedroom occupying an entire wing of the home includes a comfortable Sitting Room with fireplace looking out over pool area*

- *Cozy Library at top of stairs overlooks Foyer below*

- *Three additional bedrooms and two baths extend throughout the remainder of the second floor*

Combination Of Contemporary & New England Living

No. 92600

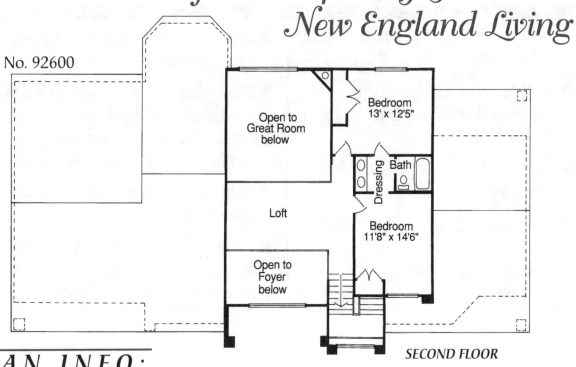

SECOND FLOOR

Loft

Open to Great Room below

Open to Foyer below

Bedroom 13' x 12'5"

Bath

Dressing

Bedroom 11'8" x 14'6"

PLAN INFO:

First Flr.	*2,245 sq. ft.*
Second Flr.	*710 sq. ft.*
Basement	*1,963 sq. ft.*
Garage	*538 sq. ft.*
Sq. Footage	*2,955 sq. ft.*
Foundation	*Basement*
Bedrooms	*Three*
Baths	*2(Full), 1(Half)*

*No materials list available

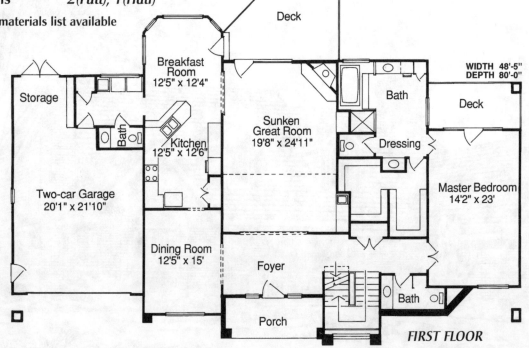

WIDTH 48'-5"
DEPTH 80'-0"

Storage

Breakfast Room 12'5" x 12'4"

Deck

Bath

Deck

Bath

Sunken Great Room 19'8" x 24'11"

Dressing

Kitchen 12'5" x 12'6"

Two-car Garage 20'1" x 21'10"

Master Bedroom 14'2" x 23'

Dining Room 12'5" x 15'

Foyer

Bath

Porch

FIRST FLOOR

- *Covered entrance leads into a large two-story Foyer and provides a view to the backyard through the Great Room*

- *Expansive, sunken Great Room includes a cozy corner fireplace, convenient wetbar and access to outdoor deck, making it a dream for entertaining*

- *Formal Dining Room, located in close proximity to the Kitchen, creates just the right atmosphere for elegant dining*

- *Efficient Kitchen equipped with an abundance of counter and storage space, has an angled work counter/snack bar connecting with a three-sided glass Breakfast Room*

- *Secluded Master Bedroom suite opens to a private deck and a luxurious Bath with a large, double walk-in closet, raised tub, shower and two vanities*

- *Two spacious bedrooms on the second floor share a divided Bath with a double vanity*

*F*amily Living On Two Levels

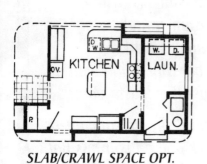

SLAB/CRAWL SPACE OPT.

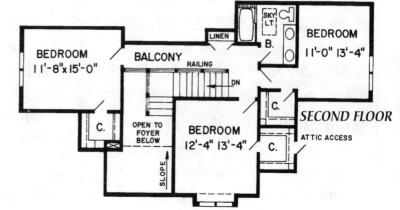

LINEN

SKY LT.

B.

BEDROOM 11'-8"x15'-0"

BALCONY

RAILING

DN

OPEN TO FOYER BELOW

SLOPE

BEDROOM 12'-4" 13'-4"

C.

C.

C.

BEDROOM 11'-0" 13'-4"

SECOND FLOOR

ATTIC ACCESS

PLAN INFO:

First Flr.	*1,933 sq. ft.*
Second Flr.	*918 sq. ft.*
Basement	*1,888 sq. ft.*
Garage	*484 sq. ft.*
Sq. Footage	*2,851 sq. ft.*
Foundation	*Bsmt, Slab, Crawl space*
Bedrooms	*Four*
Baths	*2(Full), 1(Half)*

An EXCLUSIVE DESIGN *By Karl Kreeger*

No. 20090

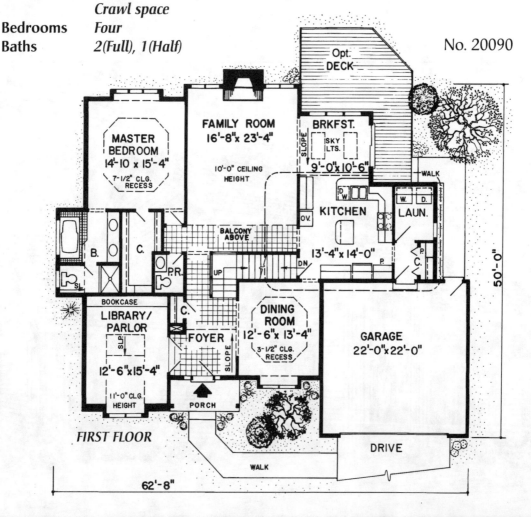

Opt. DECK

MASTER BEDROOM 14'-10 x 15'-4"

7-1/2" CLG. RECESS

FAMILY ROOM 16'-8"x 23'-4"

10'-0" CEILING HEIGHT

BRKFST.

SKY LTS.

9'-0"x10'-6"

WALK

B.

C.

PR.

BALCONY ABOVE

UP

DN

KITCHEN

13'-4"x 14'-0"

W. D.

LAUN.

P.

C.

50'-0"

BOOKCASE

LIBRARY/ PARLOR

SLP

12'-6"x15'-4"

11'-0" CLG. HEIGHT

C.

FOYER

SLOPE

DINING ROOM 12'-6"x 13'-4"

3-1/2" CLG. RECESS

GARAGE 22'-0"x22'-0"

FIRST FLOOR

PORCH

DRIVE

WALK

62'-8"

- Stacked window towers grace the facade of this more than spacious classic

- Formal Parlor and Dining Room with decorative ceilings are both located right off the Foyer

- A central work island, as well as a peninsula counter, enhance the convenience of the Kitchen

- Skylights provide natural illumination for the Breakfast Room which is surrounded by an outdoor wood deck

- A cozy fireplace in the Family Room sets the mood and adds to the atmosphere

- An elegant recess ceiling crowns the Master Suite that includes a huge walk-in closet and a private Bath

- Three additional bedrooms with walk-in closets share a roomy double vanity Bath with skylights

*B*ig Country Home Has Traditional Charm

PLAN INFO:

First Flr.	2,026 sq. ft.
Second Flr.	1,386 sq. ft.
Garage	576 sq. ft.
Sq. Footage	3,412 sq. ft.
Foundation	Basement
Bedrooms	Three
Baths	2(Full), 2(Half)

SECOND FLOOR

No. 99239

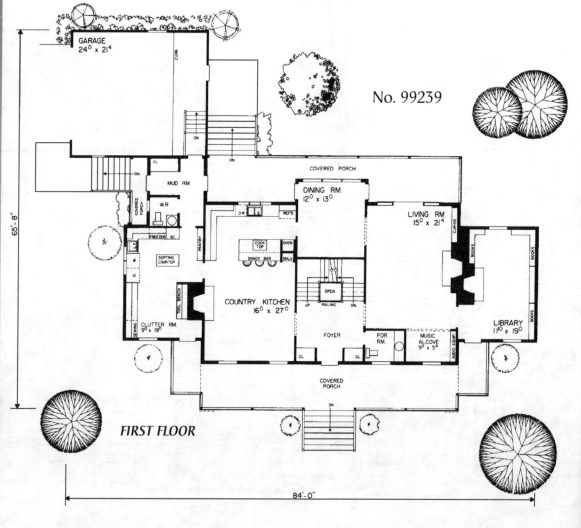

FIRST FLOOR

84'-0"

- *Covered porches on the front and back, invite friends and family to enjoy this home*

- *Back-to-back fireplaces warm the Living Room and Library*

- *Living Room also features a Music Alcove, complete with custom built-ins for audio equipment*

- *Adjoining Library offers floor-to-ceiling, built-in bookcases and a separate access to the front Porch*

- *Wall of windows opening onto the back Porch and yard beyond, adds a touch of elegance to the Dining Room*

- *Large Country Kitchen includes a fireplace in the sitting/dining area, a snack counter, and cooking layout designed for canning, baking and the preparation of gourmet meals*

- *Incredible Master Bedroom suite on the second floor offers a huge walk-in closet plus two more closets, and a combined Dressing/Bath area with a whirlpool tub*

- *Two additional bedrooms with double closets on the second floor share the full, double vanity hall Bath*

*F*ront *B*edroom *F*eatures *W*indow *S*eat

PLAN INFO:

First Flr.	2,027 sq. ft.
Second Flr.	1,476 sq. ft.
Garage	650 sq. ft.
Sq. Footage	3,503 sq. ft.
Foundation	Slab
Bedrooms	Four
Baths	Three

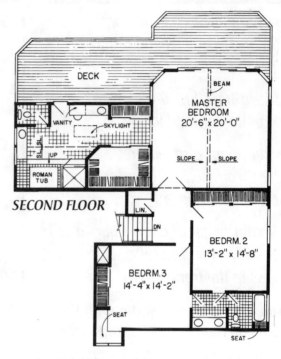

SECOND FLOOR

No. 10758

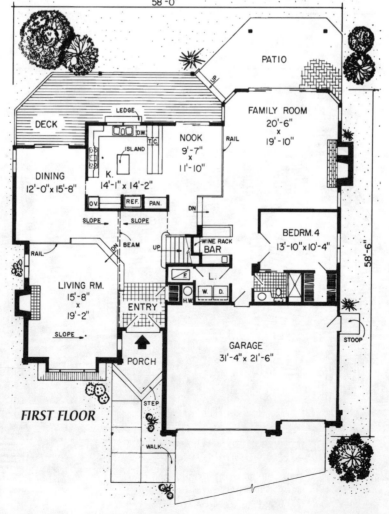

FIRST FLOOR

■ *Sloping roofline creates unusual decorating possibilities in Master Bedroom*

■ *Feel the day's cares ease away while relaxing on private deck in Master Suite after reposing in Roman tub in skylit Bath*

■ *Soaring ceilings generate airy atmosphere throughout design*

■ *Kitchen framed by formal Dining Room and cheery Eating Nook*

■ *Two additional Bedrooms on second floor have ample closet space, and share a full Bath*

■ *Open railings and single steps separate fireplaced Family and Living Rooms from Entry and Dining Areas*

■ *Sliders in Family Room and both Dining Rooms open to rear deck and patio to maximize spacious feeling*

■ *Fourth bedroom complete with full Bath tucked behind garage*

Luxury Residence For The Executive Family

PLAN INFO:

First Flr.	3,798 sq. ft.
Second Flr.	1,244 sq. ft.
Basement	3,798 sq. ft.
Garage	3-car
Sq. Footage	5,042 sq. ft.
Foundation	Basement
Bedrooms	Three
Baths	3(Full), 2(Half)

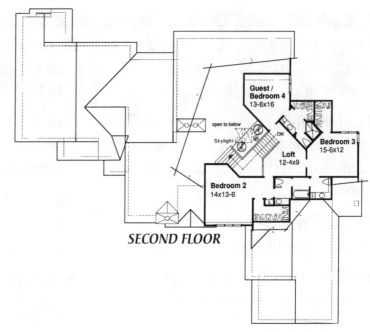

SECOND FLOOR

No. 99369

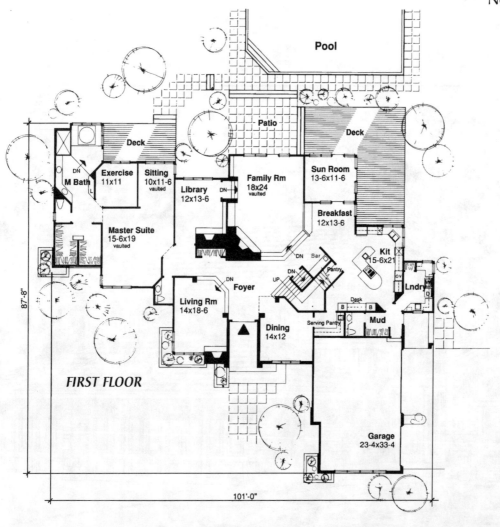

FIRST FLOOR

■ *Main floor zoned into three main living areas: formal, informal, and Master Suite*

■ *Enter formal living/entertaining area from impressive Foyer which opens into the Dining Room with an efficient serving pantry*

■ *Master Suite located in a private wing includes a vaulted Sitting Room, Exercise Room, sunken whirlpool tub, and twin walk-in closets*

■ *Second floor features a loft and three bedrooms each with personal baths and walk-in closets*

■ *Informal zone centers around a large island Kitchen with built-in desk and handy access to the 3-car Garage past the Laundry and Mudroom*

■ *Kitchen also oversees the Breakfast area and Sunroom eating areas as well as the sunken Family Room*

Bay Windows Enhance This Country Home

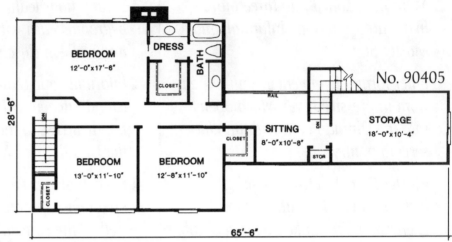

No. 90405

BEDROOM 12'-0"x17'-6"

DRESS

BATH

CLOSET

RAIL

SITTING 8'-0"x10'-8"

CLOSET

STOR

STORAGE 18'-0"x10'-4"

BEDROOM 13'-0"x11'-10"

CLOSET

BEDROOM 12'-8"x11'-10"

28'-6"

65'-6"

SECOND FLOOR

PLAN INFO:

First Flr.	2,005 sq. ft.
Second Flr.	1,063 sq. ft.
Sq. Footage	3,068 sq. ft.
Foundation	Bsmt, Crawl space*
Bedrooms	Four
Baths	2(Full), 1(Half)

*Please specify when ordering

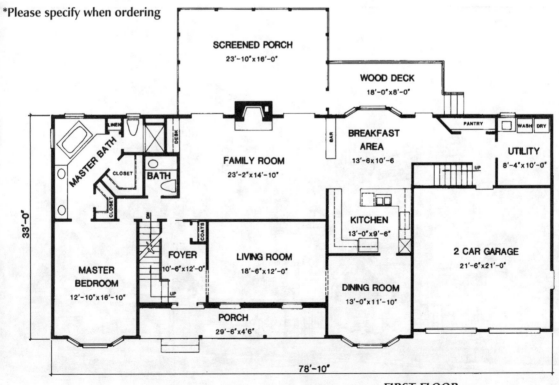

SCREENED PORCH 23'-10"x16'-0"

WOOD DECK 18'-0"x8'-0"

PANTRY

WASH **DRY**

LINEN

MASTER BATH

DESK

CLOSET

BATH

BAR

FAMILY ROOM 23'-2"x14'-10"

BREAKFAST AREA 13'-6x10'-6

UTILITY 8'-4"x10'-0"

UP

CLOSET

KITCHEN 13'-0"x9'-6"

COATS

FOYER 10'-6"x12'-0"

LIVING ROOM 18'-6"x12'-0"

2 CAR GARAGE 21'-6"x21'-0"

33'-0"

MASTER BEDROOM 12'-10"x16'-10"

UP

DINING ROOM 13'-0"x11'-10"

PORCH 29'-6"x4'6"

78'-10"

FIRST FLOOR

■ *In the center of this friendly home is the Family Room, sure to be the hub of activity with easy access to other living areas including a screened porch and outdoor deck*

■ *Large bay window floods the Breakfast Area with sunlight making it a cheery place to start your day*

■ *Between the Breakfast Area and the Dining Room is the efficient, well-appointed Kitchen that features a peninsula counter, and ample counter and cabinet space*

■ *Adjacent to the Kitchen a large pantry and separate Utility Room provide extra convenience*

■ *Large Master Bedroom Suite includes a deluxe, private Bath with a separate shower, garden tub, twin vanities and two large walk-in closets*

■ *Three additional bedrooms, located on the second floor, share a full hall Bath, a Sitting area and front and back stairways*

Surrounded By Multi-Level Decks

No. 92106

Br #2
14-6 x 12

Br #3
12-6 x 14

LINEN

OPEN TO
LIVING BELOW

OPEN TO
FOYER BELOW

DN.

SECOND FLOOR

PLAN INFO:

First Flr.	*2,358 sq. ft.*
Second Flr.	*700 sq. ft.*
Garage	*954 sq. ft.*
Sq. Footage	*3,058 sq. ft.*
Foundation	*Crawl space*
Bedrooms	*Three*
Baths	*2(Full), 1(Half)*

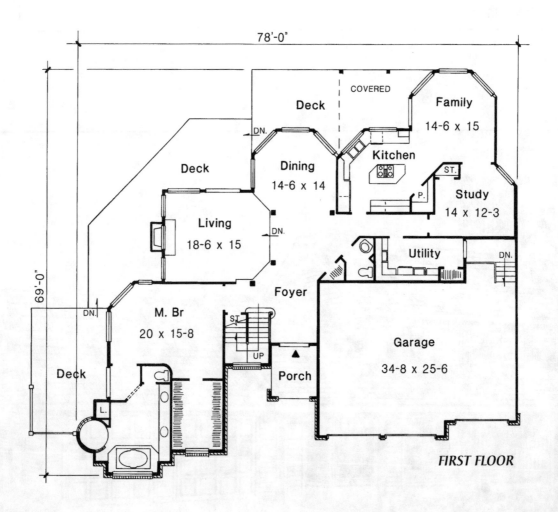

78'-0"

COVERED

Deck

Family
14-6 x 15

Deck

Dining
14-6 x 14

Kitchen

ST.

P.

Study
14 x 12-3

Living
18-6 x 15

DN.

DN.

Utility

DN.

Foyer

69'-0"

DN.

M. Br
20 x 15-8

ST.

UP

Garage
34-8 x 25-6

Deck

L.

Porch

FIRST FLOOR

■ Enter Utility Room with built-in counter and ample closet space from stucco 3-car Garage

■ Extra lighting and cabinets add to the island Kitchen that opens to a bright sunny Family Room

■ Unique octagonally-shaped Dining Room leads to immense covered deck and steps down to a fireplaced Living Room

■ Enjoy the view of the Foyer below from second floor landing with linen closet

■ Master Bedroom with personal deck features window in walk-in closet and plenty of living and decorating space

■ Master Bath has his-n-her vanity, linen closet and luxurious circular glass-walled shower

■ Bedroom Two offers a good-sized closet and breathtaking view an through extra-large window

■ Bedroom Three includes a sizeable walk-in closet and opens to a shared double vanitied Bath

Spectacular Display Of Light & Space

PLAN INFO:

First Flr.	1,786 sq. ft.
Second Flr.	1,490 sq. ft.
Basement	1,773 sq. ft.
Garage	579 sq. ft.
Sq. Footage	3,276 sq. ft.
Foundation	Basement
Bedrooms	Four
Baths	2(Full), 1(Half)

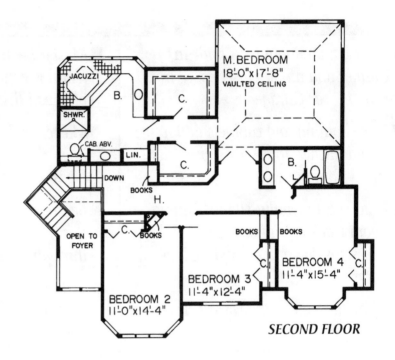

SECOND FLOOR

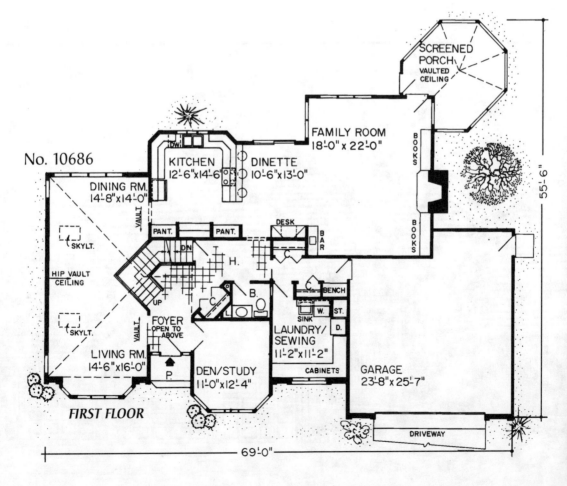

No. 10686

FIRST FLOOR

- Huge two-story Foyer features angular open staircase leading to sleeping quarters on the second floor

- Master Bedroom occupies full length of upper level, allowing many luxurious amenities to be included

- Master Bath sports a personal jacuzzi for private relaxation

- Three additional bedrooms upstairs each possess generous closet area and built-in bookshelving

- Laundry/Sewing Room provides undisturbed niche for special projects

- Wide-open family area includes Kitchen, Dinette, and fireplaced Family Room, complete with built-in bar and bookcases

- Kitchen features two pantries and lots of counter space as well as easy access to the formal Dining Room

- Well-placed skylights and abundant windows bathe every room in sunlight

A Truly Stunning Design

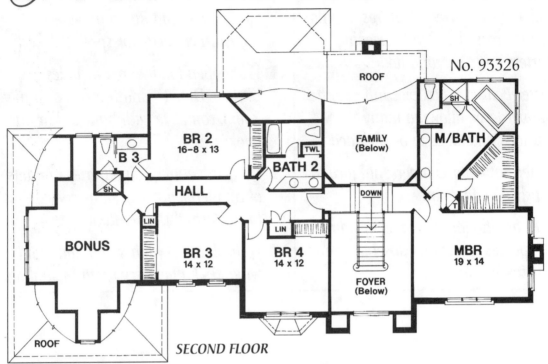

No. 93326

SECOND FLOOR

- BR 2 16-8 x 13
- B 3
- SH
- HALL
- BATH 2
- TWL
- FAMILY (Below)
- ROOF
- M/BATH
- SH
- DOWN
- T
- BONUS
- LIN
- BR 3 14 x 12
- LIN
- BR 4 14 x 12
- FOYER (Below)
- MBR 19 x 14
- ROOF

PLAN INFO:

First Flr.	2,228 sq. ft.
Second Flr.	1,625 sq. ft.
Bonus Rm.	347 sq. ft.
Basement	2,228 sq. ft.
Garage	816 sq. ft.
Sq. Footage	3,853 sq. ft.
Foundation	Basement
Bedrooms	Four
Baths	3(Full), 1(Half)

*No materials list available

- SUN RM 16 x 16 TRAY CLG
- FAMILY 15-6 x 20 TRAY CLG
- DEN 16 x 13-10
- BOOKS
- DW
- REF
- DINETTE 12 x 14
- pocket doors
- PR
- TC
- KITCHEN 14 x 16
- SNACK
- OV
- DESK
- PANTRY
- POCKET DOOR
- DN
- E
- GARAGE 24 x 34
- LDRY
- PORCH
- D W
- DINING 14 x 16
- UP
- FOYER HIGH CEIL'G
- LIVING 19 x 14
- PORCH

WIDTH — 84'-0"
DEPTH — 52'-0"
FIRST FLOOR

■ Stunning facade of this lovely home with fan-top decorative windows, blocked brick corners and two-story glass entryway attracts admiration

■ Open Foyer gives ready access to all living areas with its center staircase, pillar entrances to formal Living and Dining rooms, pocket doors into Family room and double doors into Den

■ Formal Dining Room features a bumped out decorative window and intriguing pocket doors for exclusive entertaining

■ Spacious Family Room featuring a tray ceiling and another cozy fireplace, opens into the Kitchen area and Sun Room with loads of windows

■ Gourmet Kitchen has it all; a cooktop/snack bar island, double sink, built-in pantry and desk, a comfortable Dinette area and direct access to the Dining Room, Sun Room, Family Room, Laundry and Garage

■ Indulgent Master Bedroom Suite, separated on the second floor by a balcony, has a large decorative window viewing the front yard and a lavish Bath with a huge walk-in closet, double vanity and a raised corner window tub

■ On the other end of the second floor there are three large bedrooms, one with a private bath, and a Bonus room to accommodate any need

Veranda Mirrors Two-Story Bay

PLAN INFO:

First Flr.	2,108 sq. ft.
Second Flr.	2,109 sq. ft.
Basement	1,946 sq. ft.
Garage	764 sq. ft.
Sq. Footage	4,217 sq. ft.
Foundation	Basement
Bedrooms	Four
Baths	2(Full), 1(Half)

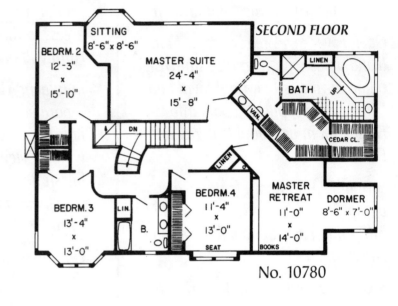

SECOND FLOOR

No. 10780

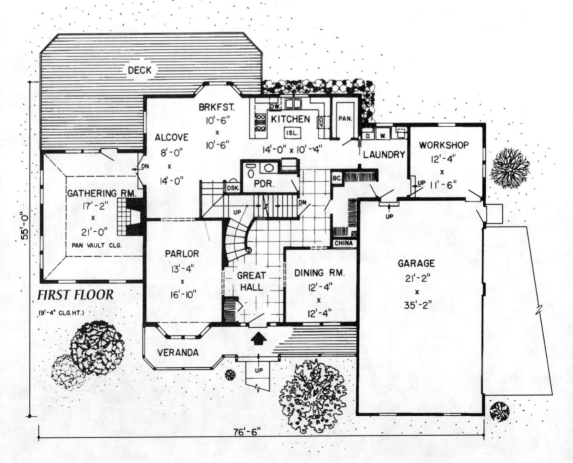

FIRST FLOOR

(9'-4" CLG. HT.)

- Elegant Victorian with modern twist celebrates classic beauty of turn-of-the-century architecture

- Eloquent Great Hall flanked by the formal Dining Room and Parlor expresses gracious welcome to all who enter

- Island Kitchen with adjoining full-sized pantry reveal plenty of cupboards and counter space

- Genial Breakfast corner opens into large Alcove with alternate route leading upstairs

- Step down into the sunken Gathering Room with fireplace, pan vault ceiling, and direct passage to wrap-around porch

- Double doors open to the Master Suite and book-lined Master Retreat with Dormer Sitting Area

- Elegant Master Bath features raised tub and adjoining cedar closet

- Other upstairs bedrooms feature distinctive shapes, huge closets, and access to full Bath with double vanities

Cathedral Entry Into This Colonial Classic

SECOND FLOOR

No. 99210

PLAN INFO:

First Flr.	2,116 sq. ft.
Second Flr.	1,848 sq. ft.
Garage	667 sq. ft.
Sq. Footage	3,964 sq. ft.
Foundation	Basement
Bedrooms	Three
Baths	3(Full), 1(Half)

FIRST FLOOR

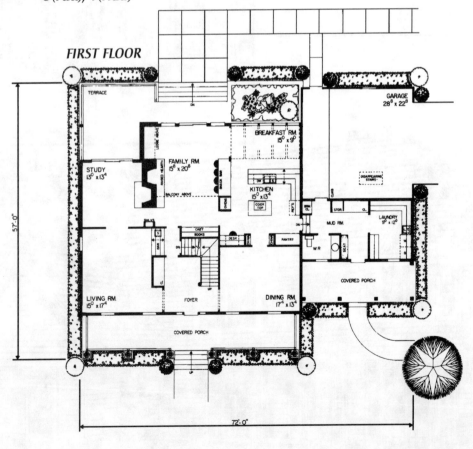

- *Spaciousness and elegance are created by the dramatic cathedral entry and balcony overlook*

- *Two covered porches are exquisite places to relax on a quiet summer evening*

- *Two fireplaces, one in the Study and the other in the first floor Family Room, add warmth and atmosphere*

- *Well-planned Kitchen opens onto a sunny "greenhouse" Breakfast Room*

- *Two Family Rooms, one up, one down, have a two-story divided window wall and are perfect for entertaining*

- *His-n-her dressing rooms and an ultra Bath add a bit of pampering to the Master Suite*

- *Three additional bedrooms on the second floor share a full hall Bath*

Stunning Manor Sure To Delight You

PLAN INFO:

First Flr.	2,745 sq. ft.
Second Flr.	2,355 sq. ft.
Garage	3-car
Sq. Footage	5,100 sq. ft.
Foundation	Slab
Bedrooms	Four
Baths	2(Full), 1(Half)

*No materials list available

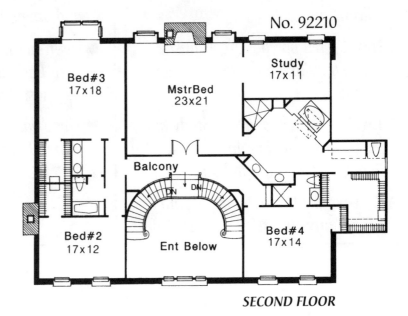

No. 92210

Bed#3
17x18

MstrBed
23x21

Study
17x11

Balcony

Bed#2
17x12

Ent Below

Bed#4
17x14

SECOND FLOOR

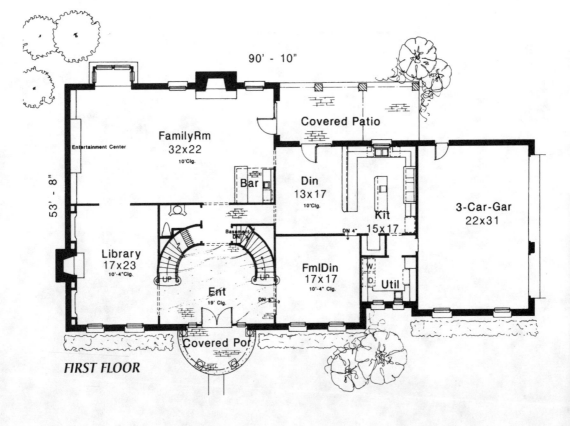

90' - 10"

53' - 8"

Covered Patio

FamilyRm
32x22
10'Clg.

Entertainment Center

Bar

Din
13x17
10'Clg.

Kit
15x17

3-Car-Gar
22x31

Library
17x23
10'-4"Clg.

Basement
DN

UP   UP

Ent
19' Clg.

FmlDin
17x17
10'-4" Clg.

W
D.

Util

Covered Por.

FIRST FLOOR

- 84 -

- *Distinctive covered porch escorts guests to the Entry highlighted by double curved staircase and 19-foot ceiling*

- *Fireplaced Library with built-in shelving for extensive collection of books*

- *Enormous Family Room extends cordial welcome to informal gatherings and private family relaxation with built-in entertainment center, fireplace, and full-sized wetbar*

- *Spacious island Kitchen with huge walk-in pantry separated from Dinette by eating bar*

- *Access to the swimming pool via the covered patio through Dinette or Family Room*

- *Enter your Master Suite through double French doors to discover a personal fireplace, private study and skylit Bath with double sink vanity*

- *Three additional bedrooms on the second floor feature adjoining Baths*

$\mathcal{H}$earth Room Highlights This Plan

No. 10527

PLAN INFO:

First Flr.	1,697 sq. ft.
Second Flr.	1,624 sq. ft.
Basement	1,697 sq. ft.
Garage	586 sq. ft.
Sq. Footage	3321 sq. ft.
Foundation	Basement
Bedrooms	Four
Baths	3(Full), 1(Half)

M. BEDROOM
19'-8" X 14'-4"

BEDROOM 2
15'-2" X 11'-10"

BEDROOM 3
16'-8" X 20'-4"

BEDROOM 4
12'-4" X 11'-4"

SECOND FLOOR

An **EXCLUSIVE DESIGN** *By Karl Kreeger*

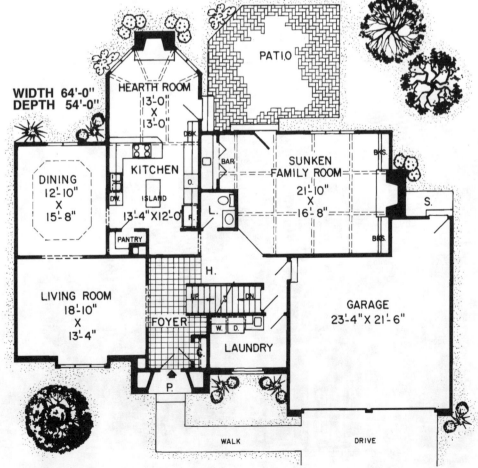

WIDTH 64'-0"
DEPTH 54'-0"

PATIO

HEARTH ROOM
13'-0" X 13'-0"

DINING
12'-10" X 15'-8"

KITCHEN
13'-4" X 12'-0"

SUNKEN FAMILY ROOM
21'-10" X 16'-8"

PANTRY

LIVING ROOM
18'-10" X 13'-4"

FOYER

LAUNDRY

GARAGE
23'-4" X 21'-6"

WALK

DRIVE

FIRST FLOOR

- *Unusual ceiling adds distinctive beauty to unique Hearth Room*

- *Spacious Kitchen features plenty of counter space with central work island*

- *Step down to the sunken Family Room for refreshments at the built-in bar*

- *Fireplace in Family Room flanked by bookcases invites informal relaxation*

- *Sizable Dining Room lends itself for formal entertaining*

- *Fireplace in Hearth Room surrounded by windows for warm cozy atmosphere*

- *Master Bedroom sports his-n-her walk-in closets plus private Bath*

- *Bedrooms two and three share a Bath but have individual basins*

- *Bedroom four has a personal Bath and ample closet space*

Ample Room To Grow As Your Needs Change

PLAN INFO:

First Flr.	1,703 sq. ft.
Second Flr.	1,739 sq. ft.
Bonus Rm.	291 sq. ft.
Garage	3-car
Sq. Footage	3,442 sq. ft.
Foundation	Daylight Bsmt
Bedrooms	Four
Baths	3(Full), 1(Half)

*No materials list available

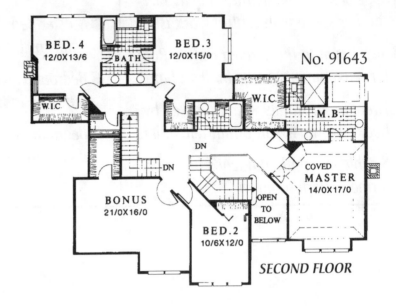

No. 91643

SECOND FLOOR

BED. 4
12/0X13/6

BED. 3
12/0X15/0

BATH

W.I.C.

W.I.C.

M.B

DN

COVED
MASTER
14/0X17/0

OPEN
TO
BELOW

DN

BONUS
21/0X16/0

BED. 2
10/6X12/0

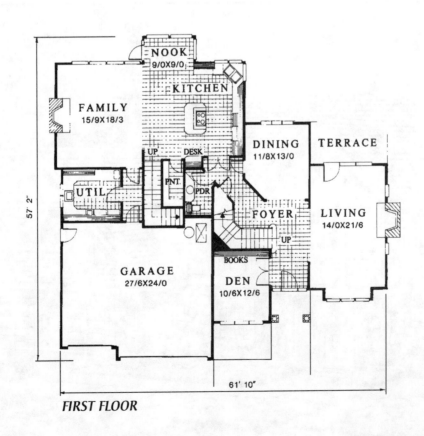

NOOK
9/0X9/0

KITCHEN

FAMILY
15/9X18/3

UP

DESK

PNT

PDR

UTIL

DINING
11/8X13/0

TERRACE

FOYER

LIVING
14/0X21/6

UP

BOOKS

GARAGE
27/6X24/0

DEN
10/6X12/6

57' 2"

61' 10"

FIRST FLOOR

■ Hip-roofed covered porch enters to Foyer with interesting staircase and open floor plan offset by a convenient Powder Room

■ Enormous island Kitchen features large Pantry, well-lighted Nook, cabinets galore and built-in desk for convenient meal-planning

■ Bedroom Three and Bedroom Four both feature plenty of windows, walk-in closet, and each have their own vanity in shared full Bath

■ Fireplaced Family Room flooded with light from extravagant window wall blends to Kitchen area

■ Master Bath with double vanities, shower, tub, and private water closet leads to walk-in closet

■ Upstairs hallway has second staircase for convenience and opens to Foyer below

■ Huge Bonus Room with walk-in closet on second floor gives space for future expansion

Luxury Is Always Popular

PLAN INFO:

First Flr.	2,579 sq. ft.
Second Flr.	997 sq. ft.
Basement	2,579 sq. ft.
Garage/Str.	1,001 sq. ft.
Sq. Footage	3,576 sq. ft.
Foundation	Basement
Bedrooms	Three
Baths	3(Full), 1(Half)

SECOND FLOOR

No. 10531

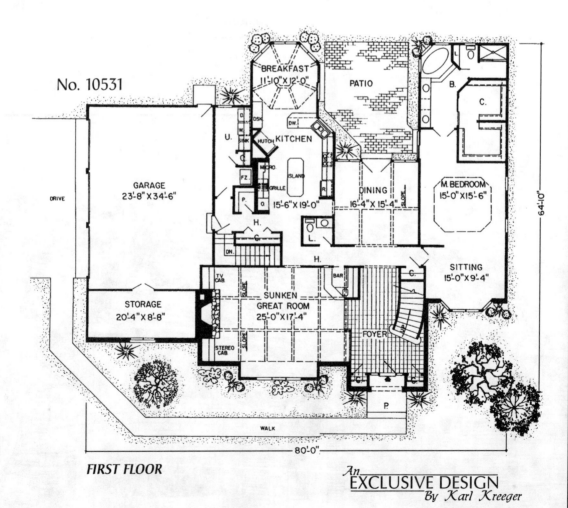

FIRST FLOOR

An
EXCLUSIVE DESIGN
By Karl Kreeger

- Step down to repose in the sunken Great Room featuring a bar, fireplace, and built-in cabinets for TV and stereo

- Fully-equipped Kitchen enjoys a sweeping view of the patio and opens to a stunning Breakfast Nook

- Unusual ceiling treatments in most rooms completes the fabulous impressiveness of this home

- Two additional bedrooms upstairs feature private baths and walk-in closets

- 3-car Garage includes extra storage space

- Bridge-like Balcony on second level overlooks Dining Room to the rear and Foyer on the front

- Luxurious Master Bedroom featuring a sunny Sitting Room with a bay window away from noisy living areas offers quiet solitude

- His-n-her walk-in closets offer plenty of storage space in Master Bedroom

PLAN INFO:

First Flr.	2,230 sq. ft.
Second Flr.	1,204 sq. ft.
Basement	2,230 sq. ft.
Garage	881 sq. ft.
Sq. Footage	3,434 sq. ft.
Foundation	Basement, Crawl space
Bedrooms	Five
Baths	3(Full), 1(Half)

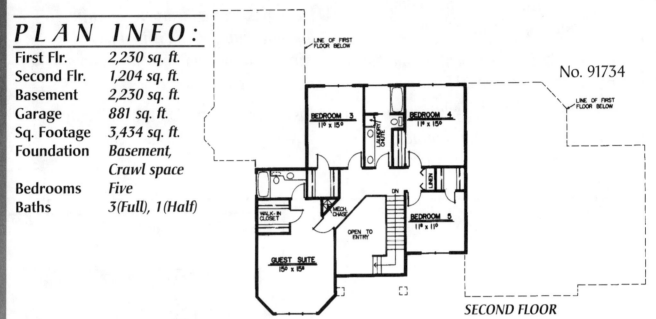

No. 91734

SECOND FLOOR

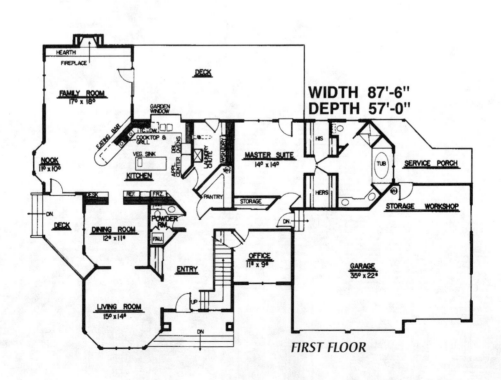

WIDTH 87'-6"
DEPTH 57'-0"

FIRST FLOOR

- *Huge Family Room bathed in beams of light streaming through skylights in high vaulted ceilings*

- *Long hearth stretching across entire far end of Family room draws attention to fireplace*

- *His-n-her walk-in closets providing sound insulation between sleeping area and water closet in Master Suite*

- *Country Kitchen features work island, long eating bar with built-in cooktop*

- *and grill, appliance center, double ovens, trash compactor and more*

- *Sliding door in toilet area maintains privacy in Master Bath, but shower, spa and double vanities are wide open*

- *Home Office located across hall from Master Suite*

- *Steps away to left of the two-story vaulted Entry takes you directly into the Living Room*

Master Bedroom Truly A Sanctuary

PLAN INFO:

First Flr.	*2,864 sq. ft.*
Garage	*607 sq. ft.*
Sq. Footage	*2,864 sq. ft.*
Foundation	*Slab*
Bedrooms	*Four*
Baths	*3(Full), 1(Half)*

No. 10451

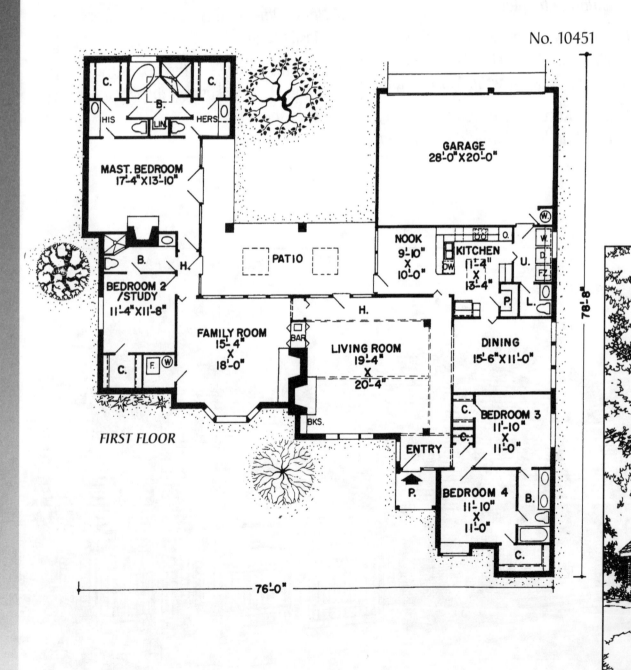

FIRST FLOOR

- *A courtyard effect is created by glassed-in living spaces overlooking the central covered patio with skylights*

- *Dual fireplace in the Family and Living Rooms and a wetbar are the touches that help to set this house apart*

- *An abundance of amenities and easy access to the Dining Room and the Nook area make the Kitchen an efficient, well-appointed room*

- *A secluded sanctuary of your own, the Master Bedroom is a generous space with its charming fireplace, individual dressing rooms, and skylit Bath*

- *Two additional bedrooms have private access to a full double vanity Bath*

$\mathcal{E}$xquisite Architectural $\mathcal{D}$etail
In $\mathcal{A}$ Single-Level $\mathcal{D}$esign

PLAN INFO:

First Flr.	3,292 sq. ft.
Garage	3-car
Sq. Footage	3,292 sq. ft.
Foundation	Slab
Bedrooms	Four
Baths	Three

*No materials list available

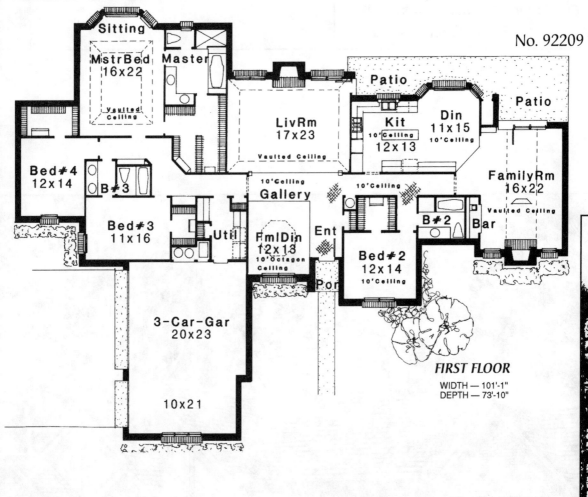

No. 92209

Sitting

MstrBed
16x22

Vaulted Ceiling

Master

Patio

Patio

LivRm
17x23

Vaulted Ceiling

Kit
12x13
10'Ceiling

Din
11x15
10'Ceiling

Bed#4
12x14

B#3

FamilyRm
16x22
Vaulted Ceiling

10'Ceiling

Gallery

10'Ceiling

Bed#3
11x16

Util

FmlDin
12x13
10'Octagon
Ceiling

Ent

B#2

Bar

Bed#2
12x14
10'Ceiling

Por

3-Car-Gar
20x23

10x21

FIRST FLOOR

WIDTH — 101'-1"
DEPTH — 73'-10"

- Walk through formal Entry to impressive Living Room with fireplace wall framed by unusual window display

- Central hallway with 10-foot ceiling escorts one through the Gallery to the quiet sleeping wing

- Master Bedroom with a vaulted ceiling enjoys a comfortable Sitting Area with bay window

- Expansive split walk-in closet in Master Suite connects to Bath with a twin basin vanity

- Two additional bedrooms with walk-in closets share a full Bath

- Just steps away from the Kitchen is the Dining Room formalized with a 10-foot octagon ceiling

- Large island Kitchen flows into Dinette with bay windows for informal family meals

- Family Room sports many amenities such as a wetbar, exclusive access to the backyard patio and uncommon windows framing the fireplace

High Impact Two-Story Angled Design

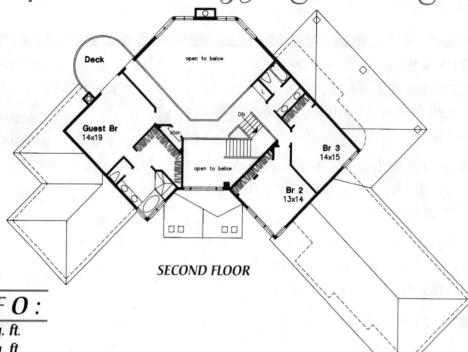

SECOND FLOOR

Deck

Guest Br
14x19

open to below

stor.

DN

Br 3
14x15

open to below

Br 2
13x14

PLAN INFO:

First Flr.	*3,158 sq. ft.*
Second Flr.	*1,374 sq. ft.*
Sq. Footage	*4,532 sq. ft.*
Foundation	*Slab*
Bedrooms	*Four*
Baths	*3(Full), 1(Half)*

*No materials list available

No. 99373

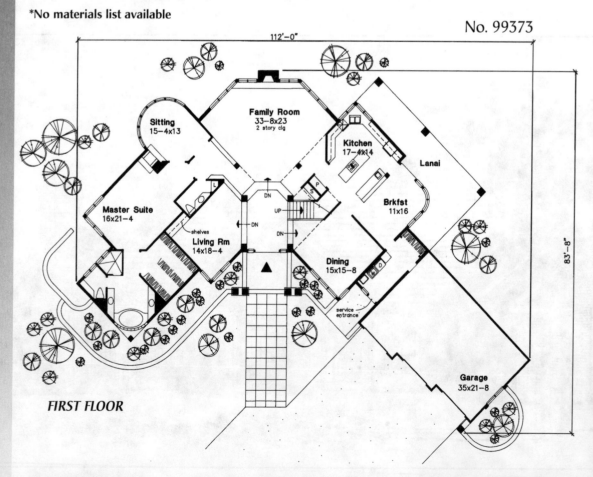

112'-0"

83'-8"

Sitting
15-4x13

Family Room
33-8x23
2 story clg

Kitchen
17-4x14

Lanai

Master Suite
16x21-4

Brkfst
11x16

shelves

Living Rm
14x18-4

DN

UP

DN

DN

Dining
15x15-8

service
entrance

Garage
35x21-8

FIRST FLOOR

- *Gracious living abounds in this high impact home with a two-story entry-way and double doors with a full transom*

- *The fireplace and window walls of the large two-story Family Room can been seen from the entrance*

- *Entertaining is a joy in the gourmet Kitchen and Breakfast area that opens to a covered Lanai*

- *Spacious and unique Master Suite has a semi-circular window wall and see-through fireplace perfect for romantic, cozy evenings*

- *A more than accommodating Guest Suite has its own private deck and a walk-in closet*

- *Two additional bedrooms with ample closet space share a full, double vanity hall Bath*

Skylit Loft Crowns Updated Traditional

PLAN INFO:

First Flr.	1,962 sq. ft.
Second Flr.	870 sq. ft.
Basement	1,962 sq. ft.
Garage	611 sq. ft.
Sq. Footage	2,832 sq. ft.
Foundation	Basement
Bedrooms	Three
Baths	2(Full), 1(Half)

SECOND FLOOR

An EXCLUSIVE DESIGN *By Karl Kreeger*

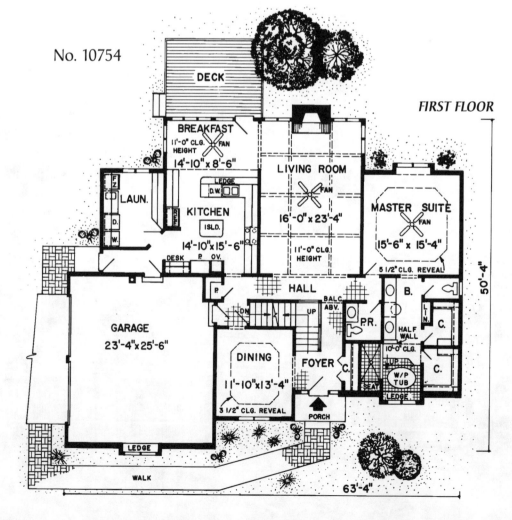

No. 10754

FIRST FLOOR

- Old and new unite with rough-hewn beams that adorn 11 foot high ceilings in the Living Room featuring a large fireplace surrounded by glass

- An efficient and large island Kitchen serves the Dining Room, Breakfast Nook and adjacent deck with ease

- Elegant recessed ceilings grace the Master Suite and the formal Dining Room adding a decorative touch

- A luxurious whirlpool tub, his-n-her walk-in closets, and double vanity add to ultra Master Bath

- Two additional bedrooms and a full bath share the second floor along with a skylit loft

Encompassed By The Warmth Of The Sun

SECOND FLOOR

- open to below
- 7'-0" high
- flue
- DINETTE AND KITCHEN BELOW
- sunken whirlpool tub
- skylights above
- seat
- shower
- up
- skylight above
- columns
- railing
- dn
- BATH
- BATH
- ROOF
- BALCONY
- fin.
- MASTER BED RM 18'-2" x 16'
- WIC
- STUDY, LIBRARY OR BED RM-5 13' x 11'
- cathedral ceiling
- cl.
- DRESSING
- cl
- cl
- ROOF

PLAN INFO:

First Flr.	1,835 sq. ft.
Second Flr.	906 sq. ft.
Lndry/Mdrm.	67 sq. ft.
Garage/Strge.	511 sq. ft.
Sq. Footage	2,808 sq. ft.
Foundation	Bsmt, Crawl space
Bedrooms	Four
Baths	3(Full), 1(Half)

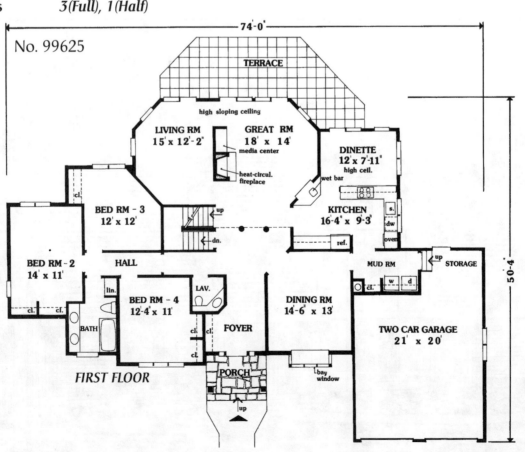

No. 99625

FIRST FLOOR

- 74'-0"
- 50'-4"
- TERRACE
- high sloping ceiling
- LIVING RM 15' x 12'-2"
- GREAT RM 18' x 14'
- media center
- heat-circul. fireplace
- DINETTE 12' x 7'-11" high ceil.
- wet bar
- BED RM - 3 12' x 12'
- up
- KITCHEN 16'-4" x 9'-3"
- s.
- dw
- oven
- BED RM - 2 14' x 11'
- HALL
- dn.
- ref.
- MUD RM
- up
- STORAGE
- lin.
- LAV.
- cl.
- w d
- BED RM - 4 12'-4" x 11'
- DINING RM 14'-6" x 13'
- TWO CAR GARAGE 21' x 20'
- BATH
- cl. cl.
- cl. cl.
- FOYER
- cl.
- PORCH
- up
- bay window

- Spacious Foyer leads to the high ceiling spaces of the Living Room/Great Room, flooded with light through French doors and clerestory windows

- Peninsula counter separates the efficient high ceiling Kitchen from the sunny and cheerful Dinette

- Dramatic balcony overlooks the Great Room below

- First floor sleeping wing contains three bedrooms and a large hall Bath

- Very private second floor Master Bedroom features a cathedral ceiling, large walk-in closet and a dressing alcove

- Luxurious Master Bath contains two sinks, a sunken whirlpool tub, a large shower stall and a separate toilet compartment

Towering Arch Graces Entry Of Spacious Design

PLAN INFO:

First Flr.	1,688 sq. ft.
Second Flr.	1,583 sq. ft.
Basement	1,688 sq. ft.
Garage	814 sq. ft.
Sq. Footage	3,271 sq. ft.
Foundation	Basement
Bedrooms	Four
Baths	2(Full), 1(Half)

No. 10781

spa
UP
linen
Dressing Rm.
Sitting 11 x 8
pan vault
lin.
linen
Br 3 11-7 x 12-4
Br 4 11-4 x 13-4
MBr 1 14-8 x 17-4
pan vault
DN
foyer below
Br 2 13-8 x 12-4

SECOND FLOOR

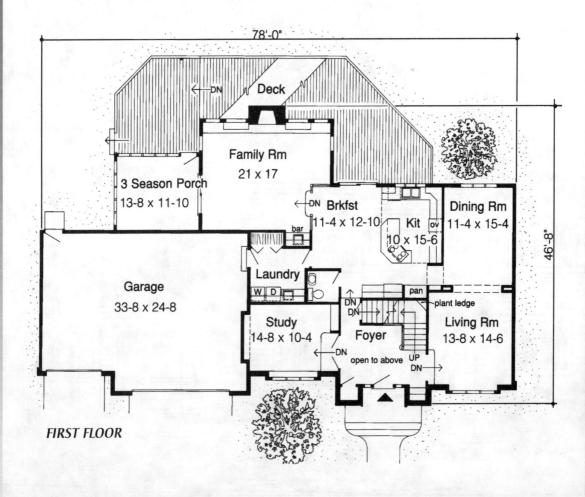

78'-0"
46'-8"

DN
Deck
Family Rm 21 x 17
3 Season Porch 13-8 x 11-10
DN Brkfst 11-4 x 12-10
bar
Kit 10 x 15-6
ov
Dining Rm 11-4 x 15-4
Laundry
W D
Garage 33-8 x 24-8
Study 14-8 x 10-4
DN
DN
Foyer
pan
plant ledge
Living Rm 13-8 x 14-6
open to above
UP
DN
DN

FIRST FLOOR

- *Towering arch provides intriguing entry for sun-filled family home*

- *Step inside the soaring Foyer with sunken Study and Living Room on either side*

- *Past the powder room, an open feeling is accentuated by glass walls of the Breakfast, Family, and Dining Rooms overlooking backyard*

- *Off the fireplaced Family Room, a Three-Season Porch opens to angular deck wrapping around active areas*

- *Efficient Kitchen with stovetop island flows into Breakfast Room and ensures ease in mealtime service*

- *Enjoy view overlooking Foyer below from balcony on second floor*

- *Grandiose Master Suite occupies entire wing and features many luxurious amenities*

- *Master Suite also includes two walk-in closets, Dressing Room, double vanities, and Sitting Room*

A *Master Suite You'll Love*

PLAN INFO:

First Flr.	*3,511 sq. ft.*
Second Flr.	*711 sq. ft.*
Garage	*841 sq. ft.*
Sq. Footage	*4,222 sq. ft.*
Foundation	*Basement*
Bedrooms	*Three*
Baths	*2(Full), 2(Half)*

SECOND FLOOR

No. 99240

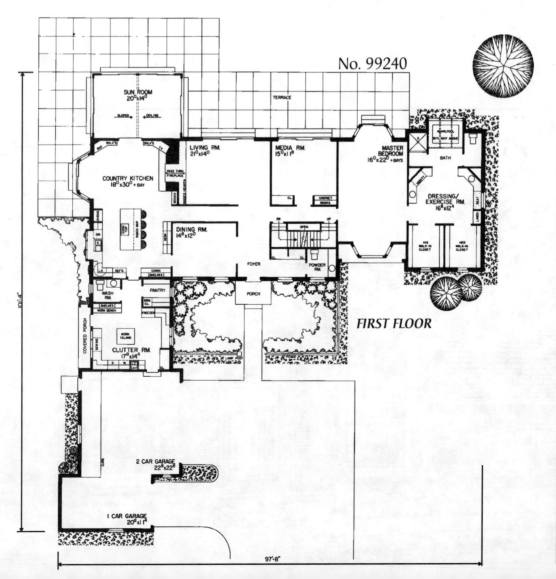

FIRST FLOOR

- *A low profile for this classic home disguises the splendid interior layout*

- *Choose a Southern exposure for passive solar benefits in the large Sun Room which features a cathedral ceiling and floor-to-ceiling windows*

- *Enormous country Kitchen with a wonderful window bay for informal dining and a fireplace with ample room for a couple of comfortable fire side rocking chairs*

- *Ease in cooking is the rule with a center range, double wall ovens and miles of counter space in the Kitchen*

- *Extras include a Clutter Room off the Kitchen and a Media Room with direct access to an expansive Terrace*

- *Double-sided fireplace opens the Kitchen to the Living Room with a wall-length raised hearth as an added accent*

- *Palatial Master Suite includes an ultra Bath with a dressing/exercise area and large his-n-her walk-in closets*

- *Two additional bedrooms and a full Bath optional located on the second floor*

Stone & Stucco Give This House Class

No. 10540

LOWER FLOOR

PLAN INFO:

Main Flr.	*2,473 sq. ft.*
Lower Flr.	*1,624 sq. ft.*
Basement	*732 sq. ft.*
Garage/Str.	*732 sq. ft.*
Sq. Footage	*4,097 sq. ft.*
Foundation	*Basement*
Bedrooms	*Four*
Baths	*Three*

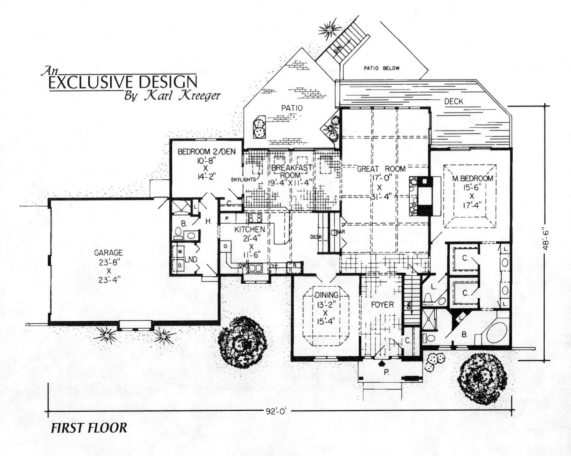

An
EXCLUSIVE DESIGN
By Karl Kreeger

FIRST FLOOR

- *Majestic Foyer creates a stunning first impression and flows into the formal Dining Room and Great Room*

- *A stone fireplace, built-in wetbar and access to a spacious deck add to the convenience and luxury of the Great Room*

- *Large Recreation Room on the lower level includes a built-in wetbar and a fireplace*

- *Dream Kitchen includes a peninsula extension counter, built-in planning center, double sink and an abundance of counter and storage space*

- *A beamed Breakfast Room includes natural illumination from skylights and access to the patio, providing a sunny way to start the morning*

- *Huge Master Suite is equipped with a dressing room with his-n-her walk-in closets and a separate whirlpool Bath*

- *Two additional bedrooms, both with walk-in closets, share a full hall Bath*

Grand Room Designs & An Elegant Facade Spell Luxury

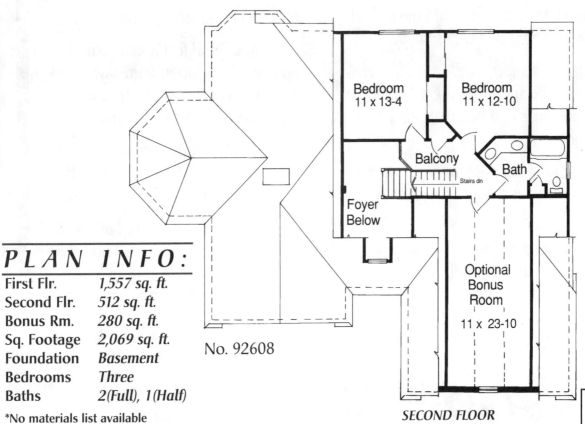

PLAN INFO:

First Flr.	*1,557 sq. ft.*
Second Flr.	*512 sq. ft.*
Bonus Rm.	*280 sq. ft.*
Sq. Footage	*2,069 sq. ft.*
Foundation	*Basement*
Bedrooms	*Three*
Baths	*2(Full), 1(Half)*

*No materials list available

No. 92608

SECOND FLOOR

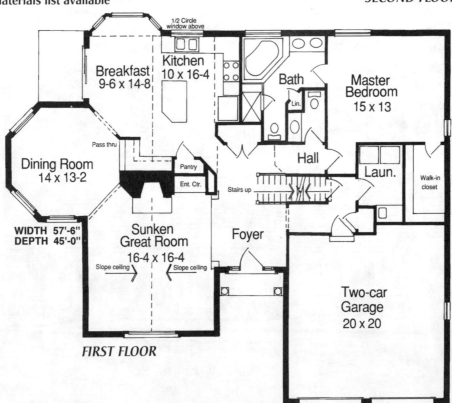

FIRST FLOOR

- *Naturally lighted by an arched dormer window, the two-story Foyer welcomes guests*

- *A grand, sunken Great Room has a cathedral ceiling and a stone fireplace*

- *Dramatic angular views can be seen from the octagonal shaped formal Dining Room*

- *Central work island, built-in pantry, abundant counter and cabinet space,* and a sunny Breakfast Room with outdoor access, make this Kitchen outstanding

- *Perfect for empty nesters or families with teenagers, the first floor Master Suite allows parents complete privacy*

- *Three additional bedrooms, located on the second floor, share a full hall Bath and a Bonus Room*

*T*wo Story *F*oyer Well-*L*it *B*y Skylights

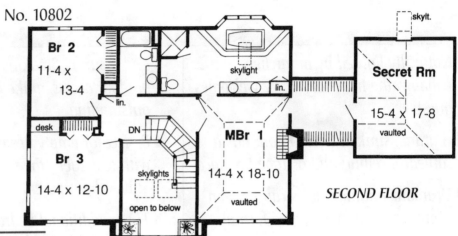

No. 10802

SECOND FLOOR

- Br 2 — 11-4 x 13-4
- lin.
- desk
- Br 3 — 14-4 x 12-10
- DN
- skylights
- open to below
- skylight
- lin.
- MBr 1 — 14-4 x 18-10
- vaulted
- skylt.
- Secret Rm — 15-4 x 17-8
- vaulted

PLAN INFO:

First Flr.	*1,522 sq. ft.*
Second Flr.	*1,545 sq. ft.*
Basement	*1,500 sq. ft.*
Garage	*3-car*
Sq. Footage	*3,067 sq. ft.*
Foundation	*Basement*
Bedrooms	*Three*
Baths	*2(Full), 1(Half)*

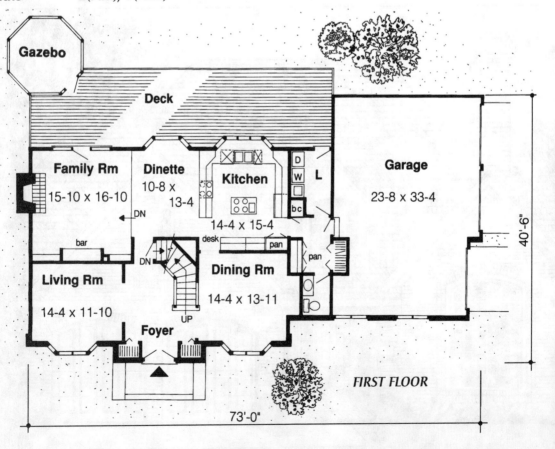

- Gazebo
- Deck
- Family Rm — 15-10 x 16-10
- Dinette — 10-8 x 13-4
- Kitchen — 14-4 x 15-4
- D W L bc
- Garage — 23-8 x 33-4
- bar
- DN
- DN
- desk
- pan
- pan
- Living Rm — 14-4 x 11-10
- Dining Rm — 14-4 x 13-11
- UP
- Foyer
- 40'-6"
- 73'-0"

FIRST FLOOR

- Central Foyer creates dazzling impression on all who enter with its towering ceilings pierced by skylights and angular staircase

- Fireplaced Master Suite with unique ceiling lines incorporates Bath, walk-in closet, and sole access to skylit "Secret" Room

- Two additional Bedrooms on second floor provide ample room for a growing family

- Enter the home via an ample Laundry Room from the 3-car Garage

- Utilize the elegant Dining Room and formal Living Room, overlooking the front yard, for entertaining

- Retire to the sunken Family Room with fireplace, built-in bar and bookcases for brief repose from busy routines

- Enjoy informal barbeques on the rear deck easily accessible from the Family Room

- Island Kitchen designed for modern family includes pantry and desk for convenient meal planning

$\mathcal{D}$esigned For Simple, Yet Elegant Living

SECOND FLOOR

PLAN INFO:

First Flr.	1,807 sq. ft.
Second Flr.	1,359 sq. ft.
Basement	1,807 sq. ft.
Garage	576 sq. ft.
Sq. Footage	3,166 sq. ft.
Foundation	Basement
Bedrooms	Three
Baths	3 (Full), 1 (Half)

No. 20353

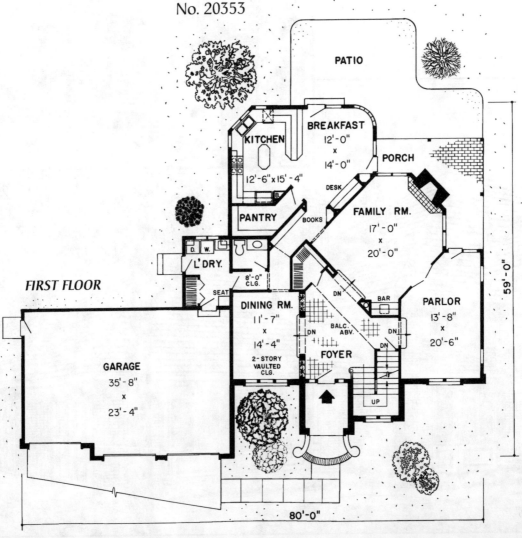

FIRST FLOOR

- *Magnificent home creates formidable impression after dark*

- *Numerous arched windows glowing with light extend warm welcome to visitors*

- *Inside find skylights, vaulted ceilings, and multiple levels rendering an interior equally as exciting as exterior*

- *Step from the skylit central Foyer into the vaulted Dining Room, cozy Parlor, and Family Room with built-in bar*

- *Walk down the book-lined hallway to the island Kitchen, Breakfast Nook with built-in desk and unique curved glass wall overlooking backyard patio*

- *Master Suite complemented by elegant pan vaulted ceiling, fireplace for romantic evenings, private deck, and garden spa*

- *At either end of the upstairs Balcony, find bedrooms each with individual baths and spacious closets*

Gable And Glass Grace Facade

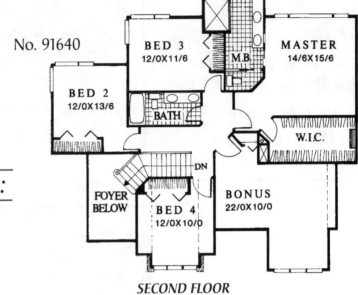

No. 91640

BED 3
12/0X11/6

MASTER
14/6X15/6

M.B.

BED 2
12/0X13/6

BATH

W.I.C.

FOYER
BELOW

DN

BONUS
22/0X10/0

BED 4
12/0X10/0

SECOND FLOOR

PLAN INFO:

First Flr.	1,540 sq. ft.
Second Flr.	1,178 sq. ft.
Bonus Room	222 sq. ft.
Sq. Footage	2,718 sq. ft.
Foundation	Post & Beam
Bedrooms	Four
Baths	2(Full), 1(Half)

*No materials list available

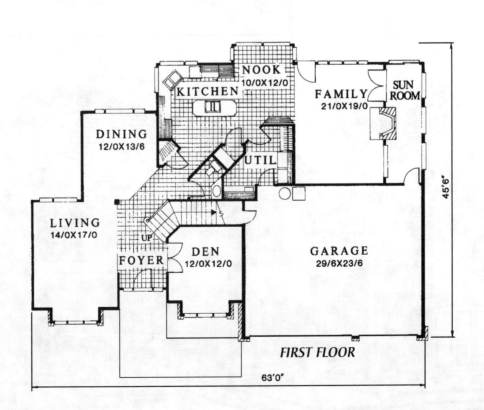

NOOK
10/0X12/0

KITCHEN

FAMILY
21/0X19/0

SUN
ROOM

DINING
12/0X13/6

UTIL

LIVING
14/0X17/0

UP

FOYER

DEN
12/0X12/0

GARAGE
29/6X23/6

45'6"

FIRST FLOOR

63'0"

DESIGN 91640

- *A stunning blend of Traditional and Contemporary styles create this gracious home*

- *A unique Sun Room opens directly into the Family Room and provides access to an over-sized three car Garage*

- *A modern wrap-around Kitchen with a central island commands the ground floor*

- *Entertaining is both enjoyable and easy because of the design of the Living and Dining Rooms*

- *The imposing Master Suite includes an elegant Bath and a large walk-in closet*

- *Three nice size, additional bedrooms share a full hall Bath*

Welcoming Foyer Makes A Lasting Impression

PLAN INFO:

First Flr.	2,419 sq. ft.
Second Flr.	926 sq. ft.
Basement	2,419 sq. ft.
Garage	615 sq. ft.
Sq. Footage	3,345 sq. ft.
Foundation	Basement
Bedrooms	Four
Baths	3(Full), 1(Half)

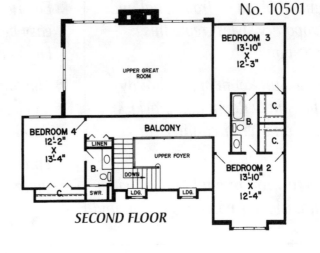

No. 10501

SECOND FLOOR

An
EXCLUSIVE DESIGN
By Karl Kreeger

FIRST FLOOR

- Massive Foyer makes a wonderful first impression in this tastefully appointed design

- Fantastic Great Room enlarged by a wrap-around deck and highlighted by a fireplace, built-in shelves and a wetbar

- An octagonal Morning Room and a central work island make the Kitchen unique and convenient

- Dinner parties will be successful in the formal Dining Room featuring a distinctive box bay window

- Inviting Master Suite equipped with a spacious dressing area and a separate and luxurious Bath

- A Balcony overlooks the Great Room and the open Foyer and provides access to three bedrooms and two full Bathrooms

Columned Porch Provides A Stately Entrance

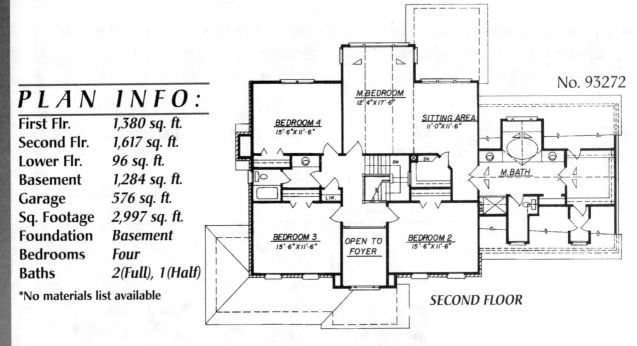

No. 93272

PLAN INFO:

First Flr.	1,380 sq. ft.
Second Flr.	1,617 sq. ft.
Lower Flr.	96 sq. ft.
Basement	1,284 sq. ft.
Garage	576 sq. ft.
Sq. Footage	2,997 sq. ft.
Foundation	Basement
Bedrooms	Four
Baths	2(Full), 1(Half)

*No materials list available

SECOND FLOOR

FIRST FLOOR

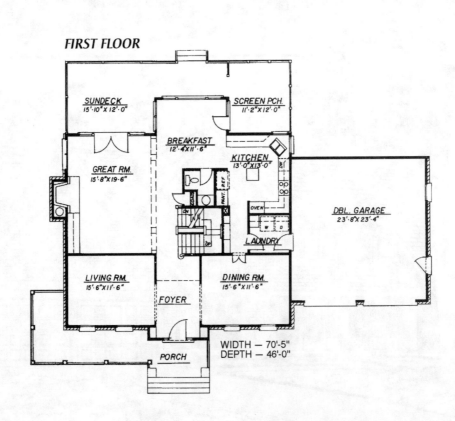

WIDTH — 70'-5"
DEPTH — 46'-0"

■ *Contrast of the spectacular stone entryway with a wrap-a-round porch and wood siding make this elegant, yet efficient home special*

■ *Formal Dining Room and Living Room flank the grand two-story Foyer that leads past wide, landing stairs into the Great Room*

■ *Grand fireplace, with built-ins and French doors to the Sundeck in the Great Room, offers a wonderful gathering place in all kinds of weather*

■ *Efficient, U-shaped Kitchen ideal for any demanding cook with a corner sink, work island, built-in pantry,* loads of counter space and cabinets as well as easy access to the Breakfast area, Dining Room and Laundry

■ *All glass Breakfast Nook with direct access to a Screen Porch is a wonderful way to start the day*

■ *Spacious Master Bedroom Suite has a private Sitting Area, three walk-in closets, and a tremendous private Bath with an oval window tub, two vanities, vaulted ceiling and loads of storage space*

■ *Three nice sized additional bedrooms share a full hall Bath*

$\mathcal{H}$eavenly Kitchen $\mathcal{F}$or The Gourmet Of The House

PLAN INFO:

First Flr.	*3,307 sq. ft.*
Second Flr.	*837 sq. ft.*
Porch/Patio	*382 sq. ft.*
Garage	*646 sq. ft.*
Sq. Footage	*4,144 sq. ft.*
Foundation	*Slab*
Bedrooms	*Five*
Baths	*4(Full), 1(Half)*

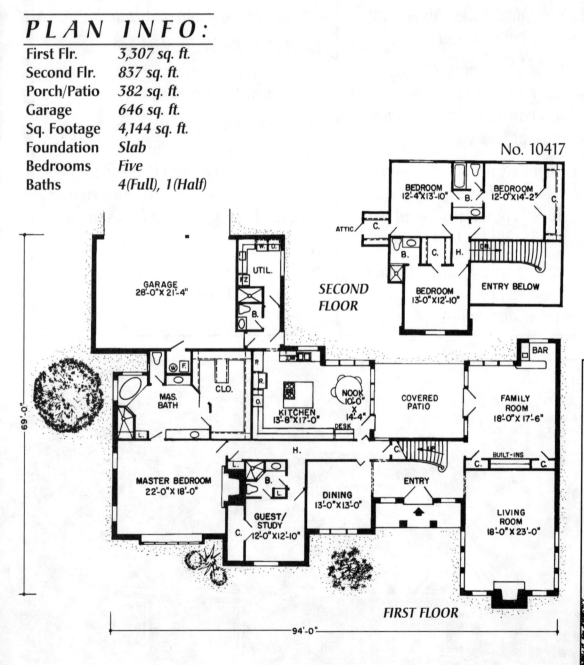

No. 10417

GARAGE
28'-0" X 21'-4"

UTIL.

B.

SECOND FLOOR

ATTIC

C.

BEDROOM
12'-4" X 13'-10"

B.

BEDROOM
12'-0" X 14'-2"

C.

B.

C.

H.

BEDROOM
13'-0" X 12'-10"

ENTRY BELOW

W. F.

CLO.

P.

R.

D.

DW

KITCHEN
13'-8" X 17'-0"

NOOK
10'-0" X 14'-4"

DESK

COVERED PATIO

BAR

FAMILY ROOM
18'-0" X 17'-6"

MAS. BATH

L.

L.

H.

C.

BUILT-INS

C.

C.

MASTER BEDROOM
22'-0" X 18'-0"

L.

B.

L.

DINING
13'-0" X 13'-0"

ENTRY

LIVING ROOM
18'-0" X 23'-0"

GUEST/ STUDY
12'-0" X 12'-10"

C.

69'-0"

94'-0"

FIRST FLOOR

- ■ *Kitchen affords 60 square feet of counter space*

- ■ *Step-saving cooking island adds more culinary area*

- ■ *Windowed Eating Nook and nearby patio extend convenience and brilliance to spacious Kitchen*

- ■ *Large Master Bedroom with walk-in closet situated away from noisy living areas*

- ■ *Study easily doubles as Guest Room*

- ■ *Ten-foot ceilings throughout lower level*

- ■ *Nine-foot ceilings upstairs add to spaciousness created by large rooms*

- ■ *Double doors usher you into two-story Entry with staircase curving gently to second-level rooms*

Country Touches Throughout
This Modern Design

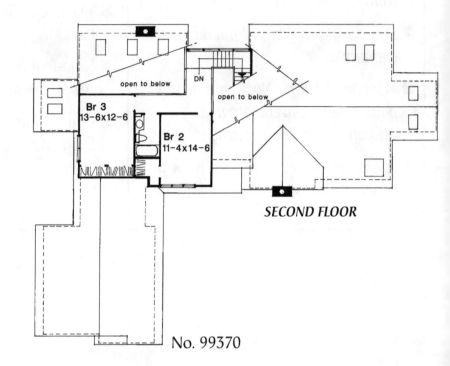

SECOND FLOOR

Br 3
13-6x12-6

Br 2
11-4x14-6

open to below

DN

open to below

No. 99370

PLAN INFO:

First Flr.	*2,389 sq. ft.*
Second Flr.	*673 sq. ft.*
Basement	*1,348 sq. ft.*
Garage	*2-car*
Sq. Footage	*3,062 sq. ft.*
Foundation	*Basement*
Bedrooms	*Three*
Baths	*Three*

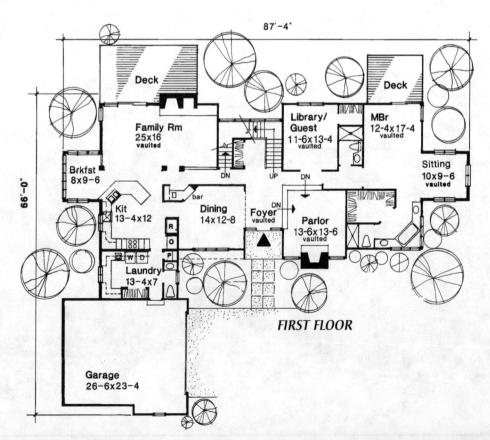

87'-4"

66'-0"

Deck

Deck

Family Rm
25x16
vaulted

Library/
Guest
11-6x13-4
vaulted

MBr
12-4x17-4
vaulted

Brkfst
8x9-6

Sitting
10x9-6
vaulted

Kit
13-4x12

DN   UP   DN

bar

Dining
14x12-8

Foyer
vaulted

DN

Parlor
13-6x13-6
vaulted

R
O
P

W D

Laundry
13-4x7

FIRST FLOOR

Garage
26-6x23-4

- *Front projections and gables give a custom look and the special interior finishes and flourishes are plentiful*

- *Impressive Foyer with a view through to the backyard features an angular staircase*

- *Invite guests to step down into your vaulted Parlor*

- *Uniquely shaped Kitchen includes many modern conveniences*

- *Breakfast alcove juts out between the island Kitchen and Family Room for early morning repast*

- *Vast Family Room with a vaulted ceiling, fireplace, and wetbar offers the perfect place for entertaining*

- *Library located in quiet side of house can double as a Guest Room with ample closet space*

- *Master Suite has an adjoining Sitting Room, secluded luxurious Bath and a walk-in wardrobe*

- *Second floor houses two additional bedrooms with individual closets and an adjoining Bath*

Stately Stucco Masterpiece You'll Love

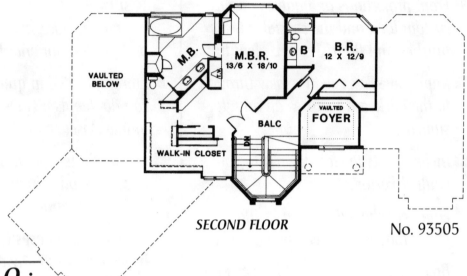

SECOND FLOOR

No. 93505

PLAN INFO:

First Flr.	*2,125 sq. ft.*
Second Flr.	*1095 sq. ft.*
Basement	*2,125 sq. ft.*
Garage	*3-car*
Sq. Footage	*3,220 sq. ft.*
Foundation	*Bsmt, Slab*
	Crawl space
Bedrooms	*Four*
Baths	*Three*

FIRST FLOOR

■ *Old world touches manifested in towering palladium windows, a columned entry, and a curving staircase*

■ *Vaulted Foyer opens to the Living Room featuring huge expanses of glass that take advantage of the rear view*

■ *Wide open Kitchen with an efficient layout flows into the Family Room*

■ *Overlook staircase and vaulted Foyer from the Balcony on the second floor*

■ *Enjoy direct access to your backyard deck via the Family Room with a vaulted ceiling, fireplace, and wetbar*

■ *Marvelous Master Suite beckons occupants to luxuriate in first-class accommodations*

■ *Design offers three additional bedrooms for the remainder of family*

■ *Formal Dining Room embellished with a built-in buffet and conveniently located adjacent to the Kitchen*

*T*raditional Elements In *A* Modern *D*esign

PLAN INFO:

First Flr.	*3,438 sq. ft.*
Garage	*610 sq. ft.*
Sq. Footage	*3,438 sq. ft.*
Foundation	*Slab*
Bedrooms	*Four*
Baths	*3(Full), 1(Half)*

No. 10749

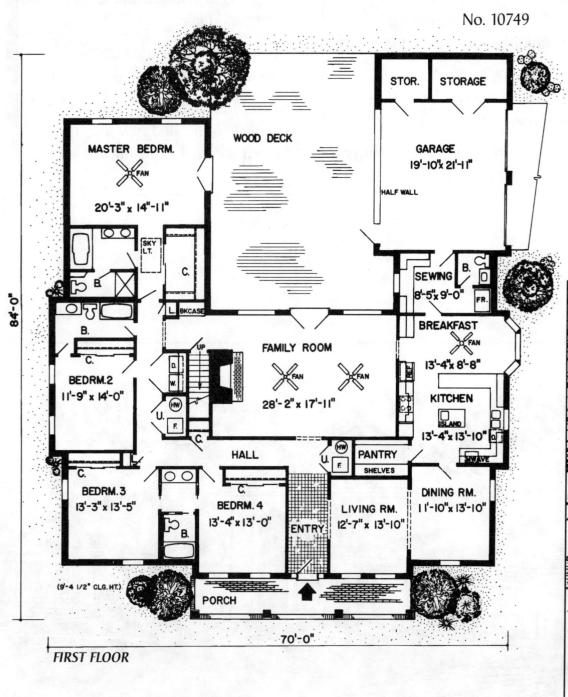

STOR.   STORAGE

GARAGE
19'-10" x 21'-11"

HALF WALL

MASTER BEDRM.
FAN
20'-3" x 14"-11"

WOOD DECK

SKY LT.

C.

B.

SEWING
8'-5" x 9'-0"

B.

FR.

BREAKFAST
FAN
13'-4" x 8'-8"

BKCASE

B.

C.

BEDRM.2
11'-9" x 14'-0"

UP

D.
W.

HW

U.

F.

C.

FAMILY ROOM
FAN   FAN
28'-2" x 17'-11"

REF.

KITCHEN
ISLAND
13'-4" x 13'-10"

HALL

HW
U.
F.

PANTRY
SHELVES

MWAVE

C.

BEDRM.3
13'-3" x 13'-5"

C.

BEDRM.4
13'-4" x 13'-0"

B.

ENTRY

LIVING RM.
12'-7" x 13'-10"

DINING RM.
11'-10" x 13'-10"

(9'-4 1/2" CLG. HT.)

PORCH

84'-0"

70'-0"

FIRST FLOOR

- *Classic elements from yesteryear: columned porch, high ceilings with cooling fans and loads of built-in storage make this home special*

- *Distinctive interior plan uses a contemporary sleeping wing and central location for family living*

- *Formal and family areas are served with equal ease from the conveniently placed island Kitchen*

- *A massive fireplace is included in the Family Room, which overlooks the outdoor wood deck*

- *Every bedroom adjoins a bath, and the skylit Master Suite enjoys access to the deck*

Design Changes As Your Needs Change

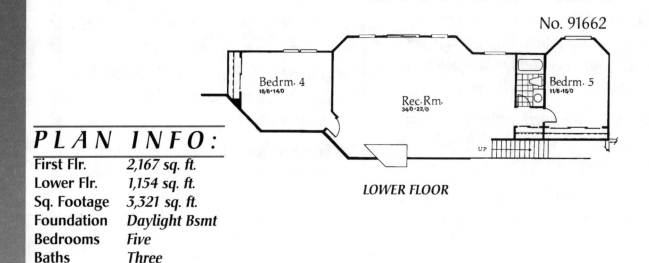

No. 91662

Bedrm. 4
16/6·14/0

Rec·Rm.
34/0·22/0

Bedrm. 5
11/6·15/0

UP

LOWER FLOOR

PLAN INFO:

First Flr.	*2,167 sq. ft.*
Lower Flr.	*1,154 sq. ft.*
Sq. Footage	*3,321 sq. ft.*
Foundation	*Daylight Bsmt*
Bedrooms	*Five*
Baths	*Three*

*No materials list available

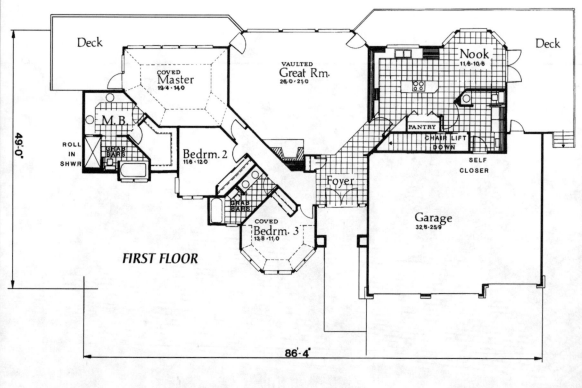

Deck

COVED
Master
19/4·14/0

VAULTED
Great Rm.
26/0·21/0

Nook
11/6·10/6

Deck

M. B.

ROLL
IN
SHWR

GRAB
BARS

Bedrm. 2
11/6·12/0

PANTRY

CHAIR LIFT
DOWN

SELF
CLOSER

GRAB
BARS

Foyer

COVED
Bedrm. 3
13/6·11/0

Garage
32/6·25/9

49'-0"

86'-4"

FIRST FLOOR

- *Wider hallways and doors, specially designed baths and kitchen, and low profile thresholds make accommodation for the permanently or temporary disabled possible*

- *A vaulted ceiling adds to the spacious feeling in the Great Room which is also enhanced by a fireplace*

- *Double sink, cook top island, built-in pantry and a sunny Breakfast Nook are just some of the many amenities gracing the Kitchen*

- *A wall of windows, access to an outdoor deck, a handicap Bath and a large walk-in closet add pleasure and convenience to the Master Suite*

- *Two additional main floor bedrooms share a full, double vanity hall Bath*

- *A chair lift to the lower floor makes getting there easy*

- *Large and expansive Recreation Room on the lower level is flanked by two more bedrooms and a full hall Bath*

Exquisite Tudor For The Nineties

PLAN INFO:

First Flr.	2,476 sq. ft.
Second Flr.	1,397 sq. ft.
Basement	2,375 sq. ft.
Garage	701 sq. ft.
Sq. Footage	3,873 sq. ft.
Foundation	Basement
Bedrooms	Three
Baths	3(Full), 1(Half)

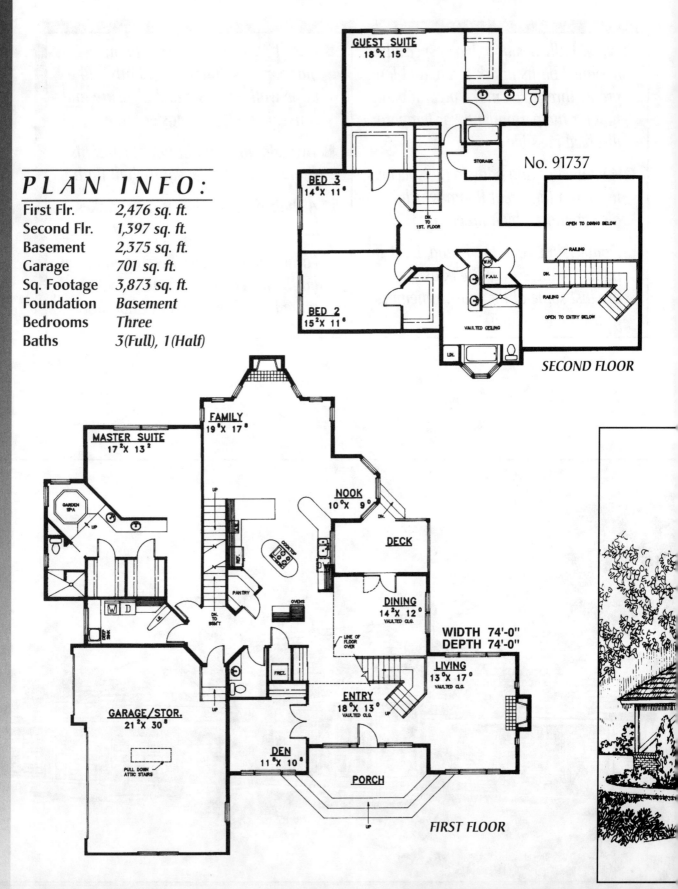

No. 91737

GUEST SUITE
18⁰ X 15⁰

BED 3
14⁸ X 11⁸

BED 2
15² X 11⁸

STORAGE

OPEN TO DINING BELOW

RAILING

DN. TO 1ST. FLOOR

W.H.
F.A.U.

DN.

RAILING

OPEN TO ENTRY BELOW

VAULTED CEILING

LIN.

SECOND FLOOR

FAMILY
19⁸ X 17⁸

MASTER SUITE
17² X 13²

GARDEN SPA

NOOK
10⁰ X 9⁰

DECK

DINING
14² X 12⁰
VAULTED CLG.

PANTRY

COOKTOP

REF.

OVENS

DN. TO BSM'T.

W D

DISP. SNK.

FREZ.

LINE OF FLOOR OVER

WIDTH 74'-0"
DEPTH 74'-0"

LIVING
13⁰ X 17⁰
VAULTED CLG.

ENTRY
18⁰ X 13⁰
VAULTED CLG.

GARAGE/STOR.
21² X 30⁸

PULL DOWN ATTIC STAIRS

DEN
11⁸ X 10⁸

PORCH

FIRST FLOOR

- ■ Expansive Entry area has a vaulted ceiling and stairway that leads to a second floor landing with a railed balcony

- ■ Fireplace centered on the far wall in the grand formal Living Room is accented by a vaulted ceiling

- ■ Formal Dining Room features another vaulted ceiling and balcony with access to an outdoor deck for elegant entertaining

- ■ Large Kitchen loaded with modern conveniences such as double ovens, island with cooktop and grill, and a walk-in pantry

- ■ Spacious and unique Master Suite with his-n-her walk-in closets, double vanity, and a beautiful garden spa tub

- ■ Two upstairs bedrooms share a bathroom with a bathing nook while the third has its own private Bathroom and may double as a Guest Suite

*S*unny *A*tmosphere *B*rightens *T*his *P*lan

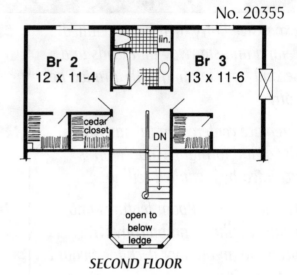

No. 20355

PLAN INFO:

First Flr.	2,424 sq. ft.
Second Flr.	638 sq. ft.
Basement	2,207 sq. ft.
Garage	768 sq. ft.
Sq. Footage	3,062 sq. ft.
Foundation	Basement
Bedrooms	Three
Baths	Three

SECOND FLOOR

Br 2
12 x 11-4

Br 3
13 x 11-6

cedar closet

lin.

DN

open to below ledge

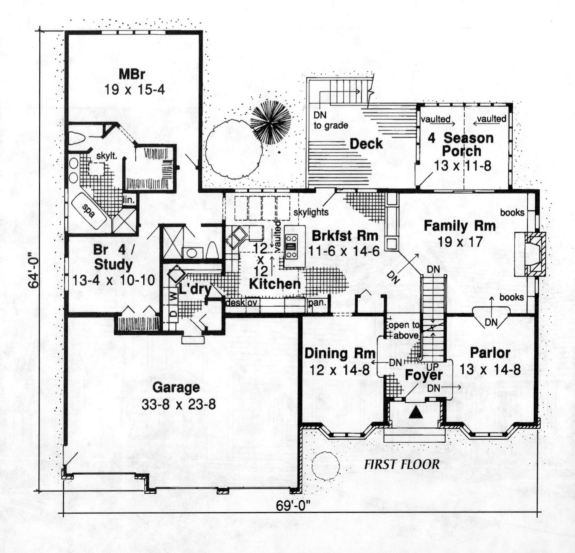

MBr
19 x 15-4

skylt.

spa

lin.

Br 4 /
Study
13-4 x 10-10

L'dry

DW

desk ov

Kitchen

12 x 12

vaulted

Brkfst Rm
11-6 x 14-6

pan.

DN to grade

Deck

skylights

4 Season Porch
13 x 11-8

vaulted   vaulted

Family Rm
19 x 17

books

books

DN

DN

open to above

DN

DN

Dining Rm
12 x 14-8

UP

Foyer

DN

Parlor
13 x 14-8

Garage
33-8 x 23-8

64'-0"

69'-0"

FIRST FLOOR

- Sunken bay-windowed Dining Room and Parlor flank gracious Foyer

- Well-appointed island Kitchen with vaulted ceiling located at rear of house

- Partake of morning coffee in the bright Breakfast Room near Kitchen

- Step down to the quaint Family Room with book-lined walls and cozy fireplace

- Retire to the four-season porch perfect for informal gatherings

- Tucked behind the Garage find a fourth Bedroom with full Bath

- Elegant Master Bedroom complete with skylit Bath featuring garden tub and double vanities

- Ascend central staircase to find two more bedrooms adorned with individual large walk-in closets

- Other amenities upstairs include a full Bath and cedar closet for out-of-season storage

Relax And Enjoy This
Magnificent Stucco Design

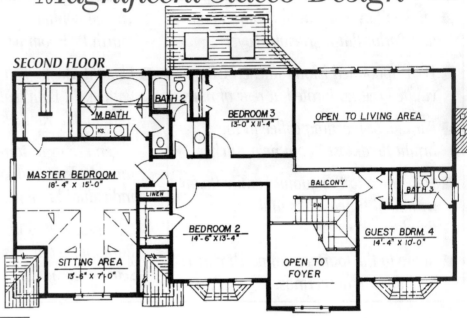

SECOND FLOOR

BATH 2

M. BATH
KS.

BEDROOM 3
13'-0" X 11'-4"

OPEN TO LIVING AREA

MASTER BEDROOM
18'-4" X 15'-0"

BALCONY

DN

BATH 3

LINEN

BEDROOM 2
14'-6" X 13'-4"

OPEN TO FOYER

GUEST BDRM. 4
14'-4" X 10'-0"

SITTING AREA
13'-6" X 7'-0"

PLAN INFO:

First Flr.	*1,695 sq. ft.*
Second Flr.	*1,620 sq. ft.*
Basement	*1,695 sq. ft.*
Garage	*572 sq. ft.*
Sq. Footage	*3,315 sq. ft.*
Foundation	*Basement*
Bedrooms	*Four*
Baths	*3(Full), 1(Half)*

*No materials list available

No. 93273

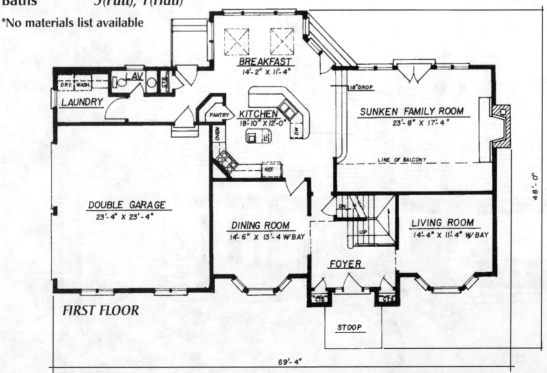

DRY. WASH

LAV

CTR.

BREAKFAST
14'-2" X 11'-4"

18" DROP

LAUNDRY

PANTRY

KITCHEN
18'-10" X 12'-0"

OVEN

DW

SUNKEN FAMILY ROOM
23'-8" X 17'-4"

LINE OF BALCONY

REF.

DOUBLE GARAGE
23'-4" X 23'-4"

DINING ROOM
14'-6" X 13'-4" W/ BAY

DN

UP

LIVING ROOM
14'-4" X 11'-4" W/ BAY

FOYER

CTR.

CTR.

FIRST FLOOR

STOOP

48'-0"

69'-4"

■ *Quiet elegance greets one and all into this classic home with a two-story, open Foyer leading to the formal Living Room and Dining Room high-lighted with bay windows*

■ *Expansive sunken Family Room offers comfort and convenience with its large, hearth fireplace, a wall of glass leading outdoors and its proximity from the kitchen*

■ *Two work islands, one with a snack bar in the Kitchen and a walk-in pantry, make this well-appointed room even more efficient*

■ *Bright and sunny Breakfast area offers a cheerful way to start the day with skylights, windows on three sides and easy access to the outdoors*

■ *Comfortable Master Bedroom Suite featuring views on three sides, contains a unique Sitting Area, a double walk-in closet, and a private Bath with window tub and double vanity*

■ *Three additional bedrooms, one with a private bath, have ample closet space*

Master Suite Dominates Second Floor

PLAN INFO:

First Flr.	1,669 sq. ft.
Second Flr.	1,450 sq. ft.
Basement	1,653 sq. ft.
Garage	823 sq. ft.
Sq. Footage	3,119 sq. ft.
Foundation	Basement
Bedrooms	Three
Baths	2(Full), 1(Half)

No. 10533

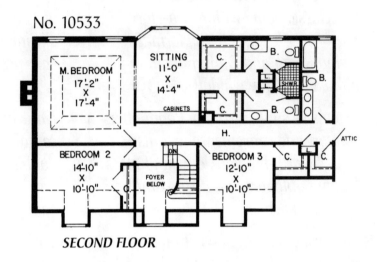

SECOND FLOOR

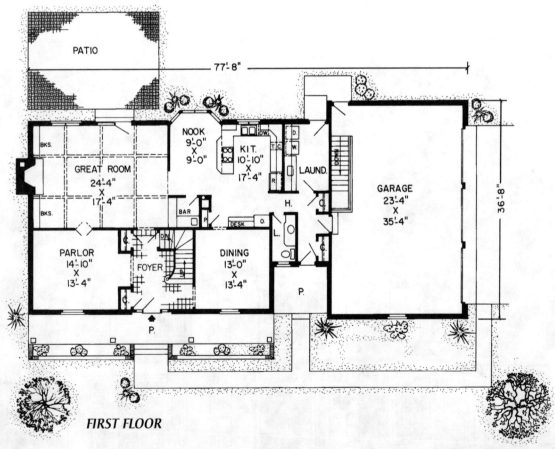

FIRST FLOOR

An
EXCLUSIVE DESIGN
By Karl Kreeger

- *Master Bedroom features a private Sitting Room dominated by a bright bay window for quiet time*

- *Master Bath includes his-n-her walk-in closets, basins, and commodes*

- *Two additional bedrooms on second floor include ample closet space and share a Bath*

- *Formal Dining Room has easy access to well-planned Kitchen*

- *U-shaped Kitchen overlooks pleasant Breakfast Nook*

- *Great Room includes beamed ceiling and bookcase-framed fireplace for welcoming warmth*

- *Relax on patio overlooking backyard on cool evenings*

- *Entrance from 3-car Garage leads to convenient half-Bath and Laundry Room*

*A*n Open Concept Floor Plan
Makes For Convenient Living

PLAN INFO:

First Flr.	*2,511 sq. ft.*
Garage	*690 sq. ft.*
Sq. Footage	*2,511 sq. ft.*
Foundation	*Slab, Crawl space***
Bedrooms	*Four*
Baths	*Two*

*No materials list available

**Please specify when ordering

No. 93050

WIDTH 69'-0"
DEPTH 63'-6"

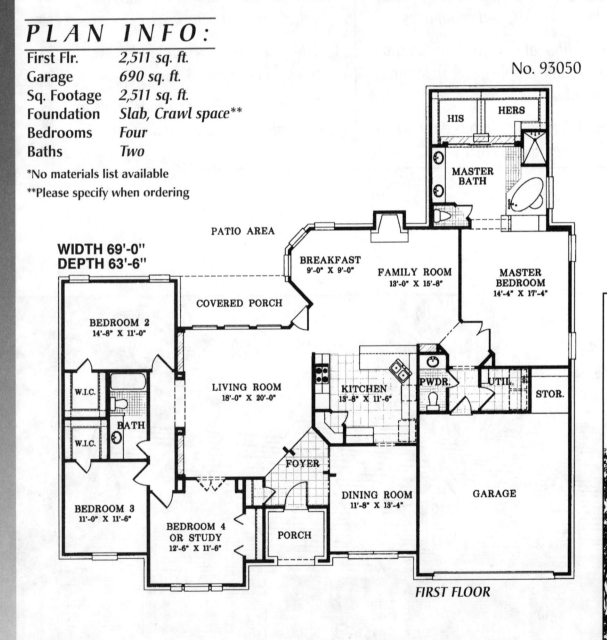

PATIO AREA

BREAKFAST
9'-0" X 9'-0"

FAMILY ROOM
13'-0" X 15'-8"

MASTER BEDROOM
14'-4" X 17'-4"

MASTER BATH

HIS

HERS

BEDROOM 2
14'-8" X 11'-0"

COVERED PORCH

LIVING ROOM
18'-0" X 20'-0"

KITCHEN
13'-8" X 11'-6"

PWDR.

UTIL.

STOR.

W.I.C.

W.I.C.

BATH

FOYER

DINING ROOM
11'-8" X 13'-4"

GARAGE

BEDROOM 3
11'-0" X 11'-6"

BEDROOM 4 OR STUDY
12'-6" X 11'-6"

PORCH

FIRST FLOOR

■ Covered front entrance to tiled Foyer leads directly to the open Living Room and formal Dining Room with a decorative front window

■ Living Room offers built-in shelves, a wall of windows and easy access to the covered Porch and Breakfast Room/Family Room

■ A well-appointed Kitchen with ample cabinet space, a peninsula counter and a walk-in pantry opens to both the Breakfast Room/Family Room and the Dining Room

■ Bay window area of the Breakfast Room and the warm, hearth fireplace in the Family Room make this area perfect for family gatherings

■ Double French doors open into the private Master Bedroom Suite highlighted by a pampering Bath with a corner whirlpool garden tub, double vanity and his-n-her walk-in closets

■ Three additional bedrooms on the same level located on the other side of the home have walk-in closets and share a full hall Bath

An Elegant Addition To Any Neighborhood

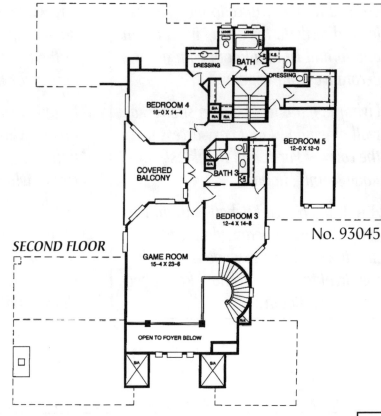

SECOND FLOOR

No. 93045

- BEDROOM 4
  16-0 X 14-4
- DRESSING
- BATH 4
- DRESSING
- BEDROOM 5
  12-0 X 12-0
- BATH 3
- COVERED BALCONY
- BEDROOM 3
  12-4 X 14-8
- GAME ROOM
  15-4 X 23-6
- OPEN TO FOYER BELOW

PLAN INFO:

First Flr.	*2,643 sq. ft.*
Second Flr.	*1,538 sq. ft.*
Garage	*661 sq. ft.*
Sq. Footage	*4,181 sq. ft.*
Foundation	*Slab, Crawl space*
Bedrooms	*Five*
Baths	*4(Full), 1(Half)*

*No materials list available

WIDTH 74-7

- MASTER BATH
  9 FT CLG
- STORAGE
- GARAGE
- MASTER BEDROOM
  21-0 X 22-8
  9 FT CLG
- SITTING AREA
- POOL AREA
- SHELVES
- CLOSET
- POWDR
- UTIL
  8-4 X 7-6
- PORTE COCHERE
- COVERED PORCH
- PAN
- BRKFST ROOM
  13-6 X 10-8
  9 FT CLG
- KITCHEN
  14-0 X 15-0
- DINING ROOM
  16-0 X 12-6
  9 FT CLG
- COVERED PORCH
- FOYER
  2 STORY CLG
- POWDR
- BATH 2
- LIVING ROOM
  21-6 X 15-0
  12 FT CLG
- PORCH
- BEDROOM 2/ STUDY
  11-0 X 15-0
  9 FT CLG

DEPTH 78-5

FIRST FLOOR

- *Two-story arched glass entrance leading to curved staircase presents an elegant introduction to this unique layout*

- *Large Living Room features a 12 foot ceiling, a central fireplace flanked by built-in bookcases and decorative casement windows*

- *Formal Dining Room enhanced by the curving staircase and French doors leads to a covered Porch*

- *Luxurious Master Suite with an elegant see-through fireplace between the bedroom and the Master Bath*

- *Ultra Master Bath with a raised tile platform showing off the angled whirlpool tub and shower*

- *Three additional bedrooms with easy access to full Baths*

- *A large Game Room with direct access to a covered balcony*

Classic Symmetry On This Columned Facade

SECOND FLOOR

PLAN INFO:

First Flr.	*3,116 sq. ft.*
Second Flr.	*1,997 sq. ft.*
Sq. Footage	*5,113 sq. ft.*
Foundation	*Basement*
Bedrooms	*Four*
Baths	*4(Full), 1(Half)*

No. 99213

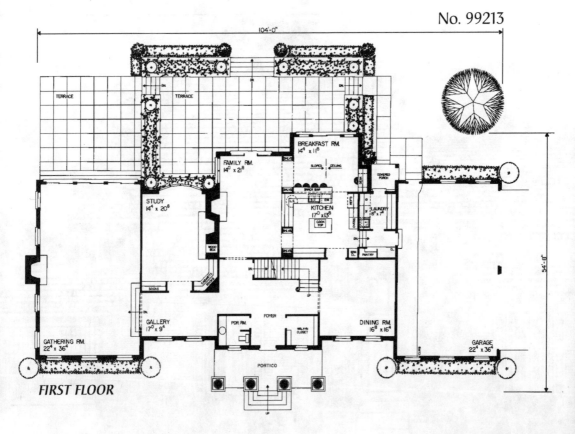

FIRST FLOOR

■ *Grand Foyer welcomes guests into the home and leads into the Gallery*

■ *Extremely spacious, yet made cozy by the large fireplace, the Gathering Room stands ready to accommodate any entertaining endeavor*

■ *Study offers a special place to sit by the fireplace and read surrounded by built-in shelves and a bow window view of the outdoor terrace*

■ *Centrally located Kitchen, with a cooktop island, built-in pantry and planning desk, plenty of counter space and snack bar easily serves both the formal Dining Room and informal Breakfast Room.*

■ *Whirlpool tub, a fourth fireplace and his-n-her closets are just a few of the reasons this second floor Master Bedroom suite will become a favorite retreat*

■ *Three additional bedrooms, each with a private bath, are also located on the second floor*

This Modern Tudor Is Hard To Resist

PLAN INFO:

First Flr.	2,457 sq. ft.
Second Flr.	1,047 sq. ft.
Sun Room	213 sq. ft.
Basement	2,457 sq. ft.
Garage	837 sq. ft.
Sq. Footage	3,504 sq. ft.
Foundation	Basement
Bedrooms	Four
Baths	3(Full), 1(Half)

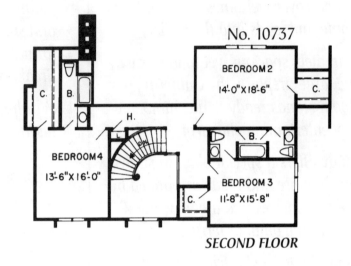

No. 10737

SECOND FLOOR

FIRST FLOOR

An EXCLUSIVE DESIGN
By Karl Kreeger

- Partake of morning coffee in the seven-sided, Breakfast Room

- Island Kitchen affords easy access to Dining Room

- Family room features exposed wood beams adding atmosphere to this impressive home

- Energy-saving Sun Room and unobtrusive Study flank Family Room for convenience

- Balcony at top of stairs overlooks grand Entry

- Master Bedroom with recessed ceiling encompasses entire wing for spacious living

- Master Bath encourages pampering with double vanity, walk-in closet, sauna, whirlpool bath, and hot tub

- Graceful curving staircase enhances exciting tiled Entry with a two-story ceiling

- Three additional bedrooms on the second floor feature individual walk-in closets for plenty of personal storage

$\mathcal{A}$ Grand Presence

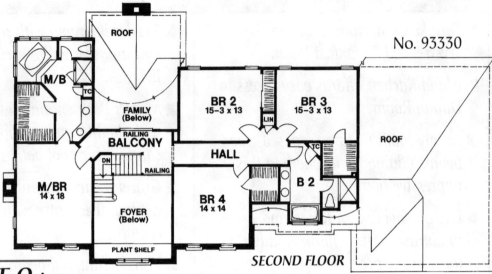

No. 93330

SECOND FLOOR

PLAN INFO:

First Flr.	*2,093 sq. ft.*
Second Flr.	*1,527 sq. ft.*
Basement	*2,093 sq. ft.*
Garage	*816 sq. ft.*
Sq. Footage	*3,620 sq. ft.*
Foundation	*Basement*
Bedrooms	*Four*
Baths	*2 (Full), 1 (Half)*

*No materials list available

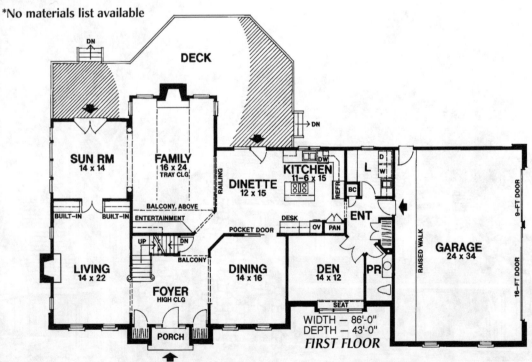

WIDTH — 86'-0"
DEPTH — 43'-0"

FIRST FLOOR

- *Imposing and symmetrical in design, this spacious home welcomes family and friends through an impressive entrance into an open Foyer leading easily into all living areas*

- *Formal Living Room offers a warm fireplace centered between two large windows and built-in shelves on each side of double doors leading into the Sun Room*

- *Pocket Door separates the formal Dining Room from the Kitchen area, providing privacy and disappearing into the wall when not needed*

- *Gourmet Kitchen is equipped with a cooktop island, built-in pantry and planning desk, and adjoining Dinette area with a glass door to the outdoor Deck*

- *Expansive Family Room has a second fireplace surrounded by windows, a built-in entertainment center, and a tray ceiling with a balcony above*

- *A luxurious Bath highlights the private Master Bedroom Suite with a raised corner window tub, step-in shower, double vanity and walk-in closet*

- *Three large, additional bedrooms share a full hall Bath with a window tub and another double vanity*

$\mathscr{F}$rench Country Design
With Elegant Amenities

No. 91658

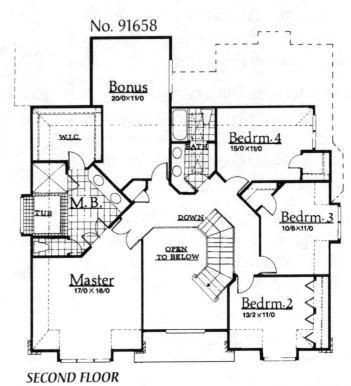

SECOND FLOOR

PLAN INFO:

First Flr.	*1,718 sq. ft.*
Second Flr.	*1,340 sq. ft.*
Bonus Rm.	*220 sq. ft.*
Sq. Footage	*3,058 sq. ft.*
Foundation	*Post & Beam*
Bedrooms	*Four*
Baths	*2(Full), 1(Half)*

*No materials list available

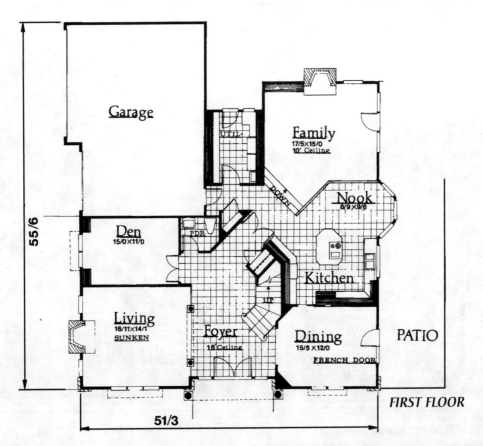

FIRST FLOOR

- Pleasant grace surrounds this corner French country home with its double front doors, two-story glass and tile Foyer, and curved stairway

- Sunken formal Living Room is enhanced by an arched Entry and a large hearth fireplace

- Formal dining takes place in the elegant Dining Room that features French doors to the Patio

- Double French doors lead to the informal living areas, including a sunken Family Room with a cozy fireplace for all to gather around on cold winter nights

- Fabulous island Kitchen includes an abundance of counter and storage space and a Nook Area for informal eating

- Master Bedroom suite highlighted by a window seat and luxurious Bath with atrium tub, double vanity and large walk-in closet

- Three additional bedrooms and a large Bonus room share the full, double vanity hall Bath

Two-Story Glass Entrance...
Need We Say More!

PLAN INFO:

First Flr.	*1,720 sq. ft.*
Second Flr.	*1,305 sq. ft.*
Basement	*1,720 sq. ft.*
Garage	*768 sq. ft.*
Sq. Footage	*3,025 sq. ft.*
Foundation	*Basement*
Bedrooms	*Four*
Baths	*2(Full),*
	1(Half)

*No materials list available

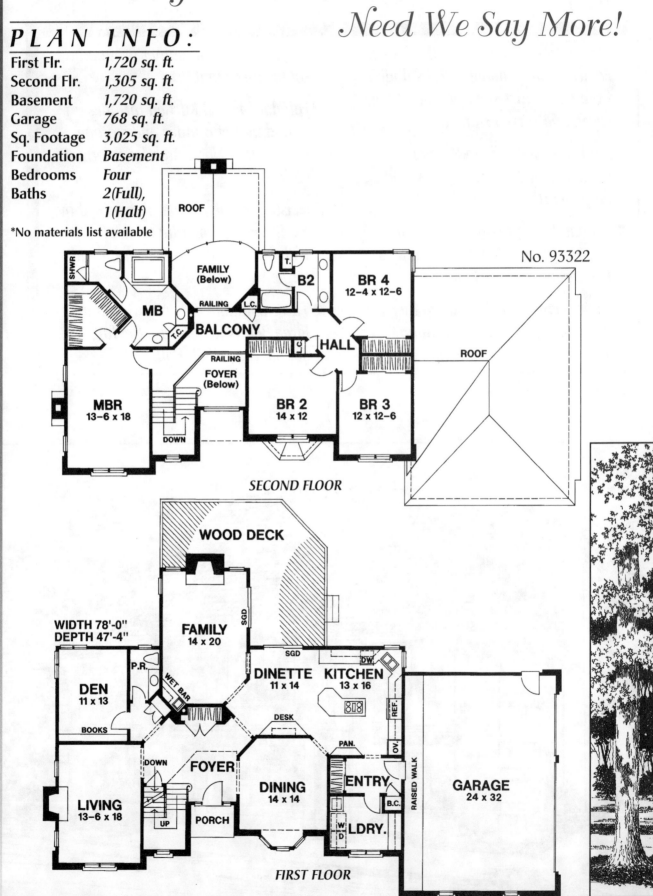

No. 93322

SECOND FLOOR

SHWR · **MB** · **T.C.** · **FAMILY (Below)** · **RAILING** · **L.C.** · **B2** · **T.** · **BR 4** 12-4 x 12-6 · **ROOF** · **BALCONY** · **HALL** · **ROOF** · **RAILING** · **C.** · **FOYER (Below)** · **BR 2** 14 x 12 · **BR 3** 12 x 12-6 · **MBR** 13-6 x 18 · **DOWN**

WIDTH 78'-0"
DEPTH 47'-4"

WOOD DECK · **FAMILY** 14 x 20 · **SGD** · **P.R.** · **WET BAR** · **SGD** · **DINETTE** 11 x 14 · **KITCHEN** 13 x 16 · **DW** · **DEN** 11 x 13 · **BOOKS** · **DESK** · **REF.** · **PAN.** · **OV.** · **DOWN** · **FOYER** · **DINING** 14 x 14 · **ENTRY** · **RAISED WALK** · **GARAGE** 24 x 32 · **LIVING** 13-6 x 18 · **UP** · **PORCH** · **W D** · **LDRY.** · **B.C.**

FIRST FLOOR

■ *Enter this gracious home through a two-story, glass entrance that leads to all living areas from the expansive Foyer*

■ *Formal Living Room features an inviting hearth fireplace to set the mood in formal entertaining*

■ *Bay window adds elegance and natural illumination to the formal Dining Room*

■ *Spacious Family Room equipped with sliders to a deck, built-in wetbar and a cozy fireplace, provides a perfect place for informal entertaining*

■ *Expansive Kitchen offers a cooktop island/eating bar, corner double sink, built-in pantry and desk as well as a Dinette area leading to the Family Room and outdoor Deck*

■ *Cozy Den offers built-in book shelves and a quiet corner on the first floor*

■ *Ultra Bath with a raised window tub and two vanities adds to the attraction of the Master Bedroom Suite*

■ *Three additional bedrooms with ample closet space share a full hall Bath with a double vanity*

Contemporary Features; Everything You Need

PLAN INFO:

First Flr.	2,188 sq. ft.
Second Flr.	1,083 sq. ft.
Basement	2,188 sq. ft.
Garage	576 sq. ft.
Sq. Footage	3,271 sq. ft.
Foundation	Basement
Bedrooms	Four
Baths	3(Full), 1(Half)

An
EXCLUSIVE DESIGN
By Karl Kreeger

No. 10500

SECOND FLOOR

- UPPER GREAT ROOM
- BEDROOM 4 10'-8" X 13'-0"
- DRESSING
- CEDAR CLOS.
- LOFT 9'-8" X 7'-8"
- C.
- H.
- B.
- BEDROOM 2 10'-8" X 15'-6"
- B.
- C.
- DOWN
- DRESSING
- C.
- UPPER FOYER
- BEDROOM 3 13'-0" X 13'-4"

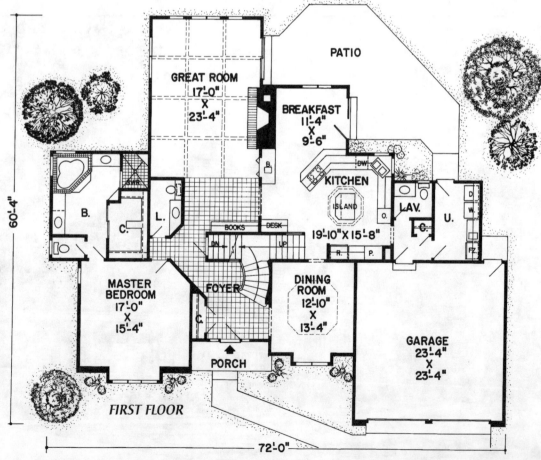

FIRST FLOOR

- GREAT ROOM 17'-0" X 23'-4"
- PATIO
- BREAKFAST 11'-4" X 9'-6"
- KITCHEN ISLAND 19'-10" X 15'-8"
- B.
- LAV.
- U.
- C.
- D. W. FZ.
- MASTER BEDROOM 17'-0" X 15'-4"
- B.
- C.
- L.
- BOOKS
- DESK
- DN
- UP
- FOYER
- C.
- DINING ROOM 12'-10" X 13'-4"
- R.
- P.
- GARAGE 23'-4" X 23'-4"
- PORCH
- 60'-4"
- 72'-0"

- *Lots of living is packed into this well organized and elegant design with backyard views*

- *Expansive Great Room is accented by a massive fireplace and a beamed, cathedral ceiling*

- *Charming and efficient, the Kitchen and Breakfast area include an angled cooking center and a work-island*

- *Conveniently located and protected from noise, the formal Dining Room provides the perfect place for entertaining*

- *Private Master Suite offers a cozy window seat, a double walk-in closet and a raised corner tub*

- *Three bedrooms, two baths and a Loft, which opens onto the Foyer, are located on the second floor*

- *Walk-in closets in each bedroom make storage the least of your worries*

$\mathcal{D}$istinctive Class Is $\mathcal{A}$ Prominent Trait

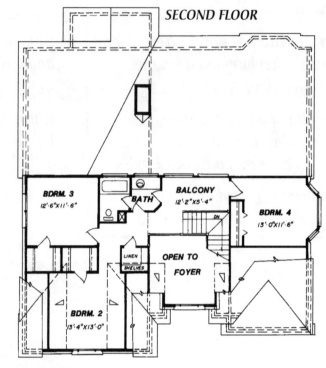

SECOND FLOOR

BDRM. 3
12'-6"X11'-6"

BATH

BALCONY
12'-2"X5'-4"

BDRM. 4
13'-0"X11'-6"

LINEN
SHELVES

OPEN TO
FOYER

DN.

BDRM. 2
13'-4"X13'-0"

No. 93248

PLAN INFO:

First Flr.	1,995 sq. ft.
Second Flr.	880 sq. ft.
Deck	392 sq. ft.
Garage	484 sq. ft.
Sq. Footage	2,875 sq. ft.
Foundation	Slab
Bedrooms	Four
Baths	2(Full), 1(Half)

*No materials list available

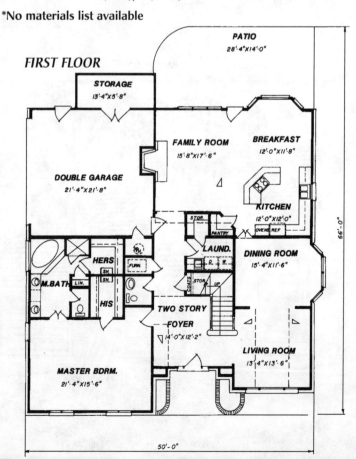

FIRST FLOOR

PATIO
28'-4"X14'-0"

STORAGE
13'-4"X5'-8"

FAMILY ROOM
15'-8"X17'-6"

BREAKFAST
12'-0"X11'-8"

DOUBLE GARAGE
21'-4"X21'-8"

KITCHEN
12'-0"X12'-0"

STOR.

OVEN REF.

HERS
SH.
SH.

FURN.

PANTRY

LAUND.

DINING ROOM
15'-4"X11'-6"

M.BATH
LIN.

HIS

COATS
STOR.
UP

TWO STORY
FOYER
14'-0"X12'-2"

LIVING ROOM
13'-4"X13'-6"

MASTER BDRM.
21'-4"X15'-6"

66'-0"

50'-0"

- Two-story Foyer, with a balcony overlooking it, adds to the impressive look of this home

- Formal Living Room and Dining Room flow together making entertaining easy as well as convenient

- Open layout between the Kitchen, Breakfast Area and Family Room creates a convenient, airy family area

- Large hearth fireplace in the Family Room can be enjoyed from the Kitchen and the sunny Breakfast Area

- Private first floor Master Suite is equipped with his-n-her walk-in closets and a luxurious Bath with a double vanity and raised corner tub

- Three additional bedrooms on the second floor share a full hall Bath

At Home On A Hillside

No. 90559

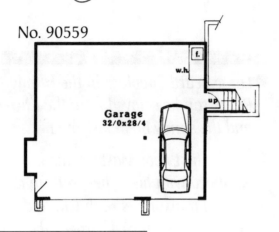

Garage
32/0x28/4

PLAN INFO:

First Flr.	2,388 sq. ft.
Second Flr.	709 sq. ft.
Basement	1,358 sq. ft.
Garage	928 sq. ft.
Sq. Footage	3,097 sq. ft.
Foundation	Bsmt, Post & Beam
Bedrooms	Three
Baths	2(Full), 1(Half)

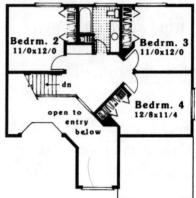

SECOND FLOOR

Bedrm. 2
11/0x12/0

Bedrm. 3
11/0x12/0

dn

Bedrm. 4
12/8x11/4

open to
entry
below

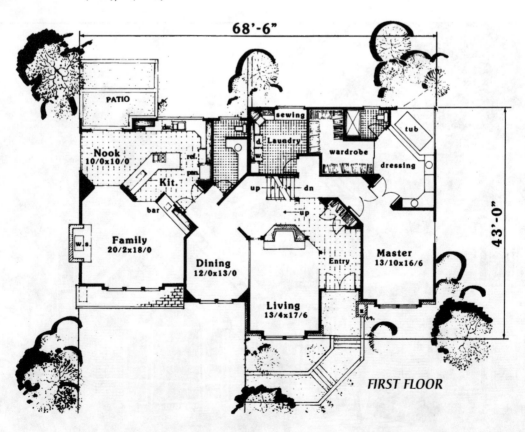

68'-6"

43'-0"

PATIO

Nook
10/0x10/0

Kit.

bar

Family
20/2x18/0

Dining
12/0x13/0

Living
13/4x17/6

Entry

sewing

Laundry

wardrobe

tub

dressing

up   dn

up

Master
13/10x16/6

FIRST FLOOR

- *Show guests into the beautiful Living Room sharing entry level with private Master Suite*

- *Dine in elegance overlooking Living Room fireplace*

- *Three additional bedrooms and a full Bath located a half-flight up away from active areas assures quiet atmosphere*

- *Master Suite features oversized Dressing Room leading into large walk-in closet*

- *Raised tub filled with silky bubbles in Master Bath induces true relaxation*

- *Comfortable Family Room with built-in bar and close proximity to Kitchen and patio provides excellent choice for casual recess*

- *Large Laundry Area with built-in sewing center located adjacent to Master Suite*

- *Kitchen and handy Powder Room just steps away for convenience*

Majestic Brickface Design

PLAN INFO:

First Flr.	*2,659 sq. ft.*
Second Flr.	*827 sq. ft.*
Garage	*552 sq. ft.*
Sq. Footage	*3,486 sq. ft.*
Foundation	*Slab*
Bedrooms	*Four*
Baths	*3(Full), 1(Half)*

*No materials list available

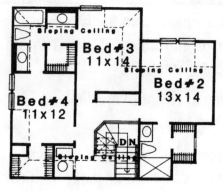

SECOND FLOOR

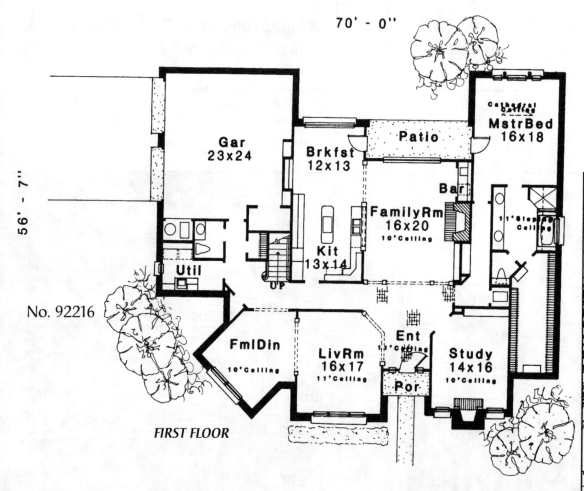

No. 92216

70' - 0''

56' - 7''

FIRST FLOOR

■ *Entryway to this luxurious but practical home reveals spacious rooms that are livable and warm*

■ *Open Family Room features easy access to an outdoor patio and Kitchen, a wetbar and fireplace for informal entertaining*

■ *Central island, double sink, an abundance of counter and storage space, and other amenities are included in the Kitchen*

■ *Flowing easily into each other, the Living Room and Formal Dining*

Room provide the perfect place for an elegant evening

■ *Study located next to the Entryway, includes a cozy fireplace framed by windows*

■ *Crowned by a cathedral ceiling, equipped with a private Bath and huge walk-in closet, the Master Suite is sure to become the owner's private retreat*

■ *Three additional bedrooms with walk-in closets and adjacent full baths are located on the second floor*

Grand Colonial Design With Entrance Court

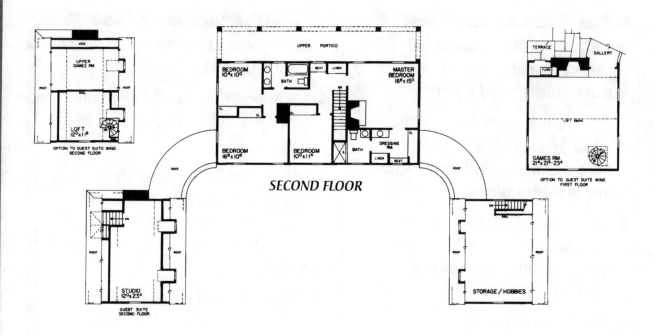

OPTION TO GUEST SUITE WING SECOND FLOOR

UPPER GAMES RM.

VOID

ROOF

LOFT
12⁰ x 11⁸

ROOF

BEDROOM
10⁴ x 10⁰

BATH

SEAT

LINEN

MASTER BEDROOM
16⁸ x 15⁰

UPPER PORTICO

BEDROOM
16⁸ x 10⁰

BEDROOM
10⁰ x 11⁴

BATH

DRESSING RM.

LINEN

SEAT

CL

ROOF

ROOF

SECOND FLOOR

TERRACE

GALLERY

FURN

LOFT ABOVE

GAMES RM.
21⁴ x 21⁴ - 23⁴

OPTION TO GUEST SUITE WING FIRST FLOOR

STUDIO
12⁰ x 23⁴

ROOF

ROOF

GUEST SUITE SECOND FLOOR

STORAGE / HOBBIES

ROOF

ROOF

PLAN INFO:

First Flr.	1,152 sq. ft.
Second Flr.	2,146 sq. ft.
Bonus Room	525 sq. ft.
Garage	483 sq. ft.
Sq. Footage	3,298 sq. ft.
Foundation	Basement
Bedrooms	Four
Baths	3(Full), 1(Half)

No. 99236

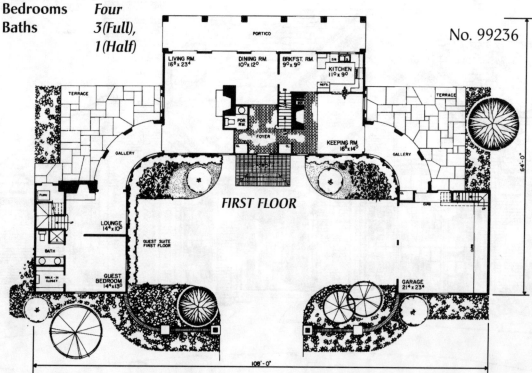

PORTICO

LIVING RM.
16⁸ x 23⁴

DINING RM.
10⁰ x 12⁰

BRKFST. RM.
9⁰ x 9⁰

KITCHEN
11⁰ x 9⁰

REFR.

TERRACE

PDR RM.

FOYER

KEEPING RM.
16⁸ x 14⁰

TERRACE

CL

GALLERY

GALLERY

FIRST FLOOR

FURN

LOUNGE
14⁴ x 10⁰

GUEST SUITE FIRST FLOOR

BATH

WALK - IN CLOSET

GUEST BEDROOM
14⁴ x 13⁰

GARAGE
21⁴ x 23⁴

64'-0"

108'-0"

■ *Courtyard entry makes an appropriate impression for the luxurious living awaiting within*

■ *Central brick floored Foyer leads into a Traditional Keeping Room equipped with a fireplace and a brick bread oven*

■ *Charming curvilinear galleries lead to a double Garage on one side, Lounge and Studio/Guest Suite on the other*

■ *Efficient Kitchen adjoins the Breakfast Room for convenient informal meals*

■ *A combined formal Living and Dining Room is extremely spacious and features a central fireplace*

■ *Large hearth fireplace and separate dressing and bath areas are highlighted in the oversized Master Suite*

■ *Three additional bedrooms share a full hall Bath*

■ *Optional ideas for guest and garage wings offered*

Convenience And Beauty Are Built In

PLAN INFO:

First Flr.	1,957 sq. ft.
Second Flr.	1,603 sq. ft.
Basement	2,238 sq. ft.
Garage	840 sq. ft.
Sq. Footage	3,560 sq. ft.
Foundation	Basement
Bedrooms	Four
Baths	4(Full), 1(Half)

No. 20358

SECOND FLOOR

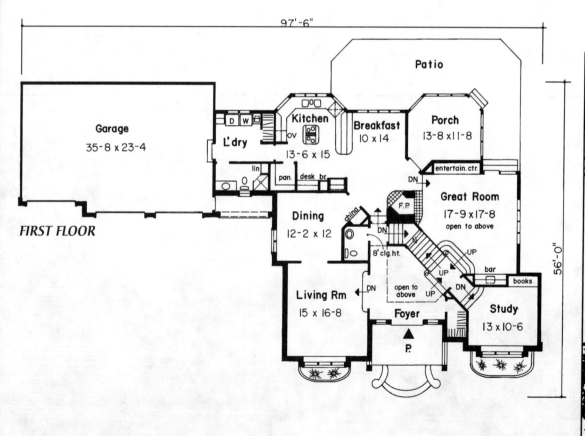

FIRST FLOOR

- *Enjoy ingenious plan of gracious brick beauty*

- *Step inside the Foyer from the covered-entry porch with open staircase leading upstairs*

- *Towering Great Room features amenities such as a built-in bar, entertainment center and direct access to rear patio*

- *Tucked away from busy areas, the book-lined Study offers the perfect place for quiet pursuits*

- *Across the Kitchen counter, the Breakfast Room is just steps away from a glass-walled sun Porch, perfect for year round activities*

- *Upstairs Master Bedroom encompasses half of second floor with two walk-in closets and spacious private Bath*

- *Guests enjoy comfort second to none in private Guest Room featuring trayed ceiling, picture window, spacious closets, and personal full Bath*

Spectacular Stucco Has Interesting Angled Design

PLAN INFO:

First Flr.	*1,924 sq. ft.*
Second Flr.	*1,438 sq. ft.*
Garage	*836 sq. ft.*
Sq. Footage	*3,362 sq. ft.*
Foundation	*Crawl space*
Bedrooms	*Three*
Baths	*2(Full), 1(Half)*

*No materials list available

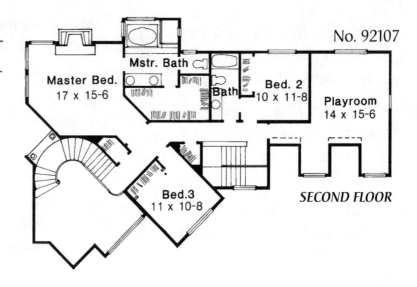

No. 92107

Mstr. Bath

Master Bed.
17 x 15-6

Bath

Bed. 2
10 x 11-8

Playroom
14 x 15-6

Bed.3
11 x 10-8

SECOND FLOOR

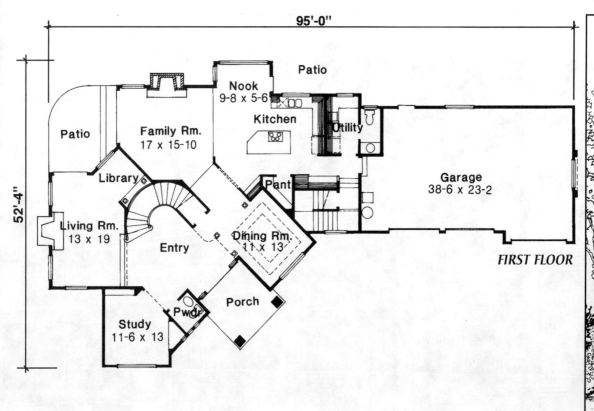

95'-0"

52'-4"

Patio

Patio

Nook
9-8 x 5-6

Kitchen

Utility

Family Rm.
17 x 15-10

Library

Living Rm.
13 x 19

Entry

Pant

Dining Rm.
11 x 13

Garage
38-6 x 23-2

Study
11-6 x 13

Pwdr

Porch

FIRST FLOOR

■ *Magnificent Entry set aglow by recessed lighting and enhanced by a curved suspended staircase*

■ *Vaulted Dining Room well-angled to obtain best available lighting*

■ *Rear staircase eases movement for family members*

■ *Quiet Library adds to elegance and charm of Living Room featuring a window over the gas fireplace*

■ *Spacious fireplaced Family Room leads out to a cleverly curved patio*

■ *Master Bedroom offers a fireplace, full luxury Bath amenities, and extra-roomy closet space*

■ *Practical Playroom with added beauty of dormers gives that just right touch for additional space*

■ *Enter house from oversized 3-car Garage through convenient Utility Room and half Bath*

■ *Open floor plan in well-equipped island Kitchen heads into brightly lighted Nook and side pantry*

An Angled Design Wrapped Around The Perfect Executive Suite

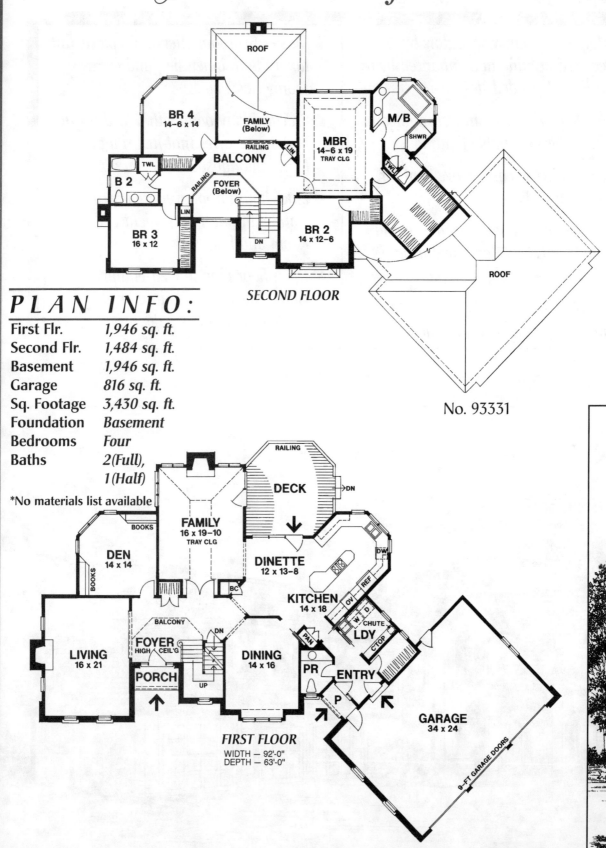

SECOND FLOOR

ROOF

BR 4
14-6 x 14

FAMILY
(Below)

M/B

RAILING

MBR
14-6 x 19
TRAY CLG

SHWR

BALCONY

B 2

FOYER
(Below)

RAILING

BR 3
16 x 12

LIN

DN

BR 2
14 x 12-6

ROOF

PLAN INFO:

First Flr.	1,946 sq. ft.
Second Flr.	1,484 sq. ft.
Basement	1,946 sq. ft.
Garage	816 sq. ft.
Sq. Footage	3,430 sq. ft.
Foundation	Basement
Bedrooms	Four
Baths	2(Full), 1(Half)

*No materials list available

No. 93331

RAILING

DECK

DN

FAMILY
16 x 19-10
TRAY CLG

BOOKS

DINETTE
12 x 13-8

DEN
14 x 14

DW

BOOKS

KITCHEN
14 x 18

REF

BC

OV

BALCONY

DN

CHUTE

LDY

CTOP

FOYER
HIGH CEIL'G

DINING
14 x 16

PAN

LIVING
16 x 21

PR

ENTRY

PORCH

UP

P

GARAGE
34 x 24

FIRST FLOOR

WIDTH — 92'-0"
DEPTH — 63'-0"

9-FT GARAGE DOORS

- *Windows around the front door, a wide landing staircase and a balcony overlooking the Foyer create a great first impression of this elegant home*

- *Hearth Fireplace centered between two windows invites company from the Foyer*

- *Formal Dining Room offers a decorative bumped out window and a quite place for elegant entertaining*

- *Unusual Den features a corner of windows overlooking the back and side yard, and surrounded by built-in book shelves*

- *Hexagon-shaped Kitchen equipped with a cooktop island/snack bar and a*

- *built-in pantry, loads of counter space and an open Dinette area with sliding glass doors to Deck, make this room ideal for cooking and entertaining*

- *A tray ceiling, a huge fireplace surrounded by windows plus access to an outdoor deck make this Family Room ideal for informal gatherings*

- *Luxurious Master Bedroom Suite features a tray ceiling, triple windows, a room-size walk-in closet, and a lavish Bath with an atrium tub, oversized shower and double vanity*

- *Three additional bedrooms with ample closets, off the balcony, share a full hall Bath*

Private Court Outside Master Bedroom

No. 10534

PLAN INFO:

First Flr.	2,486 sq. ft.
Second Flr.	954 sq. ft.
Basement	2,486 sq. ft.
Garage	576 sq. ft.
Sq. Footage	3,440 sq. ft.
Foundation	Basement
Bedrooms	Four
Baths	3(Full), 1(Half)

SECOND FLOOR

An
EXCLUSIVE DESIGN
By Karl Kreeger

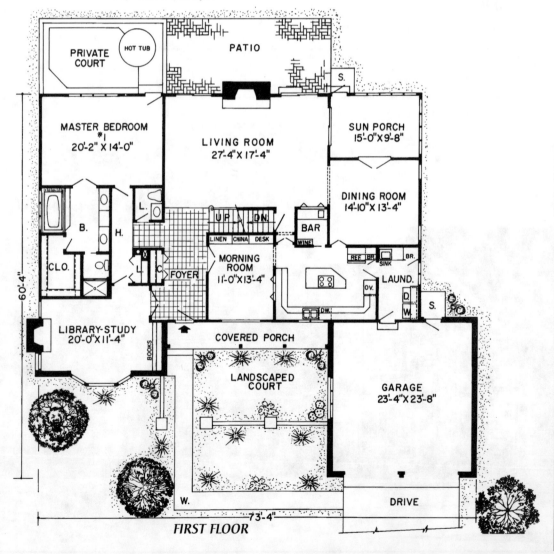

FIRST FLOOR

-170-

- Secluded from the rest of the first floor, the Master Bedroom Suite includes an oversized walk-in closet and personal Bath

- Adjoining the luxurious Master Bedroom is a private courtyard complete with hot tub

- Enter the cozy Library through French doors from Foyer

- Comfortable Morning Room features built-in linen closet, china cabinet and desk

- Focal point of spacious Living Room is the warm welcoming fireplace

- Wine storage area behind bar in Living Room for convenience

- Walk out to Sun Porch through French doors in Dining Room

- Overlook the Living Room from the second-floor railing

- Three additional bedrooms, two baths, and plenty of closet space adorn upstairs level

Complete Design With Servants' Quarters Too!

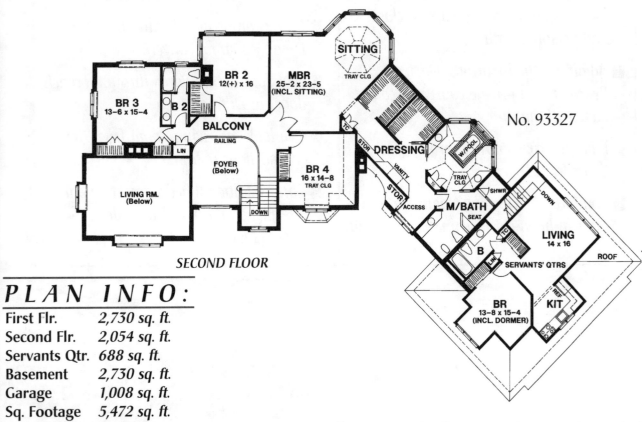

No. 93327

SECOND FLOOR

PLAN INFO:

First Flr.	2,730 sq. ft.
Second Flr.	2,054 sq. ft.
Servants Qtr.	688 sq. ft.
Basement	2,730 sq. ft.
Garage	1,008 sq. ft.
Sq. Footage	5,472 sq. ft.
Foundation	Basement
Bedrooms	Four
Baths	2(Full), 2(Half)

*No materials list available

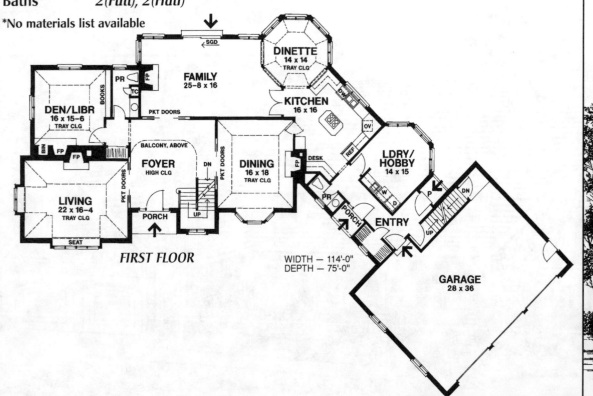

FIRST FLOOR

WIDTH — 114'-0"
DEPTH — 75'-0"

- Distinctive, luxurious and efficient, this expansive home greets one and all with a two-story Foyer leading to living areas through pocket doors and bedrooms by a wide landing staircase and curved balcony

- Tray ceilings crown the Dining Room, Living Room, Library, Dinette, Master Suite Sitting area and Master Bath

- Unique but elegant entertaining offered by a beautiful bay window and warm fireplace in Dining Room and window seat across from another fireplace in the Living Room

- Large, U-shaped Kitchen will satisfy one and all with a cooktop work island, an abundance of counter and cabinet space, and a glass, octagonal Dinette as well as easy access to the Family Room, Dining Room and Laundry/Hobby area

- Spacious Family Room with a hearth fireplace, windows on three sides and sliding doors to the backyard offers an ideal setting for informal gatherings

- Lavish Master Bedroom Suite is sure to become the owner's private retreat with a whirlpool tub, step-in shower, three separate vanities, two huge walk-in closets and a private glass, octagonal Sitting area

- Three additional bedrooms on the second floor share a full hall Bath with a double vanity

- Servant's quarters over the garage with a separate stairway provides efficient use of space and adequate privacy

Family Plan Has Everything You Need

PLAN INFO:

First Flr.	1,712 sq. ft.
Second Flr.	1,324 sq. ft.
Garage	528 sq. ft.
Sq. Footage	3,036 sq. ft.
Foundation	Basement
Bedrooms	Four
Baths	2(Full), 1(Half)

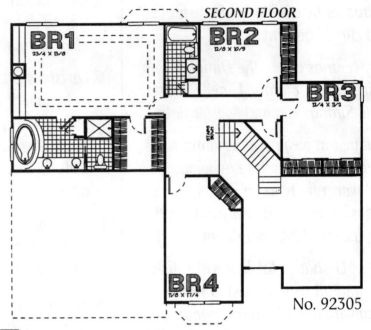

SECOND FLOOR

BR1
23/4 x 13/8

BR2
12/8 x 10/9

BR3
12/4 x 11/2

BR4
11/8 x 17/4

No. 92305

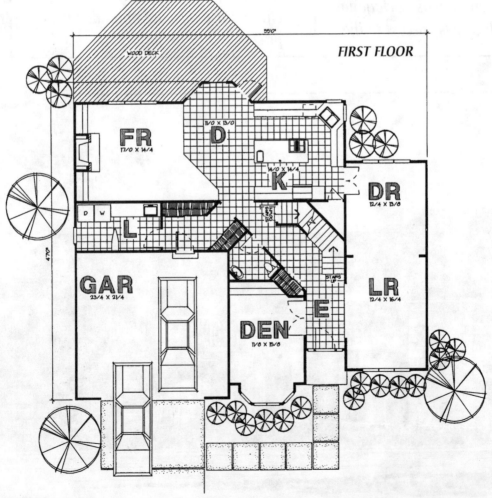

FIRST FLOOR

WOOD DECK

FR
17/0 x 14/4

D
11/0 x 13/0

K
11/0 x 14/4

DR
12/4 x 13/8

L

GAR
23/4 x 21/4

DEN
11/0 x 13/0

LR
12/4 x 16/4

E

- *An open layout between the large, country Kitchen, Dinette, and expansive Family Room gives a feeling of spaciousness*

- *Meal preparation is efficient with the convenient center island, amenity packed Kitchen*

- *A formal Living and Dining Room merge together forming a perfect spot for entertaining*

- *An expansive Family Room with a cozy fireplace provides a relaxing atmosphere for family togetherness and informal gatherings*

- *Coffered ceilings and a private Bath are featured in this superb Master Suite*

- *Three additional bedrooms share a full hall Bath and have ample closet space*

Contemporary Drama

No. 99366

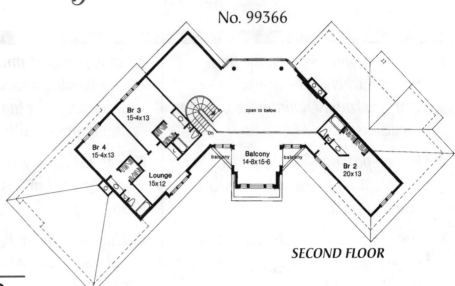

SECOND FLOOR

PLAN INFO:

First Flr.	*3,900 sq. ft.*
Second Flr.	*1,720 sq. ft.*
Basement	*2,505 sq. ft.*
Garage	*3-car*
Sq. Footage	*5,620 sq. ft.*
Foundation	*Basement*
Bedrooms	*Four*
Baths	*4(Full), 1(Half)*

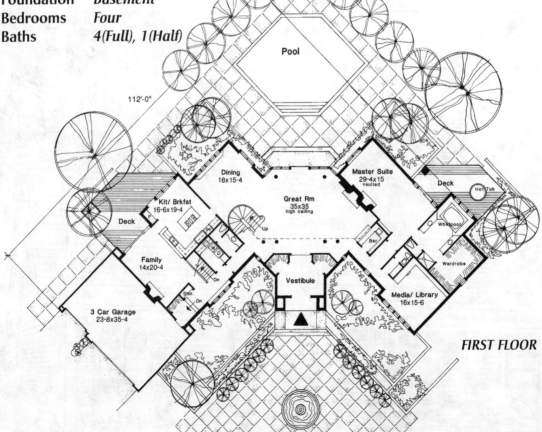

FIRST FLOOR

- Special dramatics focused on the grand stairway and balcony above Great Room

- Columned arcade directs traffic from Vestibule to Master Suite and Library wing on left; Family and Kitchen areas on right

- Entrance offers impressive view of the double-height Great Room with a detailed fireplace wall

- Vast Master Suite has walk-in closet and whirlpool tub with twin vanities in the Master Bath

- Private access through the Master Suite allows intimate evenings relaxing in your hot tub on the deck

- Dining Room is open, yet in its own alcove, to savor same spatial elegance

- L-shaped Kitchen opens to the Breakfast area with sliding glass doors to the second deck

- Three additional bedrooms on the second level each sport personal baths and plenty of closet space

Spacious Loft Ideal As A Playroom, Library, Etc.

PLAN INFO:

First Flr.	*2,887 sq. ft.*
Second Flr.	*1,488 sq. ft.*
Basement	*2,888 sq. ft.*
Garage	*843 sq. ft.*
Sq. Footage	*4,375 sq. ft.*
Foundation	*Basement*
Bedrooms	*Four*
Baths	*3(Full), 2(Half)*

BEDROOM 2
14'-2"X16'-0"

BEDROOM 3
13'-8"X16'-0"

C.

B.

BEDROOM 4
15'-0"X22'-10"

C.

SLOPE

DN

B.

C.

LOFT
16'-4"X 24'-0"

SECOND FLOOR

No. 10734

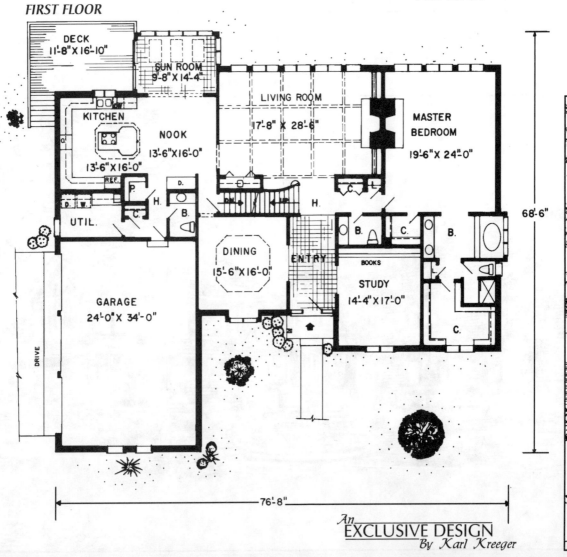

FIRST FLOOR

DECK
11'-8"X16'-10"

SUN ROOM
9'-8"X14'-4"

KITCHEN

NOOK
13'-6"X16'-0"

13'-6"X16'-0"

REF.

P.

D.

LIVING ROOM
17'-8" X 28'-6"

MASTER
BEDROOM
19'-6"X 24'-0"

C.

D.W.

H.

C.

B.

DN

H.

B.

C.

B.

UTIL.

GARAGE
24'-0"X 34'-0"

DRIVE

DINING
15'-6"X16'-0"

ENTRY

BOOKS

STUDY
14'-4"X17'-0"

C.

68'-6"

76'-8"

An EXCLUSIVE DESIGN
By Karl Kreeger

- *Large, tiled Entry provides easy access to spacious upstairs Loft, offering the perfect playroom for children*

- *Informal meals are enjoyable in the Sun Room, Nook or on the outdoor wood deck*

- *An adjacent Kitchen is designed for efficiency, equipped with a cook top island, more than ample counter space and a built-in pantry*

- *Wood beams and a glowing fireplace in the Living Room make for a cozy escape*

- *First floor Master Suite provides a relaxing atmosphere with its own fireplace and a whirlpool bath*

- *Children's rooms are equipped with their own baths and a double vanity*

Two Story Living Areas Lend A Spacious Air To This Home

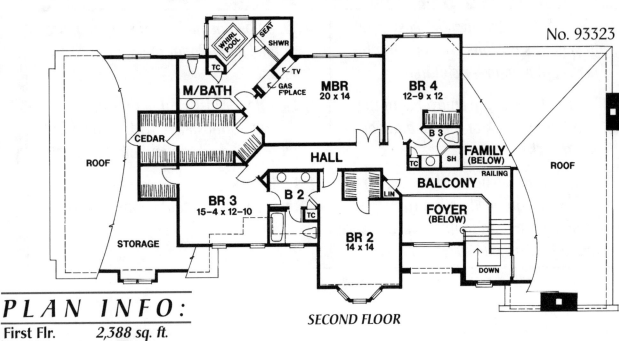

No. 93323

SECOND FLOOR

PLAN INFO:

First Flr.	2,388 sq. ft.
Second Flr.	1,660 sq. ft.
Basement	2,338 sq. ft.
Garage	816 sq. ft.
Sq. Footage	4,048 sq. ft.
Foundation	Basement
Bedrooms	Four
Baths	4(Full), 1(Half)

*No materials list available

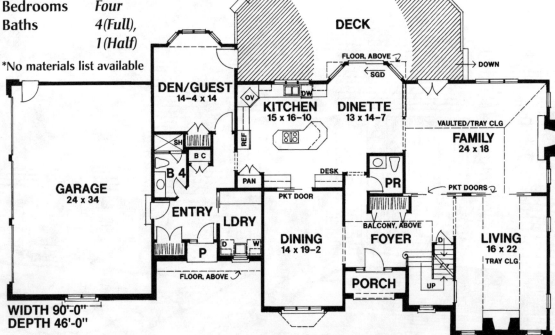

FIRST FLOOR

WIDTH 90'-0"
DEPTH 46'-0"

- *Grand entrance created by a detailed door with sidelights and window transom lead into an open Foyer with window stair landing*

- *Decorative ceiling treatments add drama and fireplaces add warmth to the Living Room and the Family Room*

- *Formal Dining Room enhanced by expansive front window and pocket door leads directly to the Kitchen*

- *Family Room provides access to the Foyer and Living Room with pocket doors, to the outdoor deck by French doors and to the Kitchen area with sliding doors*

- *Efficient Kitchen offers a cooktop island and eating bar, a built-in pantry and planning desk open to a Dinette area with a bay access to outdoor deck*

- *Luxurious second floor Master Bedroom suite has a gas fireplace, a huge walk-in closet, separate cedar closet and large storage area, and a private Bath with a whirlpool, corner tub, over-sized shower and double vanity*

- *Three additional bedrooms, one with a private Bath, the other two sharing a Bath with private accesses*

Spacious Style And Elegant Room Designs

No. 92614

PLAN INFO:

First Flr.	2,231 sq. ft.
Second Flr.	838 sq. ft.
Sq. Footage	3,069 sq. ft.
Foundation	Basement
Bedrooms	Four
Baths	3(Full), 1(Half)

*No materials list available

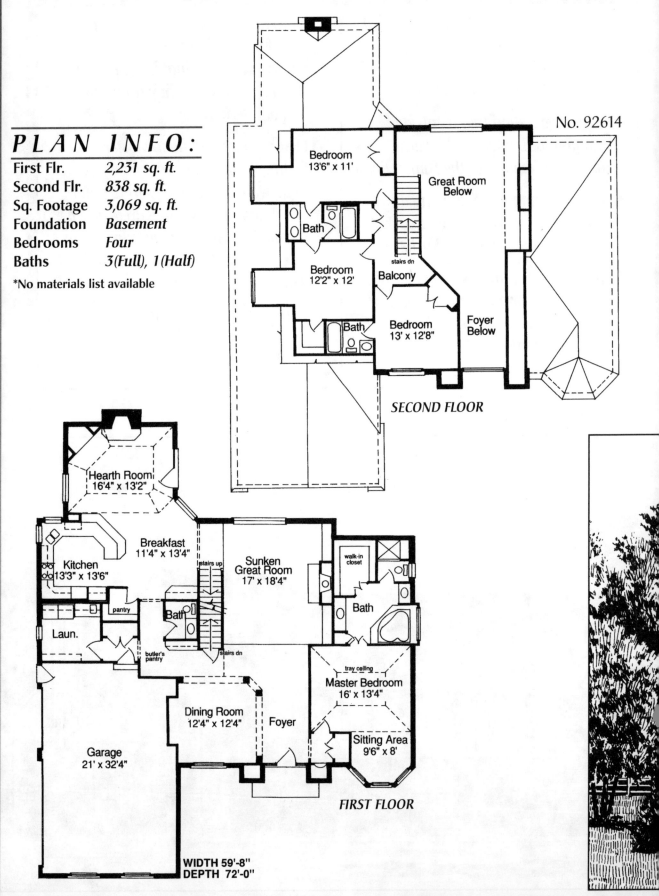

Bedroom
13'6" x 11'

Great Room
Below

Bath

Bedroom
12'2" x 12'

Balcony

stairs dn

Bath

Bedroom
13' x 12'8"

Foyer
Below

SECOND FLOOR

Hearth Room
16'4" x 13'2"

Breakfast
11'4" x 13'4"

Kitchen
13'3" x 13'6"

Sunken
Great Room
17' x 18'4"

walk-in
closet

pantry

Bath

stairs up

Bath

Laun.

butler's
pantry

stairs dn

Master Bedroom
16' x 13'4"

tray ceiling

Dining Room
12'4" x 12'4"

Foyer

Garage
21' x 32'4"

Sitting Area
9'6" x 8'

FIRST FLOOR

WIDTH 59'-8"
DEPTH 72'-0"

- *Two-story Foyer leads to a spacious, sunken Great Room with a super fireplace and vaulted ceiling*

- *Formal Dining Room presents an impressive setting with columns and custom moldings*

- *Butler's Pantry leads to the modern Kitchen/Breakfast area equipped with a peninsula counter, double sink and a built-in pantry*

- *Cozy Hearth Room adjacent to Kitchen area provides a special place for intimate family gatherings with a large hearth fireplace, built-in entertainment center and easy access to the backyard*

- *Private Master Suite includes a bay window sitting area, tray ceiling, and lavish Bath featuring a large walk-in closet, two vanities, a raised garden tub and private shower*

- *Three additional bedrooms on the second floor have easy access to two full baths and overlook the Great Room*

Enjoy The Skylit Sunporch And Backyard Views

PLAN INFO:

First Flr.	2,069 sq. ft.
Second Flr.	821 sq. ft.
Basement	2,045 sq. ft.
Garage	562 sq. ft.
Sq. Footage	2,890 sq. ft.
Foundation	Basement
Bedrooms	Four
Baths	3(Full), 2(Half)

No. 10550

BEDROOM 3
11'-8" X 13'-10"

BEDROOM 4
11'-10" X 11'-2"

BEDROOM 2
12'-10" X 11'-4"

B.

C.

H.

C.

L.

B.

DN.

FOYER BELOW

SECOND FLOOR

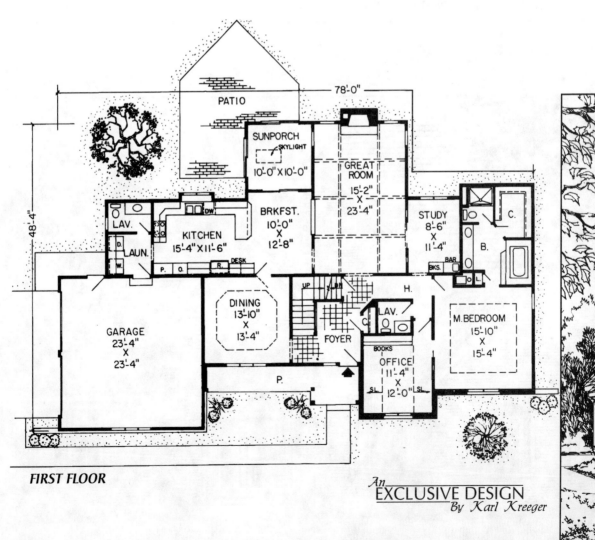

78'-0"

48'-4"

PATIO

SUNPORCH
SKYLIGHT
10'-0" X 10'-0"

GREAT ROOM
15'-2" X 23'-4"

BRKFST.
10'-0" X 12'-8"

STUDY
8'-6" X 11'-4"

C.

B.

LAV.

KITCHEN
15'-4" X 11'-6"

LAUN.

DW

D.

W.

P. Q.

R. DESK

BAR

BKS.

DINING
13'-10" X 13'-4"

UP

FOYER

LAV.

H.

M. BEDROOM
15'-10" X 15'-4"

L.

GARAGE
23'-4" X 23'-4"

BOOKS

OFFICE
11'-4" X 12'-0"

SL

SL

P.

FIRST FLOOR

An **EXCLUSIVE DESIGN**
By Karl Kreeger

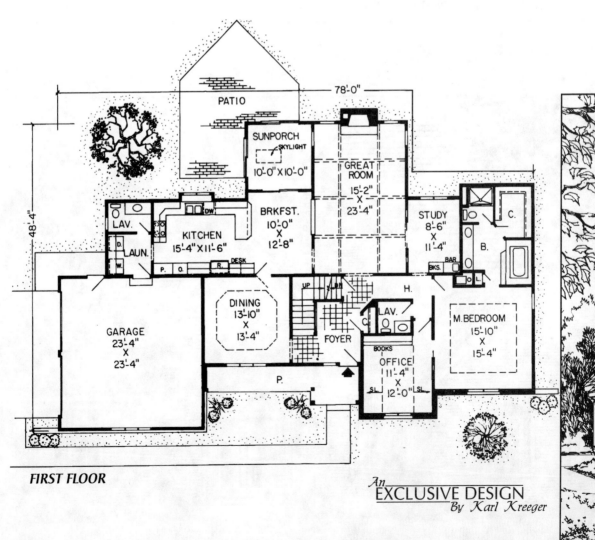

- *Skylit Sunporch leading to backyard patio offers peaceful relaxation while enjoying backyard beauty*

- *Large Kitchen provides ample counter space, pantry, and desk*

- *Easy access to Breakfast Nook and Dining Room from Kitchen*

- *Fireplaced Great Room exhibits warm characteristics with its wood-beamed ceiling*

- *Private Study affords quiet solitude*

- *Recessed ceilings in Dining Room and Master Bedroom create distinctive angles throughout the first floor*

- *Master Bedroom includes oversized personal Bath with double basins*

- *Office area adjacent to Master Bedroom situated to induce minimum disturbance for working at home*

- *Second floor contains three additional bedrooms, two full baths and lots of closet space*

Striking, Notable And Very Impressive

No. 91670

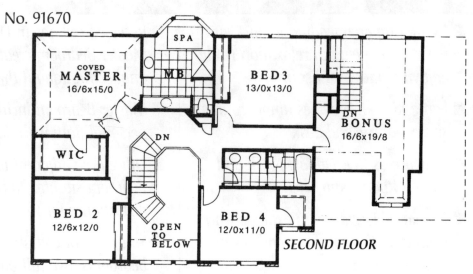

SECOND FLOOR

PLAN INFO:

First Flr.	*1,586 sq. ft.*
Second Flr.	*1,433 sq. ft.*
Bonus Rm.	*305 sq. ft.*
Garage	*632 sq. ft.*
Sq. Footage	*3,019 sq. ft.*
Foundation	*Crawl space*
Bedrooms	*Four*
Baths	*2(Full), 1(Half)*

*No materials list available

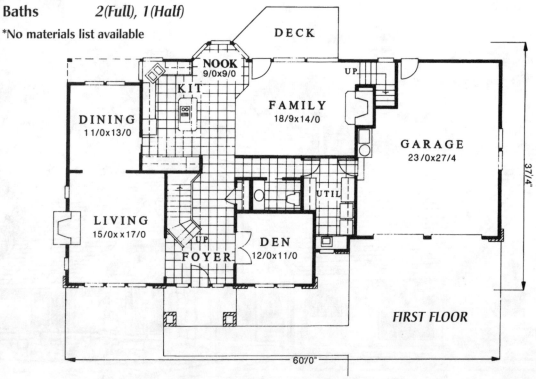

FIRST FLOOR

- *Exciting French Contemporary exterior conceals a simple building form*

- *Spacious formal Living Room, located off the Foyer, includes a large hearth fireplace as a terrific focal point*

- *Formal dining is a delight in the elegant Dining Room that flows from the Living Room and is located next to the Kitchen*

- *Large and expansive Kitchen is equipped with a center, cooktop island, more than ample counter and storage space, plus a sunny Breakfast Nook*

- *Open to the Kitchen and Nook, the Family Room feels even more spacious and includes another great fireplace as well as direct access to the outdoor deck*

- *Cozy Den provides a private area for late night work or just time alone*

- *A coved ceiling crowns the Master Suite that includes a large walk-in closet, and lavish Bath with a spa tub, separate shower and two vanities*

- *Three additional second floor bedrooms share a full, double vanity hall Bath*

Dignified Drama Exudes From This Charmer

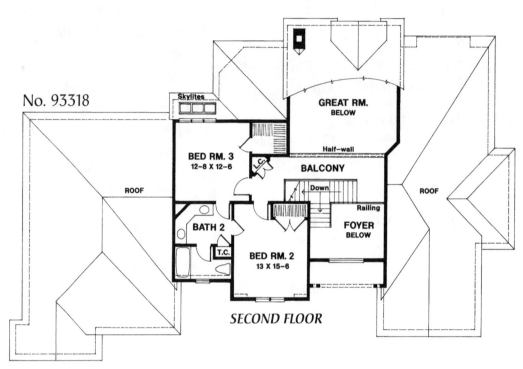

No. 93318

SECOND FLOOR

- GREAT RM. BELOW
- Skylites
- BED RM. 3 — 12-8 X 12-6
- L.C.
- BALCONY
- Half-wall
- ROOF
- Down
- Railing
- FOYER BELOW
- ROOF
- BATH 2
- T.C.
- BED RM. 2 — 13 X 15-6

PLAN INFO:

First Flr.	*1,984 sq. ft.*
Second Flr.	*633 sq. ft.*
Basement	*1,984 sq. ft.*
Garage	*884 sq. ft.*
Sq. Footage	*2,617 sq. ft.*
Foundation	*Basement*
Bedrooms	*Three*
Baths	*2(Full), 1(Half)*

*No materials list available

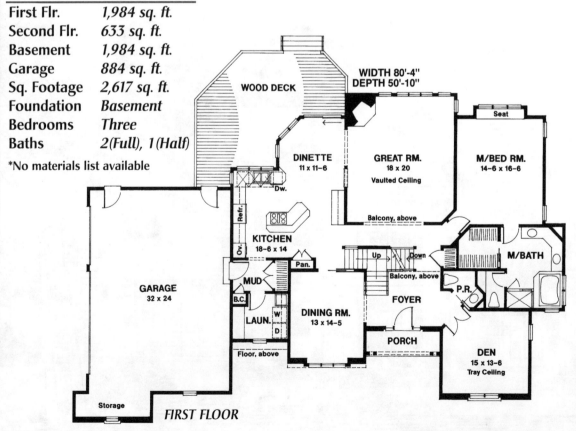

FIRST FLOOR

- WOOD DECK
- WIDTH 80'-4" / DEPTH 50'-10"
- Seat
- DINETTE — 11 x 11-6
- GREAT RM. — 18 x 20 — Vaulted Ceiling
- M/BED RM. — 14-6 x 16-6
- Balcony, above
- Dw.
- Refr.
- KITCHEN — 18-6 x 14
- Ov.
- Up / Down
- Balcony, above
- M/BATH
- Pan.
- MUD
- B.C.
- GARAGE — 32 x 24
- LAUN. — W / D
- DINING RM. — 13 x 14-5
- FOYER
- P.R.
- PORCH
- Floor, above
- DEN — 15 x 13-6 — Tray Ceiling
- Storage

■ Columned entrance invites guests into a bright two-story Foyer with a split stairway and impressive balcony

■ Vaulted ceiling, glass wall and a corner fireplace in the Great Room provides a spacious but cozy place for family gatherings

■ Brightened by skylights above the sink and made convenient by a built-in pantry, center island with cooktop and abundant cabinet space, this Kitchen is sure to please the any gourmet cook

■ Quiet corner Den with tray ceiling and decorative front window presents a getaway for daytime projects and late night reading

■ Romantic window seat, walk-in closet, luxurious Bath with a double vanity, and a raised window tub allow the Master Suite to become a personal hide-away

■ Two additional bedrooms share a large, segmented Bath on second floor

Classic Beauty With A Distinctive Air

PLAN INFO:

First Flr.	*2,065 sq. ft.*
Second Flr.	*970 sq. ft.*
Basement	*2,047 sq. ft.*
Garage	*524 sq. ft.*
Sq. Footage	*3,035 sq. ft.*
Foundation	*Basement*
Bedrooms	*Four*
Baths	*3(Full), 1(Half)*

SECOND FLOOR

BEDROOM 12'-0"x13'-4"

BATH

1/2 WALL

1/2 WALL

C.

BALCONY

TO ATTIC

RAIL

DN

FOYER BELOW

L.

BEDROOM 13'-0"x11'-6"

C.

B.

C.

BEDROOM 13'-4"x14'-4"

LEDGE

No. 20094

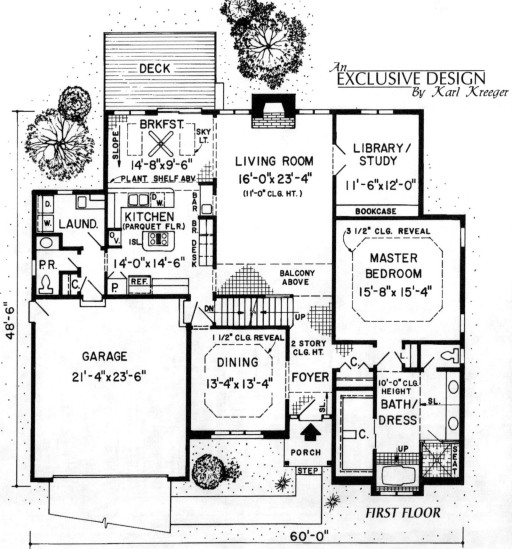

DECK

An EXCLUSIVE DESIGN *By Karl Kreeger*

BRKFST. 14'-8"x9'-6"

SKY LT.

SLOPE

PLANT SHELF ABV.

LIVING ROOM 16'-0"x 23'-4" (11'-0" CLG. HT.)

LIBRARY/ STUDY 11'-6"x12'-0"

BOOKCASE

D.

W.

LAUND.

KITCHEN (PARQUET FLR.) 14'-0"x14'-6"

D.W.

O.V.

ISL

BAR BR DESK

3 1/2" CLG. REVEAL

MASTER BEDROOM 15'-8"x 15'-4"

P.R.

C.

P.

REF.

BALCONY ABOVE

DN

UP

48'-6"

GARAGE 21'-4"x23'-6"

1 1/2" CLG. REVEAL

DINING 13'-4"x13'-4"

2 STORY CLG. HT.

FOYER

C.

L.

10'-0" CLG. HEIGHT

BATH/ DRESS

SL.

SL.

C.

PORCH

STEP

UP

SEAT

FIRST FLOOR

60'-0"

■ *Master Suite situated away from family areas features many extra amenities such as double vanities and walk-in closet, 10-foot ceiling in Bath, raised tub, and shower stall with seat*

■ *Built-in bookcase in Library allows quiet sanctuary for study and deep meditation*

■ *Comfortable Breakfast Room invites informal mealtime enjoyment with ceiling fan, plant shelf, skylights, and sliding glass doors to deck in backyard*

■ *Beautiful Kitchen with parquet floor, stove top island, pantry, and desk affords easy access to both dining areas*

■ *A recessed ceiling in the Dining Room offers formality to more solemn occasions*

■ *Three additional Bedrooms contain special features to make each room unique*

■ *Fireplaced Living Room shares a wetbar with the Kitchen for easy stocking and clean-up*

Two-Story Daylight Basement Design

PLAN INFO:

First Flr.	1,888 sq. ft.
Second Flr.	1,613 sq. ft.
Basement	1,365 sq. ft.
Garage	955 sq. ft.
Sq. Footage	4,866 sq. ft.
Foundation	Bsmt, Crawl space
Bedrooms	Four
Baths	3(Full), 1(Half)

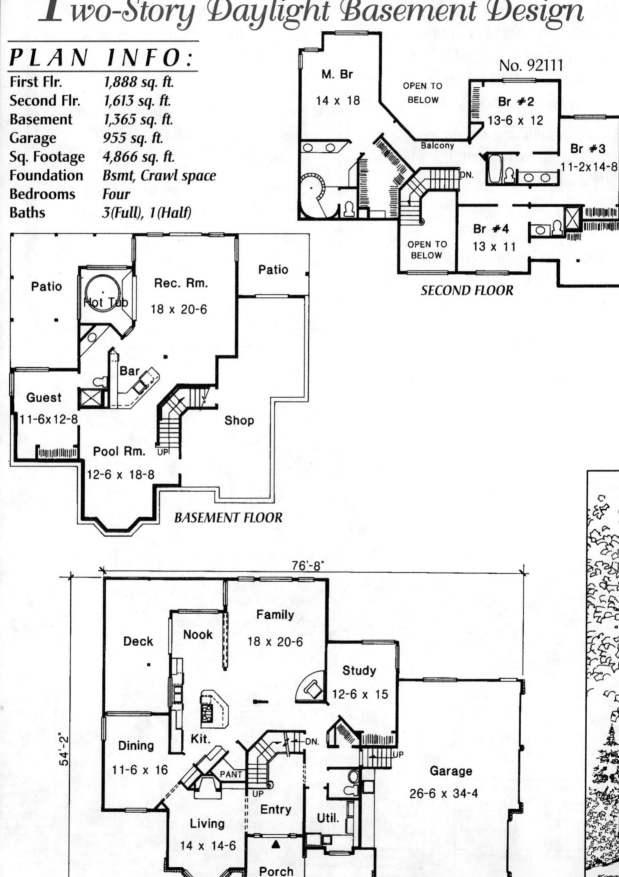

No. 92111

SECOND FLOOR

M. Br
14 x 18

OPEN TO BELOW

Br #2
13-6 x 12

Br #3
11-2x14-8

Balcony

DN.

OPEN TO BELOW

Br #4
13 x 11

Patio

Hot Tub

Rec. Rm.
18 x 20-6

Patio

Bar

Guest
11-6x12-8

Shop

Pool Rm.
12-6 x 18-8

UP

BASEMENT FLOOR

76'-8"

54'-2"

Deck

Nook

Family
18 x 20-6

Study
12-6 x 15

Dining
11-6 x 16

Kit.

PANT

UP

DN.

UP

Garage
26-6 x 34-4

Entry

Util.

Living
14 x 14-6

Porch

FIRST FLOOR

- Step-down to the 3-car Garage hidden by a graceful arched window treatment

- Secluded Study with corner window affords peaceful atmosphere

- Exceptional Family Room has elegant corner fireplace and additional light floods in from door to deck

- Private Guest room with ample closet space opens to expansive patio

- Island Kitchen features a pantry for extra storage and bright sunny Nook with access to rear deck

- Recreation Room with wetbar, private Bath including convenient shower stall, luxurious hot tub, and angled vanity features a Pool Room

- Basement complemented by a handy-man Shop located next to the Recreation Room with access to a backyard patio

Come Inside And Experience
Luxurious Living

PLAN INFO:

First Flr.	2,277 sq. ft.
Second Flr.	1,838 sq. ft.
Basement	2,277 sq. ft.
Garage	1,196 sq. ft.
Sq. Footage	4,115 sq. ft.
Foundation	Basement
Bedrooms	Four
Baths	3(Full), 1(Half)

*No materials list available

No. 93328

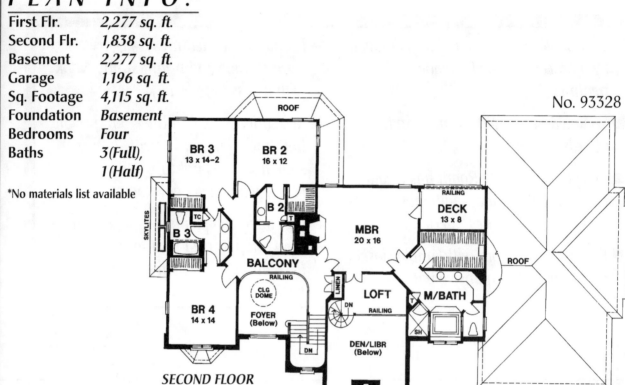

SECOND FLOOR

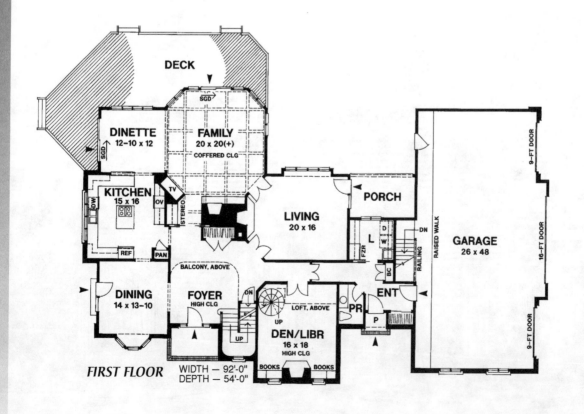

FIRST FLOOR

WIDTH — 92'-0"
DEPTH — 54'-0"

■ *Graceful and imposing, this home presents intricate brick detailing, fan top windows and a double front door topped with a arched transom window inviting everyone to come inside*

■ *Formal Living Room, accessed by French doors from the Foyer and Family Room, features a huge fireplace, expansive view of the backyard and a private covered Porch to expand living space in warmer weather*

■ *Formal Dining Room with a bay window, glass door to the side yard, and adjacent Kitchen allows elegant but efficient entertaining*

■ *Convenient Den/Library offers a cozy fireplace set between windows and built-in book shelves, and a unique spiral staircase to a reading Loft*

■ *Expansive Family Room provides a wonderful gathering place with a coffered ceiling, huge fireplace, built-in entertainment center, a wall of window with a sliding glass door to the backyard, and open to Dinette area*

■ *Gourmet Kitchen located between the Dining Room and Dinette is equipped with a cooktop island, built-in pantry and an abundance of counter and cabinet space*

■ *Lavish Master Bedroom Suite includes a cozy fireplace, private deck, large walk-in closet, exclusive access to reading Loft, and an ideal Bath with a raised window tub, step-in shower and double vanity*

■ *Three additional large bedrooms have private access to full baths*

Elegance From Any Direction

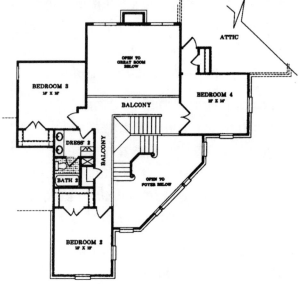

SECOND FLOOR

PLAN INFO:

First Flr.	*1,966 sq. ft.*
Second Flr.	*872 sq. ft.*
Garage	*569 sq. ft.*
Sq. Footage	*2,838 sq. ft.*
Foundation	*Slab, Crawl space*
Bedrooms	*Four*
Baths	*Three*

*No materials list available

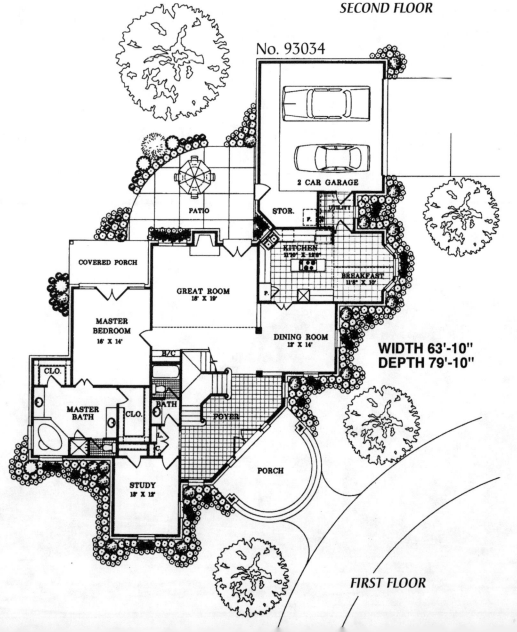

No. 93034

WIDTH 63'-10"
DEPTH 79'-10"

FIRST FLOOR

- Designed for a corner or pie-shaped lot, this beautiful brick home provides lots of natural light and comfort

- Spectacular split staircase moves upward floor from the two-story, glass and tile Foyer

- Entrance to the Dining Room features square columns accenting the elegance of the room

- Cook top work island and angled window sink help to make this well equipped Kitchen even more efficient

- Distinctive Breakfast area accented by a vaulted ceiling and expansive bay window

- Sumptuous retreat for the homeowner, the Master Suite includes his-n-her closets and vanities, and a corner whirlpool tub with a separate shower

- Three additional bedrooms on the second floor share a double vanity Bath

$\mathscr{F}$amily Preferred Features In Tudor Design

PLAN INFO:

First Flr.	2,167 sq. ft.
Second Flr.	755 sq. ft.
Basement	2,224 sq. ft.
Garage	690 sq. ft.
Sq. Footage	2,922 sq. ft.
Foundation	Basement
Bedrooms	Three
Baths	3 (Full), 1 (Half)

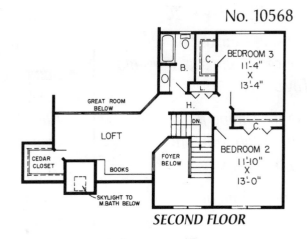

No. 10568

SECOND FLOOR

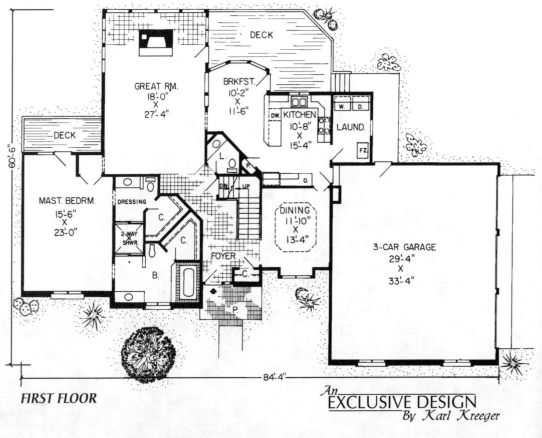

FIRST FLOOR

An
EXCLUSIVE DESIGN
By Karl Kreeger

- Energy-efficient Foyer leads into an expansive Great Room, featuring a wood-burning fireplace and easy access to the Breakfast Nook and a large deck

- A U-shaped Kitchen efficiently located close to both the sunny Breakfast Nook and the elegant formal Dining Room

- Deluxe Master Suite includes a private wood deck, two way shower and his and her bathroom, space with separate facilities

- Terrific cedar closet located on the second floor is an easy solution to the storage of winter clothing

- Special Loft area serves as a balcony over the Great Room

- Two additional bedrooms share a full hall Bath

All The Luxury You Want & Need

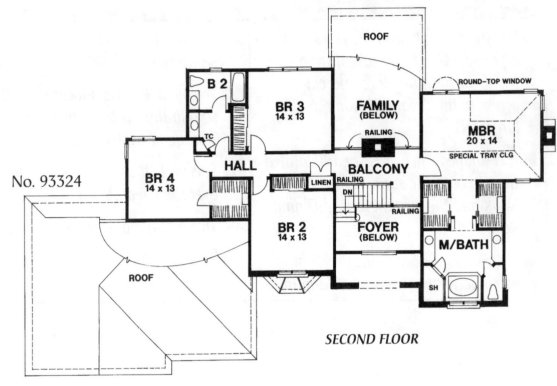

No. 93324

ROOF

B 2

BR 3
14 x 13

FAMILY
(BELOW)

RAILING

ROUND-TOP WINDOW

MBR
20 x 14
SPECIAL TRAY CLG

HALL

BR 4
14 x 13

LINEN

BALCONY
RAILING

DN

BR 2
14 x 13

FOYER
(BELOW)

RAILING

M/BATH

SH

ROOF

SECOND FLOOR

PLAN INFO:

First Flr.	*1,880 sq. ft.*
Second Flr.	*1,465 sq. ft.*
Basement	*1,880 sq. ft.*
Garage	*900 sq. ft.*
Sq. Footage	*3,345 sq. ft.*
Foundation	*Basement*
Bedrooms	*Four*
Baths	*2(Full), 1(Half)*

*No materials list available

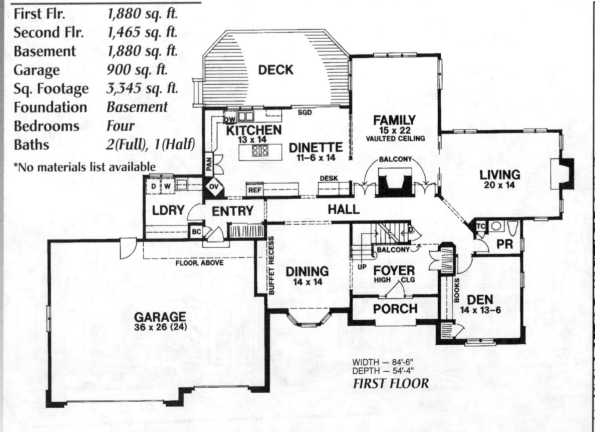

DECK

SGD

FAMILY
15 x 22
VAULTED CEILING

KITCHEN
13 x 14

DINETTE
11-6 x 14

BALCONY

LIVING
20 x 14

DESK

PAN

REF

HALL

LDRY

ENTRY

TC

PR

BC

BALCONY

FLOOR, ABOVE

BUFFET RECESS

UP

FOYER
HIGH CLG

BOOKS

DEN
14 x 13-6

DINING
14 x 14

GARAGE
36 x 26 (24)

PORCH

WIDTH — 84'-6"
DEPTH — 54'-4"
FIRST FLOOR

■ *Elegant entrance created by an alcove Porch, windows surrounding the front door and a two-story Foyer with a landing staircase and direct access to all living areas*

■ *Buffet recess and splendid bay window in Dining Room add beauty and convenience for entertaining*

■ *A splendid fireplace accents the formal Living Room that also has views on three sides and pocket doors into the Family Room area*

■ *Vaulted ceiling, a second fireplace, double French doors and windows all around make the Family Room perfect for informal gatherings*

■ *Efficient and well-appointed Kitchen is equipped with a built-in pantry, work island and Dinette area with sliding glass doors to an outdoor deck*

■ *First floor Den offers built-in book shelves and a quiet corner for relaxing or working*

■ *Second floor Master Bedroom Suite has its own wing and includes a special tray ceiling, his-n-her closets and a secluded Bath with two vanities and a raised window tub*

■ *Three additional large bedrooms share a full hall Bath*

Sleek $\mathcal{F}$rench Contemporary

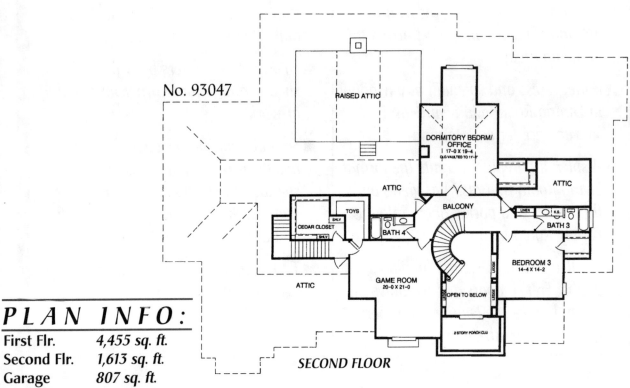

No. 93047

RAISED ATTIC

DORMITORY BEDRM/
OFFICE
17-0 X 19-4
CLG VAULTED TO 11-F

ATTIC

BALCONY

ATTIC

CEDAR CLOSET   TOYS   SHLV

BATH 4

LINEN   K.S.

BATH 3

GAME ROOM
20-0 X 21-0

OPEN TO BELOW

BEDROOM 3
14-4 X 14-2

ATTIC

2 STORY PORCH CLG

SECOND FLOOR

PLAN INFO:

First Flr.	*4,455 sq. ft.*
Second Flr.	*1,613 sq. ft.*
Garage	*807 sq. ft.*
Sq. Footage	*6,068 sq. ft.*
Foundation	*Slab, Crawl space*
Bedrooms	*Four*
Baths	*4(Full), 2(Half)*

*No materials list available

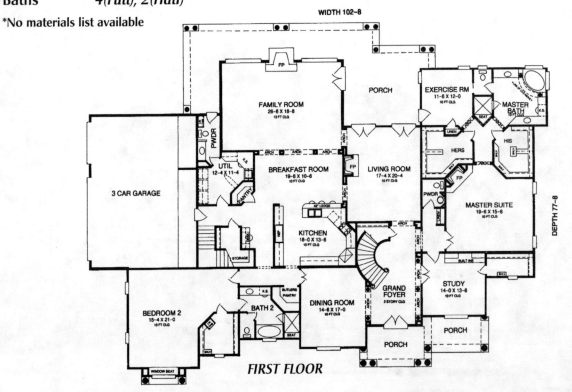

WIDTH 102-8

FP

FAMILY ROOM
26-6 X 18-8
13 FT CLG

PORCH

EXERCISE RM
11-6 X 12-0
10 FT CLG

MASTER
BATH

3 CAR GARAGE

PWDR

UTIL
12-4 X 11-4

BREAKFAST ROOM
19-6 X 10-6
10 FT CLG

FP

LIVING ROOM
17-4 X 20-4
10 FT CLG

LINEN

HERS

HIS

FP

PWDR

MASTER SUITE
19-6 X 15-6
10 FT CLG

PANTRY

42" LEDGE

KITCHEN
18-0 X 13-6
10 FT CLG

BUILT INS

STORAGE

BEDROOM 2
15-4 X 21-0
10 FT CLG

BATH 2

BUTLERS
PANTRY

DINING ROOM
14-6 X 17-0
10 FT CLG

GRAND
FOYER
2 STORY CLG

STUDY
14-0 X 13-6
10 FT CLG

SEAT

PORCH

PORCH

DEPTH 77-8

WINDOW SEAT

FIRST FLOOR

- Grand Foyer offers a gracefully, curved staircase, and elegant curved arches into the Formal Dining Room, Study and Living Room

- Formal Living Room features a center fireplace with arches to the Breakfast and Family Rooms as well as direct access to an expansive Porch

- Kitchen, Breakfast Room and an enormous Family Room open to one another to provide a great place for family gatherings

- Luxurious Master Suite with a cozy corner fireplace, his-n-her walk-in closets, an Exercise Room, and elegantly appointed Master Bath will pamper your every need

- A first floor Bedroom with a private large Bath and walk-in closet accommodates guests with privacy

- Two additional bedrooms on the second floor with walk-in closets have access to a full Bath

Timeless Elegance Exudes From This Design

PLAN INFO:

First Flr.	*2,080 sq. ft.*
Second Flr.	*1,051 sq. ft.*
Basement	*2,080 sq. ft.*
Garage	*666 sq. ft.*
Sq. Footage	*3,131 sq. ft.*
Foundation	*Basement*
Bedrooms	*Four*
Baths	*3(Full), 1(Half)*

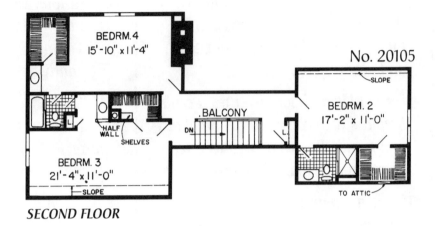

No. 20105

BEDRM. 4
15'-10" x 11'-4"

SLOPE

BEDRM. 2
17'-2" x 11'-0"

BALCONY

DN

HALF WALL

SHELVES

BEDRM. 3
21'-4" x 11'-0"

SLOPE

TO ATTIC

SECOND FLOOR

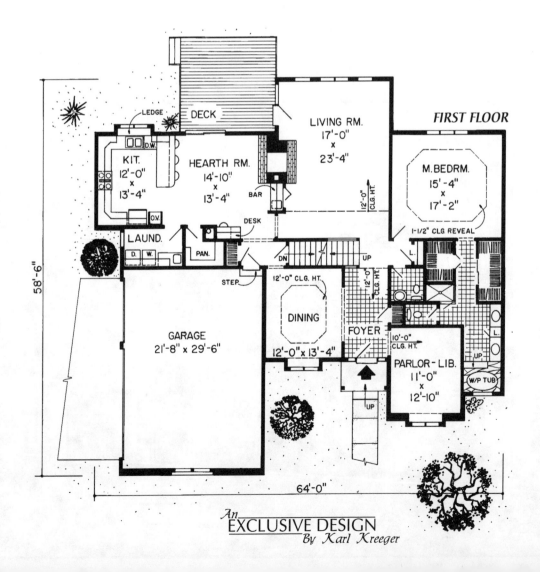

FIRST FLOOR

LEDGE

DECK

KIT.
12'-0"
x
13'-4"

HEARTH RM.
14'-10"
x
13'-4"

LIVING RM.
17'-0"
x
23'-4"

BAR

DESK

M. BEDRM.
15'-4"
x
17'-2"

12'-0" CLG. HT.

1-1/2" CLG REVEAL

LAUND.

D. W.

PAN.

STEP

DN

UP

L.

12'-0" CLG. HT.

12'-0" CLG. HT.

DINING

FOYER

10'-0"
CLG. HT.

GARAGE
21'-8" x 29'-6"

12'-0" x 13'-4"

PARLOR - LIB.
11'-0"
x
12'-10"

W/P TUB

UP

UP

58'-6"

64'-0"

An
EXCLUSIVE DESIGN
By Karl Kreeger

- Step through the Foyer past stairway into the massive Living Room characterized by high ceiling, abundant windows, and access to private rear deck

- Both Living and Hearth Rooms share easy entertaining and cozy atmosphere with two-way access to the wetbar and fireplace

- Steal away to quiet solitude in the Parlor/Library for serious contemplation or light conversation with good friends

- Recessed ceiling, twin walk-in closets and a luxurious Bath adorn first floor Master Suite

- Three ample bedrooms enjoy walk-in closets and neighboring baths upstairs

- Overlook the tiled Foyer and Living Room from balcony above

- Revealed ceiling in Dining Room adds sophistication to formal meals

- Adjoining Kitchen with handy breakfast bar and nearby pantry is marvel of convenience

Two Story Farmhouse With A Wrap-Around Porch

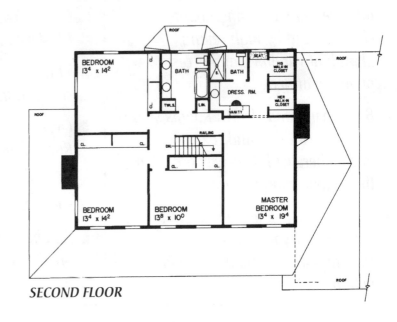

SECOND FLOOR

PLAN INFO:

First Flr.	1,590 sq. ft.
Second Flr.	1,344 sq. ft.
Basement	1,271 sq. ft.
Garage	2-car
Sq. Footage	2,934 sq. ft.
Foundation	Basement
Bedrooms	Four
Baths	2(Full), 1(Half)

No. 99205

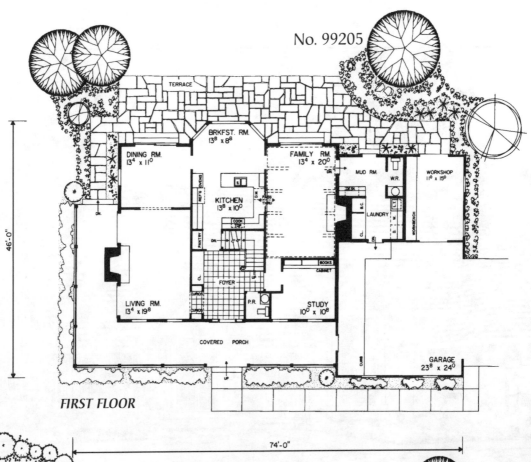

FIRST FLOOR

- *Wrap-around covered porch gives good old-fashioned air of comfort and relaxation*

- *Welcoming Foyer features angled staircase, huge closet, built-in curio shelves and access to a convenient Powder Room*

- *Extra-large Workshop has a built-in workbench for tool organization*

- *Oversized Master Bedroom opens to a Dressing Room with make-up vanity, old-fashioned window seat and his-n-her walk-in closets*

- *Spacious Kitchen with plenty of cabinet and counter space and a cook-top opens to bright sunny Breakfast Room overlooking the backyard terrace*

- *Exceptionally large Family Room with a fireplace and convenient pass-thru to the Kitchen exits to the patio or steps down to Mudroom with a Washroom and handy built-in desk*

- *Three Bedrooms share a full Bath with a double vanity, tub, linen closet and extra towel storage*

Columned Entrance Greets Your Visitors

No. 93040

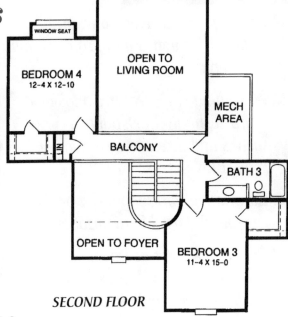

BEDROOM 4
12-4 X 12-10

WINDOW SEAT

OPEN TO LIVING ROOM

MECH AREA

BALCONY

BATH 3

OPEN TO FOYER

BEDROOM 3
11-4 X 15-0

SECOND FLOOR

PLAN INFO:

First Flr.   *2,266 sq. ft.*
Second Flr.   *609 sq. ft.*
Garage   *589 sq. ft.*
Sq. Footage   *2,875 sq. ft.*
Foundation   *Slab, Crawl space*
Bedrooms   *Four*
Baths   *Three*

*No materials list available

WIDTH 70-6

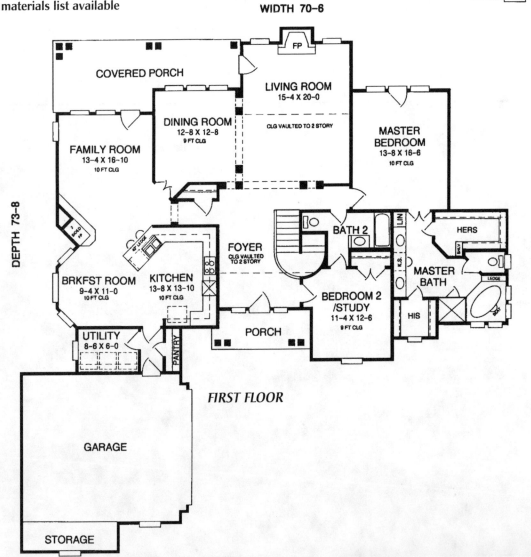

DEPTH 73-8

COVERED PORCH

FP

LIVING ROOM
15-4 X 20-0
CLG VAULTED TO 2 STORY

DINING ROOM
12-8 X 12-8
9 FT CLG

FAMILY ROOM
13-4 X 16-10
10 FT CLG

MASTER BEDROOM
13-8 X 16-6
10 FT CLG

BATH 2

HERS

FOYER
CLG VAULTED TO 2 STORY

BRKFST ROOM
9-4 X 11-0
10 FT CLG

KITCHEN
13-8 X 13-10
10 FT CLG

MASTER BATH

LEDGE

BEDROOM 2 /STUDY
11-4 X 12-6
9 FT CLG

HIS

UTILITY
8-6 X 6-0

PANTRY

PORCH

GARAGE

STORAGE

FIRST FLOOR

- *Impressive columns frame the stately front entrance featuring decorative windows, a vaulted Foyer and a lovely curved stairway*

- *Expansive Living room crowned by a two-story vaulted ceiling features more columns from Foyer and into formal Dining Room, an inviting hearth fireplace and access to a covered back Porch for easy entertaining*

- *Unusual two-sided fireplace accents both the Family Room and the Breakfast Room creating warm and space for informal gatherings*

- *Efficient Kitchen has a peninsula sink and snack bar, a sunny Breakfast Room, a walk-in pantry and Utility Room*

- *Private Master Bedroom Suite offers access to the backyard and a lavish Bath with two walk-in closets, two vanities and a raised corner atrium tub*

- *Another first floor Bedroom/Study with access to a full hall Bath could also double as a home office*

- *Two additional bedrooms on the second floor have walk-in closets and share a full Bath*

Vaulted Ceilings Make This Home Special

PLAN INFO:

First Flr.	4,014 sq. ft.
Second Flr.	727 sq. ft.
Garage	657 sq. ft.
Sq. Footage	4,741 sq. ft.
Foundation	Slab
Bedrooms	Five
Baths	Five

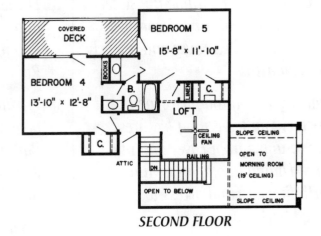

SECOND FLOOR

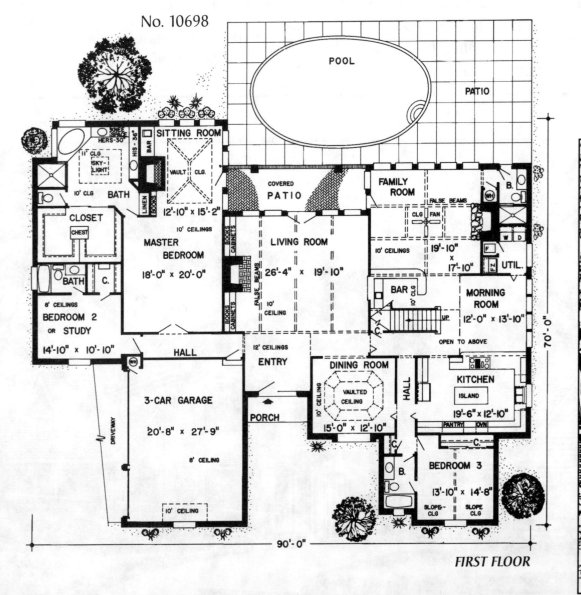

No. 10698

FIRST FLOOR

- Survey two-story Morning Room and yard beyond from vantage point upstairs

- Stately Dining Room displays special ceiling works

- Island Kitchen separated from Morning Room by counter bar

- Delight in pool vistas from covered patio

- Master Suite opens into spacious king-size Bedroom flowing into awesome Sitting Room with built-in bar and fireplace

- Two bedrooms adjoining full bath and covered deck share upper level with Loft

- Skylit Master Bath features his-n-her basins and leads directly into double walk-in closet

- Additional Bedroom adjacent to Master Suite doubles as Study

- Both Family Room and Living Room include beamed, ten-foot ceilings, massive fireplaces, and share a wetbar and access to patio

$\mathcal{F}$ive Fireplaces Add A Distinctive Flair

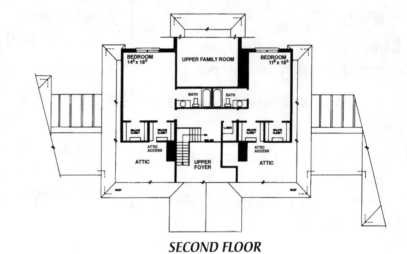

SECOND FLOOR

PLAN INFO:

First Flr.	4,104 sq. ft.
Second Flr.	979 sq. ft.
Basement	2,110 sq. ft.
Garage	2-car
Sq. Footage	5,083 sq. ft.
Foundation	Basement
Bedrooms	Four
Baths	4(Full), 1(Half)

No. 99204

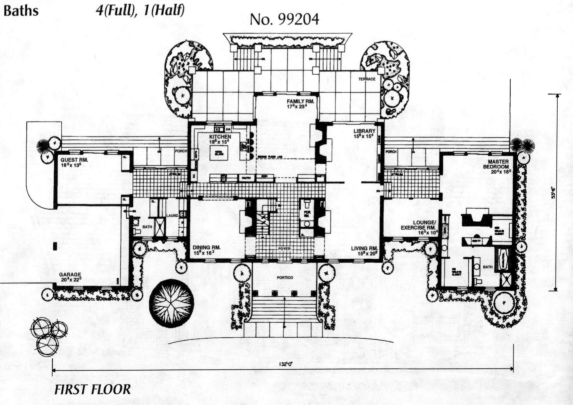

FIRST FLOOR

- Sprawling portico opens to a two-story Foyer with a sweeping view of the overhead balcony

- Fireplaced Dining and Living Rooms allow for formal entertaining

- Towering Family Room leads out to an expansive rear terrace

- Rear-facing rooms linked to the backyard by charming atrium doors

- Centrally located island Kitchen for easy service to active areas

- Huge Master suite has a fireplace, luxurious walk-in closets, plush Bath, and extends into a unique exercise room

- Upstairs bedrooms feature twin walk-in closets and private baths

- Design topped with decorative glass-walled cupola to reflect air of elegance

- Guest room has desirable privacy and the added comfort of an adjoining Bath – perfect for entertaining visitors

$\mathscr{P}$lan Separates Formal & Family Areas

No. 20359

PLAN INFO:

First Flr.	2,516 sq. ft.
Second Flr.	1,602 sq. ft.
Basement	2,516 sq. ft.
Garage	822 sq. ft.
Sq. Footage	4,118 sq. ft.
Foundation	Basement
Bedrooms	Four
Baths	3(Full), 1(Half)

SECOND FLOOR

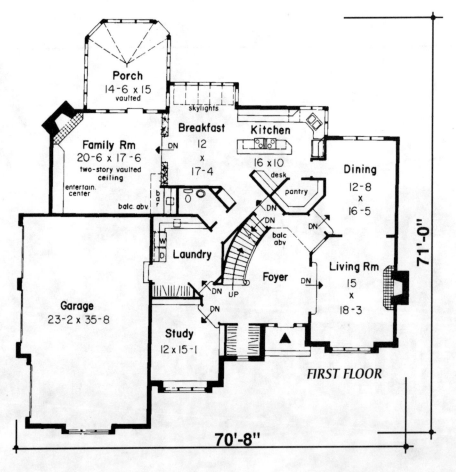

FIRST FLOOR

- Elegant home easily entertains without dislocating children

- Sunken Study, Living Room, and Dining Room surround central Foyer

- Informal areas in rear of house include the island Kitchen with large walk-in pantry

- Pantry adjacent to skylit Breakfast room and convenient Laundry Room

- Guest Room features a spacious walk-in closet and private Bath

- Family Room with vaulted ceiling, built-in bar and entertainment center includes direct access to vaulted Porch

- Ascend curving staircase to find wide-open Balcony Loft for semi-private contemplation

- Master Suite features tray ceiling, large walk-in closet, private Bath, and deck overlooking backyard vista

- Two additional Bedrooms upstairs connected by adjoining Bathroom

Skylights Brighten Rooms Throughout This Home

PLAN INFO:

First Flr.	2,314 sq. ft.
Basement	1,302 sq. ft.
Garage	1,017 sq. ft.
Sq. Footage	3,616 sq. ft.
Foundation	Basement
Bedrooms	Four
Baths	Three

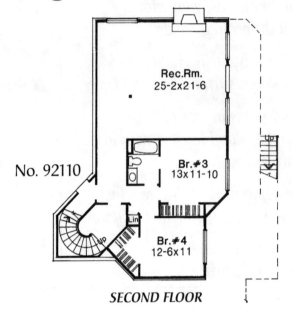

No. 92110

Rec.Rm.
25-2x21-6

Br.#3
13x11-10

Br.#4
12-6x11

SECOND FLOOR

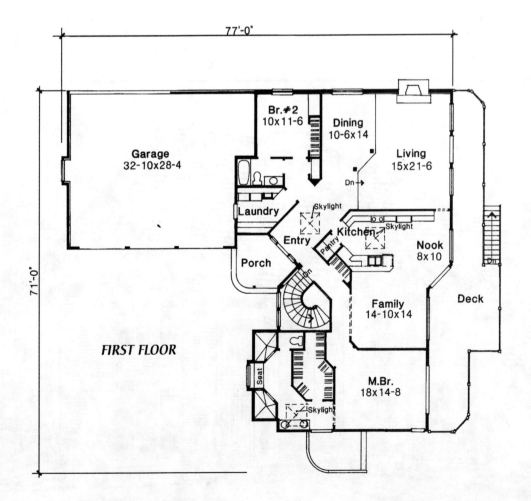

77'-0"

71'-0"

Garage
32-10x28-4

Br.#2
10x11-6

Dining
10-6x14

Living
15x21-6

Laundry

Skylight

Dn

Entry

Kitchen

Skylight

Pantry

Nook
8x10

Porch

Family
14-10x14

Deck

FIRST FLOOR

Seat

M.Br.
18x14-8

Skylight

■ Rounded covered porch leads to aesthetically pleasing Entry with skylight for extra brightness and elegant circular staircase

■ Kitchen features a skylight, plenty of cabinet space, eat-in Nook and exits to an extra-long double deck

■ Sunken fireplaced Living Room flooded with light from two large windows has access to deck

■ Convenient first-floor Laundry Room has built-in shelving and ample space for appliances

■ Master Bedroom has added luxury of private high-walled deck

■ Master Bath offers skylight, double vanity, elegant window seat, his-n-her showers, and enormous walk-in closet

■ Recreation Room with fireplace has interesting window works and includes easy access to top deck

■ Three-car Garage has decorative window allowing added light and attractiveness

Bridge Over Foyer Is A Unique Feature Of This Home

No. 10535

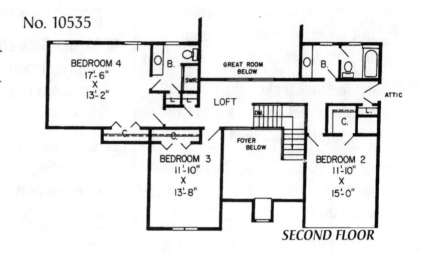

SECOND FLOOR

PLAN INFO:

First Flr.	2,335 sq. ft.
Second Flr.	1,157 sq. ft.
Basement	2,281 sq. ft.
Garage	862 sq. ft.
Sq. Footage	3,492 sq. ft.
Foundation	Basement
Bedrooms	Four
Baths	3(Full), 2(Half)

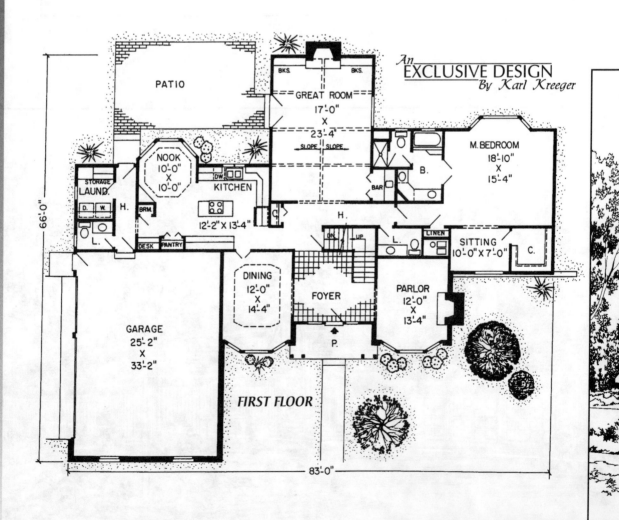

An EXCLUSIVE DESIGN *By Karl Kreeger*

FIRST FLOOR

■ *A dramatic, two-story Foyer opens into a Great Room with a cathedral ceiling and a cozy fireplace framed with built-in bookcases*

■ *Both a formal Parlor, with its own fireplace, and an elegant Dining Room with a decorative ceiling provide a view of the front yard through inviting bay windows*

■ *An octagonal Breakfast Nook adds to the already spacious and well-appointed Kitchen*

■ *A cooktop work island, double sink, built-in pantry, built-in desk and a broom closet are just a few of the amenities awaiting you in the efficient Kitchen*

■ *The first floor Master Bedroom is equipped with a quaint sitting room, private compartmented Bath and a walk-in closet*

■ *Three additional bedrooms share the second floor with a Loft and two full Baths*

Curved Staircase Highlights Design

PLAN INFO:

First Flr.	2,036 sq. ft.
Second Flr.	1,554 sq. ft.
Garage	533 sq. ft.
Sq. Footage	3,590 sq. ft.
Foundation	Basement
Bedrooms	Three
Baths	2(Full), 1(Half)

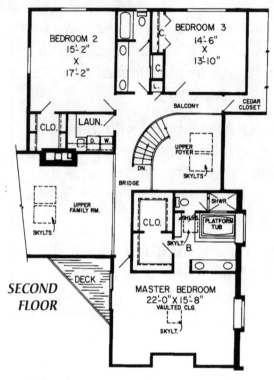

SECOND FLOOR

No. 10587

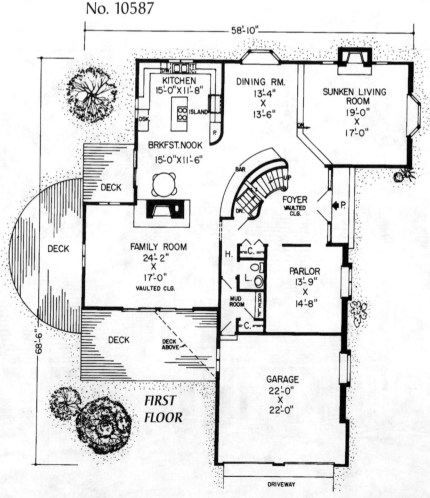

FIRST FLOOR

- Sweeping staircase and skylit sloped ceiling in Foyer create elegant sophistication

- Step down to fireplaced Living Room off grand Foyer

- Large Kitchen features centralized food preparation island and desk for meal planning

- Enjoy informal meals in your bright Breakfast Nook overlooking backyard deck

- Dining Room affords exquisite environment for formal dining

- Vaulted ceiling in the Family Room and expansive fireplace extend warm welcome

- Spacious Master Bedroom includes private bath with double walk-in closets, basins, and raised tub

- Enjoy summer evenings on the private deck outside your Master Bedroom

- Two additional bedrooms on second floor share full Bath

- Cedar closet provides exclusive storage area for valuable items

*M*agnificent Style With
Loads Of Convenience

PLAN INFO:

First Flr.	*2,397 sq. ft.*
Second Flr.	*1,612 sq. ft.*
Basement	*2,397 sq. ft.*
Garage	*1,187 sq. ft.*
Sq. Footage	*4,009 sq. ft.*
Foundation	*Basement*
Bedrooms	*Four*
Baths	*3(Full),*
	1(Half)

*No materials list available

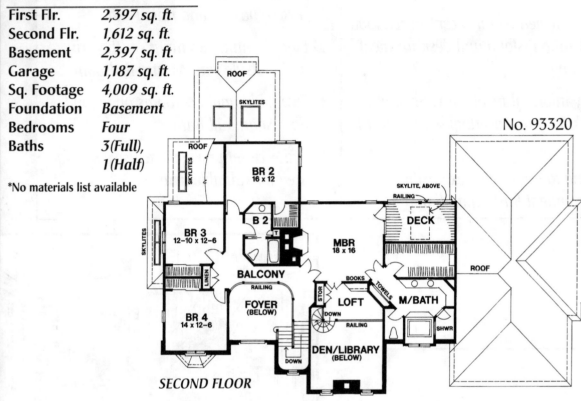

No. 93320

SECOND FLOOR

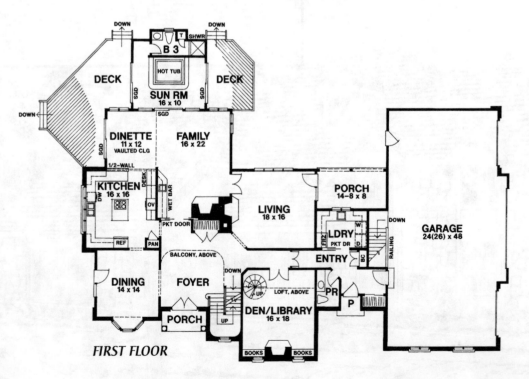

FIRST FLOOR

- *Impressive two-story entrance leads into the Foyer with an angled staircase and curved balcony*

- *Elegant formal Dining Room with a beautiful bay window facing front yard and glass doors to side yard*

- *Library features a spiral staircase to the Loft above and a cozy fireplace flanked by built-in shelves*

- *Family Room flows from the Dinette to the Living Room for easy entertaining and features a window wall, fireplace and wetbar*

- *U-shaped Kitchen equipped with a cooktop island, loads of counter space,*

- *built-in pantry and desk makes this room a joy to use*

- *Vaulted ceiling crowns the Dinette Area and sliding glass doors provide direct access to the wooden deck*

- *Get-away from the cares of the day in the hot tub in the Sun Room*

- *Scrumptious Master Bedroom Suite creates another world with its own fireplace, outdoor deck, raised atrium tub and direct access to the Library Loft*

- *Three additional bedrooms with ample closets share a full hall, segmented Bath*

Contemporary Two-Story With Secluded Sleeping Area

PLAN INFO:

First Flr.	1,712 sq. ft.
Second Flr.	1,387 sq. ft.
Basement	1,548 sq. ft.
Garage	831 sq. ft.
Sq. Footage	3,099 sq. ft.
Foundation	Basement
Bedrooms	Four
Baths	3(Full), 1(Half)

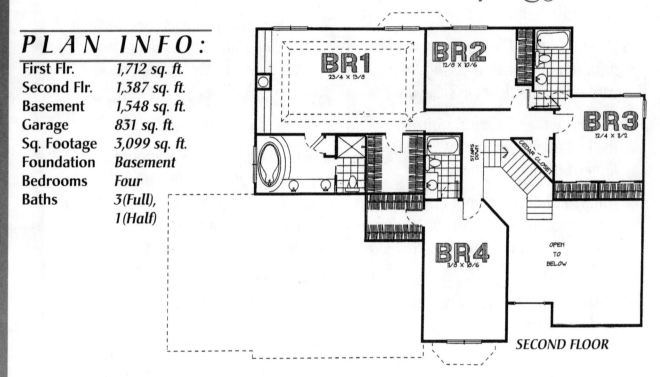

SECOND FLOOR

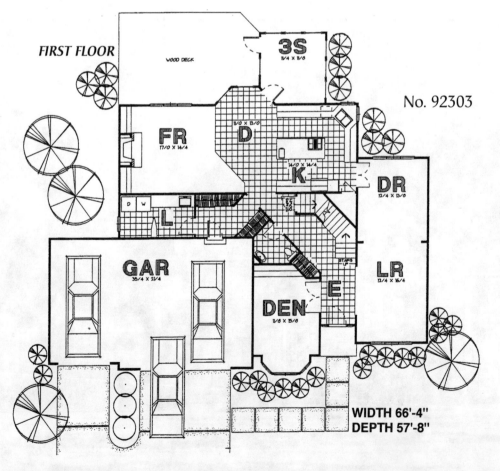

FIRST FLOOR

No. 92303

WIDTH 66'-4"
DEPTH 57'-8"

- Beautiful Den with built-in book-shelves located off curved Entry features picturesque bay window

- Fireplaced Family Room merges with a sunny Dinette and large Kitchen creating an open airy feeling

- Country Kitchen features large center island with vegetable sink and stove top and corner sink

- Atrium doors open from Kitchen into formal Dining Room and vaulted Living Room

- First-floor Laundry Room conveniently situated off the 3-car Garage doubles as a mudroom

- Master suite on upper level has coffered ceilings, massive walk-in closet and luxurious bath with whirlpool tub

- Three additional bedrooms sharing a full Bath and Cedar Closet occupy remainder of second level

- Three-season porch just off Dinette offers protected outdoor relaxation

*R*elax On Your Own Private Veranda

PLAN INFO:

First Flr.	*3,051 sq. ft.*
Garage	*646 sq. ft.*
Sq. Footage	*3,051 sq. ft.*
Foundation	*Crawl space*
Bedrooms	*Three*
Baths	*3(Full), 1(Half)*

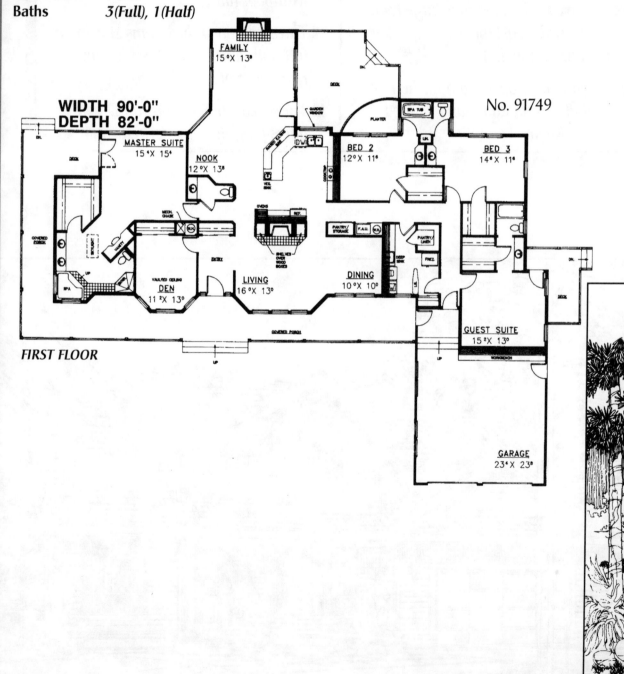

WIDTH 90'-0"
DEPTH 82'-0"

No. 91749

FAMILY
15⁰X 13⁸

MASTER SUITE
15⁴X 15⁴

NOOK
12⁰X 13⁸

BED 2
12⁰X 11⁶

BED 3
14⁸X 11⁶

DEN
11²X 13⁰

LIVING
16⁰X 13⁰

DINING
10⁰X 10⁰

GUEST SUITE
15²X 13⁰

GARAGE
23⁴X 23⁸

FIRST FLOOR

- *Inspired by warm climates this friendly home features a wrap-around porch accessible from most of the living areas and the Master Suite*

- *Both the Living Room/Dining Room area and the Family Room feature hearth fireplaces to chase evening chill away*

- *More than accommodating Guest room has a private Bath*

- *Skylit Master Suite has an elevated custom spa, double vanity, walk-in closet, and an additional vanity outside of the bathroom*

- *Each of the three additional bedrooms have walk-in closets and share a full Bath*

$\mathcal{P}$erfect For Large Parties
Or Intimate Gatherings

PLAN INFO:

First Flr.	*2,310 sq. ft.*
Second Flr.	*866 sq. ft.*
Garage	*679 sq. ft.*
Sq. Footage	*3,176 sq. ft.*
Foundation	*Slab*
Bedrooms	*Three*
Baths	*3(Full), 1(Half)*

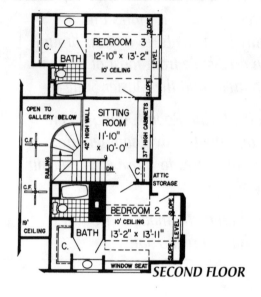

SECOND FLOOR

No. 10663

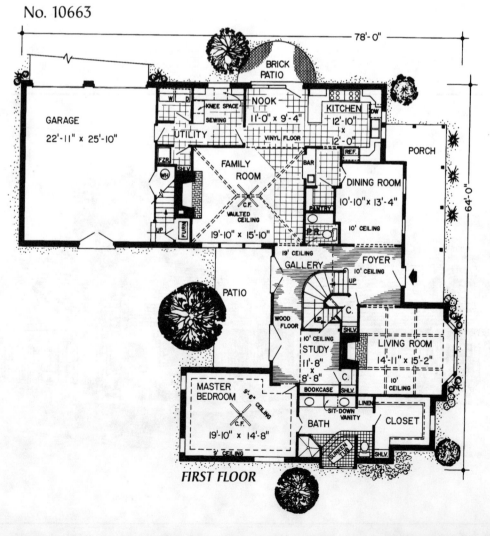

FIRST FLOOR

- *Greet guests in this fabulous Foyer adorned with an impressive two-story gallery behind a beautiful curving stairway*

- *Leisurely unwind with family and friends in this Family Room with a vaulted ceiling, large windows, built-in bar, and lots of space*

- *Entertain guests in the Dining Room for more formal occasions*

- *Lovely Sitting Room between two second-floor Bedrooms overlooks Gallery below*

- *Master Bedroom with paddle fan offers cool comfort for a good night's rest*

- *Lavish Bath in Master Suite features sunken tub to soak away the day's cares*

- *Two bedrooms on upper floor include individual baths and walk-in closets*

- *Cheerful Eating Nook has easy approach to efficient Kitchen*

- *Wood beams on ceiling of Living Room exudes warm welcome*

Colonial Tradition In A Very Neat Layout

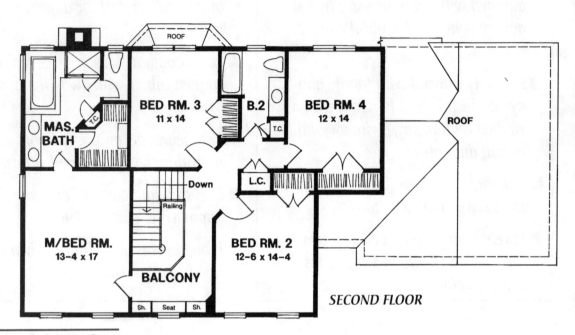

BED RM. 3
11 x 14

BED RM. 4
12 x 14

B.2

MAS. BATH

T.C.

ROOF

Down

Railing

L.C.

M/BED RM.
13-4 x 17

BED RM. 2
12-6 x 14-4

BALCONY

Sh. | Seat | Sh.

SECOND FLOOR

PLAN INFO:

First Flr.	1,228 sq. ft.
Second Flr.	1,191 sq. ft.
Basement	1,228 sq. ft.
Garage	528 sq. ft.
Sq. Footage	2,419 sq. ft.
Foundation	Basement
Bedrooms	Four
Baths	2(Full), 1(Half)

*No materials list available

No. 93319

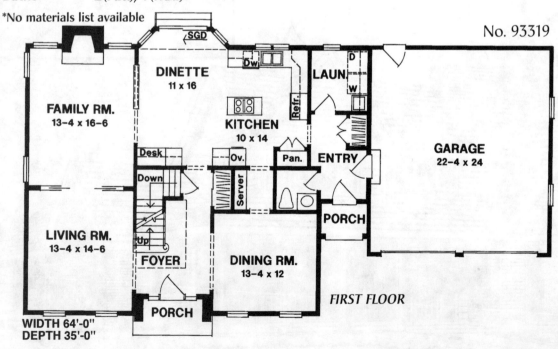

SGD

DINETTE
11 x 16

Dw

LAUN

D

W

FAMILY RM.
13-4 x 16-6

KITCHEN
10 x 14

Refr.

Desk

Ov.

Pan.

ENTRY

GARAGE
22-4 x 24

Down

Server

Up

FOYER

DINING RM.
13-4 x 12

PORCH

LIVING RM.
13-4 x 14-6

PORCH

FIRST FLOOR

WIDTH 64'-0"
DEPTH 35'-0"

- Recessed entrance leads guests into a classic Foyer with a wrap-around stairway, balcony and easy access to all main floor rooms

- Large formal Living Room and Dining Room make entertaining a breeze

- Expansive Kitchen features a cooktop island, built-in pantry, double sink, planning area, and a warm, open Dinette area with alcove sliding doors to the outdoors

- Spacious Family Room, open on all sides, offers convenience and warmth with a hearth fireplace corner

windows, and sliding doors to the living room and Kitchen area

- Luxurious, front-to-back Master Bedroom Suite with a private, segmented Bath offers a large walk-in closet, double vanity and raised window tub

- Balcony area has a built-in window seat to cuddle up and read a book or just enjoy the view

- Three additional bedrooms, each with ample closet space, share a full hall Bath

With A Large Family In Mind

No. 91710

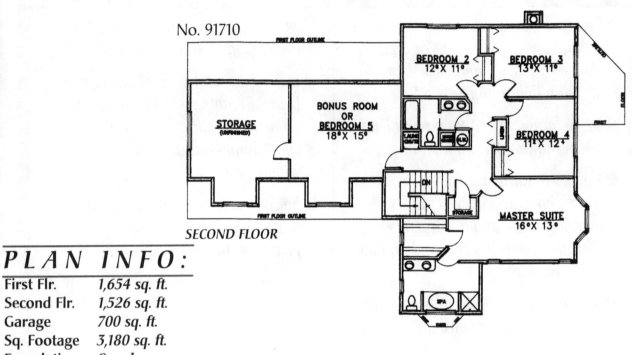

SECOND FLOOR

PLAN INFO:

First Flr.	1,654 sq. ft.
Second Flr.	1,526 sq. ft.
Garage	700 sq. ft.
Sq. Footage	3,180 sq. ft.
Foundation	Crawl space
Bedrooms	Five
Baths	Three

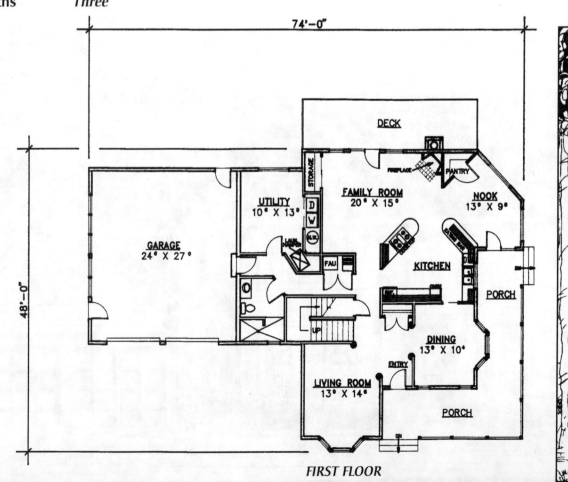

FIRST FLOOR

- An expansive stylish home with a wide country-style, wrap-around Porch provides a lot of comfortable living space

- An efficient, well-appointed Kitchen serves as a nucleus to the living areas of the home, equipped with a cook top extension counter, snack bar and a Nook area with built-in pantry

- Corner fireplace, storage closet and French doors to an outdoor deck add convenience and class to the large Family Room

- Elegant formal dining takes place in a Dining Room that includes a bay window and easy access to the Kitchen area

- Inventive chute from the second floor feeds into the laundry hamper in the corner of the Utility Room

- Ultra private Bath with a spa and double vanity highlight the Master Suite, which also includes a walk-in closet

- Four additional bedrooms share a full, segmented, double vanity Bath

$\mathcal{D}$ignified Traditional Brick Design

PLAN INFO:

First Flr.	2,292 sq. ft.
Garage	526 sq. ft.
Sq. Footage	2,292 sq. ft.
Foundation	Slab, Crawl space**
Bedrooms	Four
Baths	2(Full), 1(Half)

*No materials list available

**Please specify when ordering

WIDTH 80-7

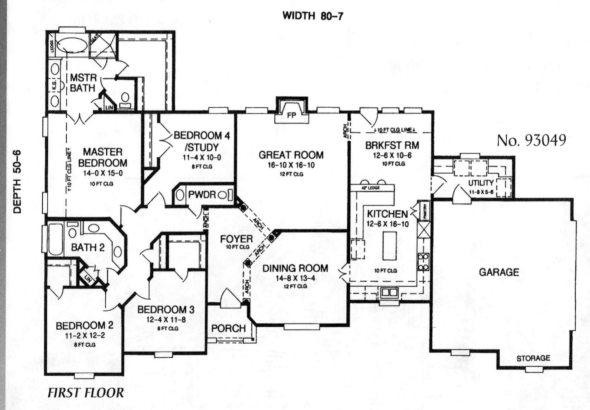

No. 93049

DEPTH 50-6

MSTR BATH

MASTER BEDROOM
14-0 X 15-0
10 FT CLG

BEDROOM 4 /STUDY
11-4 X 10-0
8 FT CLG

GREAT ROOM
16-10 X 16-10
12 FT CLG

BRKFST RM
12-6 X 10-6
10 FT CLG

UTILITY
11-8 X 5-6

BATH 2

PWDR

FOYER
10 FT CLG

KITCHEN
12-6 X 16-10

GARAGE

DINING ROOM
14-8 X 13-4
12 FT CLG

BEDROOM 2
11-2 X 12-2
8 FT CLG

BEDROOM 3
12-4 X 11-8
8 FT CLG

PORCH

STORAGE

FIRST FLOOR

- *Covered entrance leads into the open Foyer accented by dramatic columns farming entrance to the elegant Dining Room and the expansive Great Room*

- *Convenient floor plan separates living area and sleeping areas all on one level*

- *Spacious, gourmet Kitchen made efficient by an abundance of counter and cabinet space, a built-in pantry, work island and snack bar as well as direct access to Dining Room, Utility Room and Breakfast Room*

- *Entertaining is a delight in the Great Room with a hearth fireplace framed by windows and adjacent to the kitchen area*

- *Lavish Master Bedroom Suite includes an enormous walk-in closet and a ultra Bath with a window tub, extra-large shower and double vanity*

- *Three additional bedrooms with huge closets share a full Bath with a double vanity*

$\mathcal{B}$ay Windows Top Impressive Design

PLAN INFO:

First Flr.	2,136 sq. ft.
Second Flr.	873 sq. ft.
Basement	2,130 sq. ft.
Garage	720 sq. ft.
Sq. Footage	3,009 sq. ft.
Foundation	Basement
Bedrooms	Four
Baths	Three

No. 20138

SECOND FLOOR

Br 4
10-8 x 12

Br 3
13-2 x 12-8

DN

DN Balcony chute

DN

open to below

Br 2
13 x 12

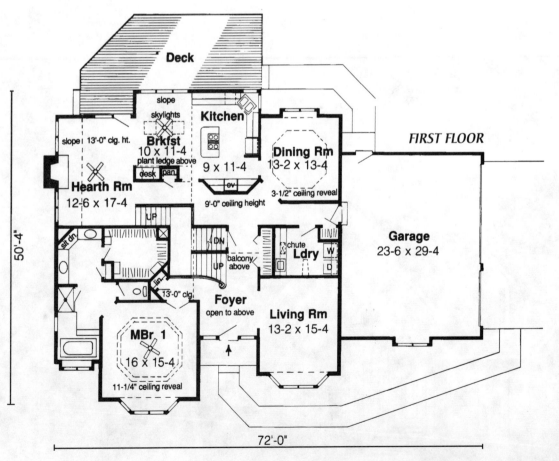

FIRST FLOOR

Deck

slope

skylights

Kitchen

slope 13'-0" clg. ht.

Brkfst
10 x 11-4
plant ledge above
desk pan

9 x 11-4
ov

9'-0" ceiling height

Hearth Rm
12-6 x 17-4

Dining Rm
13-2 x 13-4
3-1/2" ceiling reveal

Garage
23-6 x 29-4

UP

sit dn

DN

balcony above

chute **Ldry**
W
D

50'-4"

lin
13'-0" clg.

UP

Foyer
open to above

Living Rm
13-2 x 15-4

MBr 1
16 x 15-4
11-1/4" ceiling reveal

72'-0"

- ■ *Facade of this impressive home includes bay windows that hint at classic beauty found upon entering*

- ■ *Two-story Foyer flanked by formal Living Room and Master suite*

- ■ *Adjoining Breakfast Room abuts cozy fireplaced Hearth Room*

- ■ *Master Suite contains amenities such as a spacious walk-in closet and amazing Bathroom*

- ■ *Efficient gourmet Kitchen complete with range-top island for simple meal preparation*

- ■ *Step past staircase in Foyer to rear of home to find the formal Dining Room with a bump-out window overlooking the backyard*

- ■ *Ascend two-way staircase from either the Hearth Room or Foyer to find three more Bedrooms*

- ■ *Each bedroom has a walk-in closet and two adjoining Baths*

- ■ *Note the convenient laundry chute that will deliver clothes to first floor Laundry Room effortlessly*

Unique Brick Treatment
Enhances This Facade

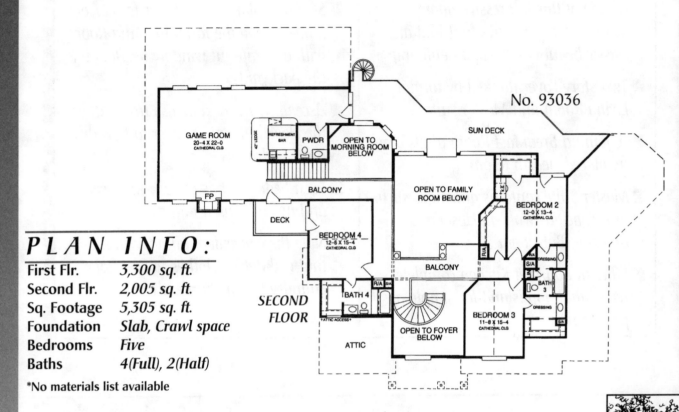

No. 93036

GAME ROOM
20-4 X 22-0
CATHEDRAL CLG

FP

42" LEDGE

REFRESHMENT BAR

PWDR

OPEN TO MORNING ROOM BELOW

SUN DECK

BALCONY

DECK

OPEN TO FAMILY ROOM BELOW

BEDROOM 2
12-0 X 13-4
CATHEDRAL CLG

BEDROOM 4
12-6 X 15-4
CATHEDRAL CLG

BALCONY

DRESSING

BATH 4

R/A   S/A

BATH 3

DRESSING

BEDROOM 3
11-8 X 15-4
CATHEDRAL CLG

S/A

SECOND FLOOR

ATTIC ACCESS

OPEN TO FOYER BELOW

ATTIC

PLAN INFO:

First Flr.	3,300 sq. ft.
Second Flr.	2,005 sq. ft.
Sq. Footage	5,305 sq. ft.
Foundation	Slab, Crawl space
Bedrooms	Five
Baths	4(Full), 2(Half)

*No materials list available

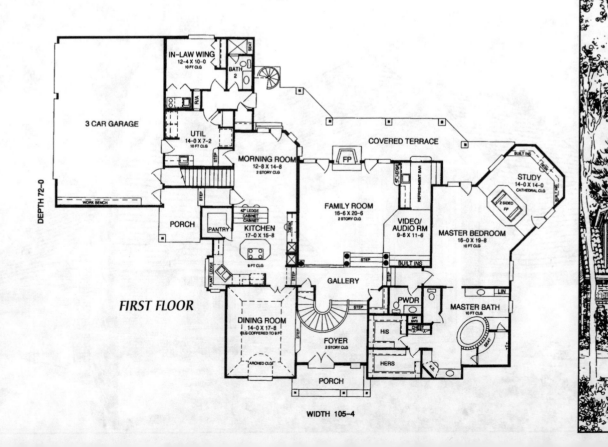

IN-LAW WING
12-4 X 10-0
10 FT CLG

BATH 2

3 CAR GARAGE

UTIL
14-0 X 7-2
10 FT CLG

COVERED TERRACE

BUILT INS

STUDY
14-0 X 14-0
CATHEDRAL CLG

FP

MORNING ROOM
12-8 X 14-8
2 STORY CLG

2 SIDED FP

DEPTH 72-0

WORK BENCH

PORCH

PANTRY

42" LEDGE
CABINET
CABINET

KITCHEN
17-0 X 15-8

9 FT CLG

FAMILY ROOM
16-6 X 20-6
2 STORY CLG

REFRESHMENT BAR

42" LEDGE

VIDEO/ AUDIO RM
9-6 X 11-6

MASTER BEDROOM
16-0 X 19-8
10 FT CLG

BUILT INS

STEP

GALLERY

STEP

LIN

FIRST FLOOR

DINING ROOM
14-0 X 17-8
CLG COFFERED TO 9 FT

ARCHED CLG

FOYER
2 STORY CLG

STEP

PWDR

HIS

HERS

MASTER BATH
10 FT CLG

SEAT

PORCH

WIDTH 105-4

- *Two-story Foyer with a dramatic cascading staircase*

- *Large two-story Family Room opening off the Gallery area includes a video/audio area and a conveniently placed refreshment bar*

- *Decorative ceiling in the elegant Dining Room adds a sense of style and elegance*

- *Master Suite with a private Study that is crowned with a cathedral ceiling and separated from the Bedroom by a see-through fireplace*

- *Master Bath with a centerpiece whirlpool accented by glass blocking is a great retreat after a grueling day*

- *An In-Law Wing with a Bath and kitchenette affords privacy for its occupants*

- *Three additional bedrooms, two with deck access, and two full baths on the second floor*

- *An oversized Game Room with a refreshment bar, powder room and fireplace also on the second floor*

Stucco, Brick & Arched Windows
Enhance Facade

SECOND FLOOR

PLAN INFO:

First Flr.	1,973 sq. ft.
Second Flr.	1,060 sq. ft.
Garage	531 sq. ft.
Sq. Footage	3,034 sq. ft.
Foundation	Slab, Crawl space
Bedrooms	Five
Baths	2(Full), 1(Half)

*No materials list available

No. 93041

FIRST FLOOR

WIDTH 64-4
DEPTH 53-4

- *A stucco design accented by an impressive arched two-story entry*

- *All major living areas provide views to the rear grounds, terrific for "on the golf course" location*

- *Kitchen, Breakfast Room and Family Room are adjacent and open to one another*

- *An island cook top and double sinks along with an abundance of storage space makes the Kitchen even more convenient*

- *Fantastic Master Suite has an angled whirlpool tub, separate shower and his-n-her vanities*

- *The three additional bedrooms are located on the second floor*

Garden Room & Abundant Windows Add Warmth

PLAN INFO:

First Flr.	2,527 sq. ft.
Second Flr.	1,115 sq. ft.
Garage, Ldry & Workshop	884 sq. ft.
Sq. Footage	3,642 sq. ft.
Foundation	Crawl space
Bedrooms	Three
Baths	2(Full), 1(Half)

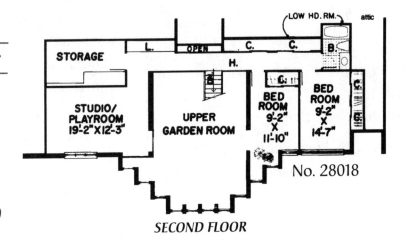

No. 28018

SECOND FLOOR

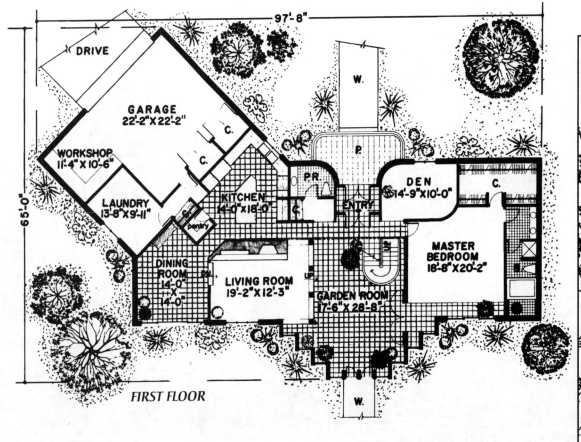

FIRST FLOOR

- *Passive solar design for front Southern exposure provides much of the heating requirements for this home*

- *Elegant balcony overlooks the glorious Garden Room on the main floor*

- *Glimmering fires in the fireplace add a cozy touch to the formal Living Room which flows easily into the formal Dining Room creating a relaxing and easy layout for entertaining*

- *Expansive Kitchen has a built-in pantry area and food preparation island making it the gourmet's preference*

- *Private Master Suite includes large walk-in closet and personal Bath with an atrium window*

- *Upper level contains two bedrooms and a Bath on the east side and a Studio/Playroom and Storage area on the west*

Everything You Could Possibly Ask For In A Home

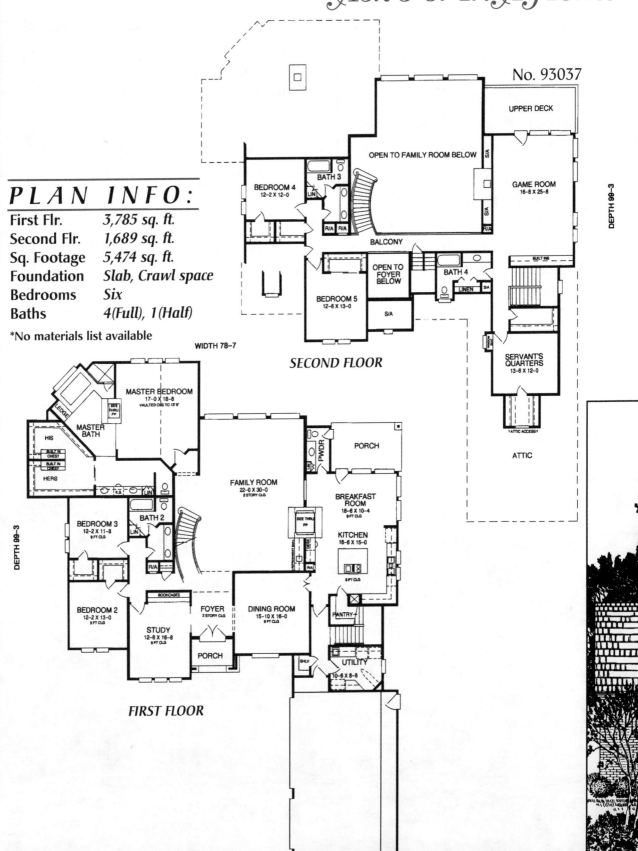

No. 93037

PLAN INFO:

First Flr.	3,785 sq. ft.
Second Flr.	1,689 sq. ft.
Sq. Footage	5,474 sq. ft.
Foundation	Slab, Crawl space
Bedrooms	Six
Baths	4(Full), 1(Half)

*No materials list available

UPPER DECK

OPEN TO FAMILY ROOM BELOW

BEDROOM 4
12-2 X 12-0

BATH 3

GAME ROOM
16-8 X 25-8

DEPTH 99-3

BALCONY

OPEN TO FOYER BELOW

BATH 4

LINEN

BEDROOM 5
12-6 X 13-0

SERVANT'S QUARTERS
13-6 X 12-0

WIDTH 78-7

SECOND FLOOR

ATTIC

ATTIC ACCESS

MASTER BEDROOM
17-0 X 18-6
VAULTED CLG to 13'6"

SEE THRU FP

MASTER BATH

HIS

BUILT IN CHEST

BUILT IN CHEST

HERS

PORCH

DEPTH 99-3

FAMILY ROOM
22-0 X 30-0
2 STORY CLG

PWDR

BREAKFAST ROOM
18-6 X 10-4
9 FT CLG

BEDROOM 3
12-2 X 11-8
9 FT CLG

BATH 2

SEE THRU FP

KITCHEN
18-6 X 15-0

9 FT CLG

BOOKCASES

FOYER
2 STORY CLG

DINING ROOM
15-10 X 16-0
9 FT CLG

PANTRY

BEDROOM 2
12-2 X 13-0
9 FT CLG

STUDY
12-6 X 16-8
9 FT CLG

PORCH

SHLV

UTILITY
10-6 X 8-8

FIRST FLOOR

- *Grand and impressive two-story Foyer with curved staircase welcomes guests*

- *Enormous two-story Family Room that includes a masonry see-through fireplace*

- *Large efficient Kitchen with a built-in pantry, cook-top island and a Breakfast Room that is enhanced by the other side of the see-through fireplace in the Family Room*

- *Second see-through fireplace in the Master Suite that provides a cozy feel in the Master Bedroom and Master Bath*

- *His-n-her walk-in closets, his-n-her vanities, an atrium-style whirlpool tub*

- *and separate shower gives this Master Bath pizzazz*

- *Two secondary bedrooms with walk-in closets on the first floor share a full hall Bath with a double vanity*

- *Two additional family bedrooms on the second floor that share a full hall Bath*

- *Large Game Room provides a super place to relax and access to a rear deck on the second floor*

- *An additional bedroom provided for Servant's Quarters*

*F*loor To Ceiling *W*indow
*T*reatment *E*nhances *D*esign

SECOND FLOOR

Study
11 x 14-8

M. Bath

L.C

DN.

OPEN TO BELOW

M.Bedroom
14 x 20-6

Deck

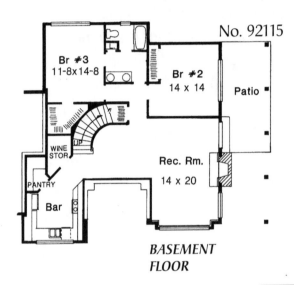

No. 92115

Br #3
11-8x14-8

Br #2
14 x 14

Patio

WINE STOR

UP

PANTRY

Rec. Rm.
14 x 20

Bar

BASEMENT FLOOR

PLAN INFO:

First Flr.	1,587 sq. ft.
Second Flr.	905 sq. ft.
Basement	1,289 sq. ft.
Garage	1,020 sq. ft.
Sq. Footage	3,781 sq. ft.
Foundation	Basement
Bedrooms	Three
Baths	3(Full), 1(Half)

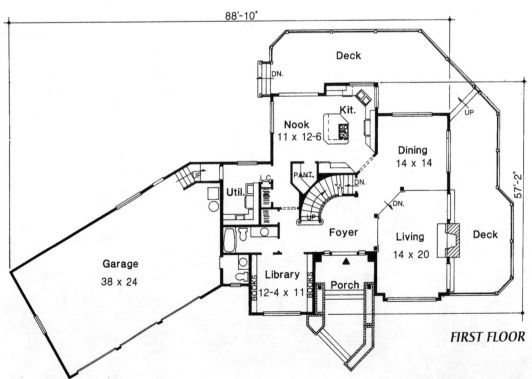

88'-10"

Deck

DN.

Kit.

UP

Nook
11 x 12-6

Dining
14 x 14

57'-2"

Util.

L.C

PANT.

DN.

UP

DN.

Foyer

Living
14 x 20

Deck

Garage
38 x 24

BOOKS

Library
12-4 x 11

BOOKS

Porch

FIRST FLOOR

- *Unique front porch with elegant brick angled wall makes for a grand entrance to the gracious Foyer*

- *Recreation Room affords efficient uniqueness of full Kitchen, Bar, and Wine Storage, and exit to a spacious patio*

- *Curved staircase from another era in Foyer combines with open concept allowing for ease in entertaining*

- *Kitchen with island surrounded by cabinets features a Pantry and opens*

to the sunny Nook which steps onto a wrap-around bi-level Deck

- *Book-shelved Library has interesting window treatment and extends to Bath*

- *Master Bedroom features a fireplace, double windows and a sliding glass door leading to a private deck*

- *Three-car angled Garage steps up to enter roomy Utility Area with separate linen closet*

Surround Yourself With Luxury

PLAN INFO:

First Flr.	*4,075 sq. ft.*
Second Flr.	*1,179 sq. ft.*
Garage	*633 sq. ft.*
Sq. Footage	*5,254 sq. ft.*
Foundation	*Slab*
Bedrooms	*Five*
Baths	*Five*

No. 10615

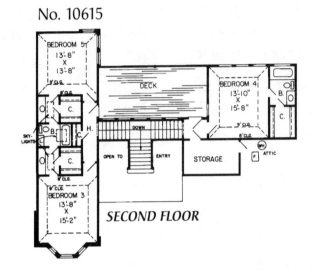

SECOND FLOOR

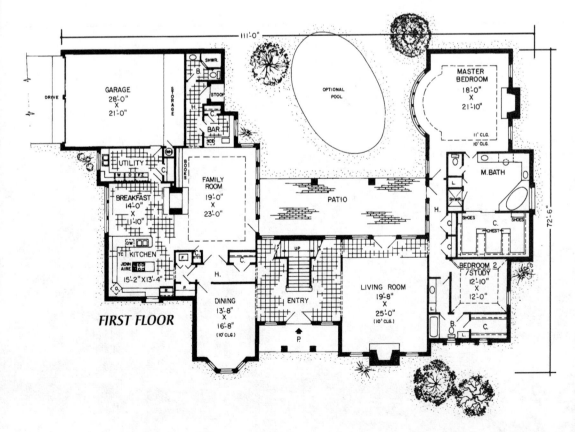

FIRST FLOOR

- Master Bedroom complex with huge walk-in closet featuring double shoe storage areas, chests, and plenty of clothes space

- Staircase landing splits ascent into separate wings creating aura of seclusion in fourth Bedroom

- Spacious Family Room enables vast Living Room to be reserved for more formal entertaining

- Two more bedrooms on the second level retain personal walk-in closets and basins, but share lavatory facilities

- Courtyard area isolates Master Bedroom and second Bedroom from busy living areas

- Kitchen design allows easy access to Breakfast Area and formal Dining Room

Intricate Details Highlight A Spectacular Design

No. 92504

PLAN INFO:

First Flr.	2,553 sq. ft.
Second Flr.	1,260 sq. ft.
Garage	714 sq. ft.
Sq. Footage	3,813 sq. ft.
Foundation	Slab, Crawl space
Bedrooms	Four
Baths	3(Full), 1(Half)

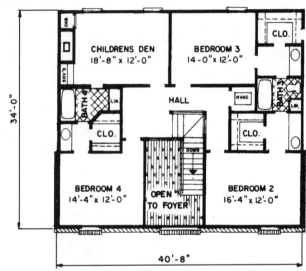

SECOND FLOOR

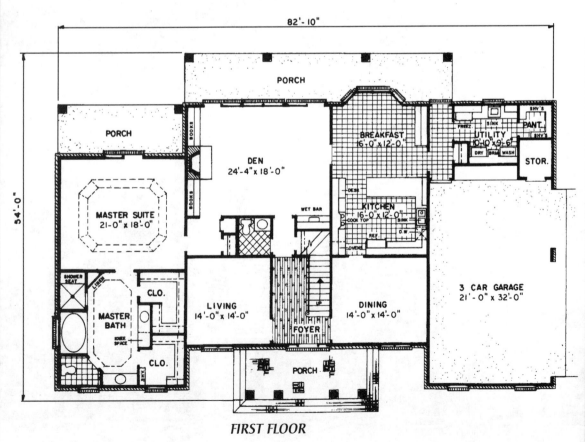

FIRST FLOOR

- An intricately detailed entrance leads into a magnificent two-story Foyer

- Formal Living Room and Dining Room, located on each side of Foyer, feature large decorative windows

- Amenities abound in the efficient Kitchen equipped with a peninsula counter and Breakfast Area

- Beyond the Foyer, the large Den equipped with a fireplace, built-in shelves and wetbar provides a spacious relaxing atmosphere for informal gatherings

- Decorative ceilings add more elegance to the grand Master Suite and the Master Bath which includes two walk-in closets, two vanities, an oversized shower and window tub

- Three additional bedrooms located on the second floor offer walk-in closets, adjacent full baths and a terrific Children's Den

$\mathcal{F}$amily Living Is At The Heart Of This Design

No. 91751

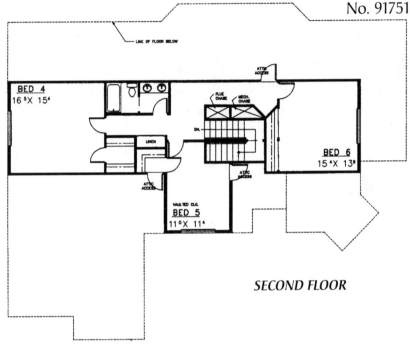

PLAN INFO:

First Flr.	2,199 sq. ft.
Second Flr.	999 sq. ft.
Basement	2,199 sq. ft.
Garage	606 sq. ft.
Sq. Footage	3,198 sq. ft.
Foundation	Crawl space
Bedrooms	Four
Baths	3(Full), 1(Half)

SECOND FLOOR

WIDTH 70'-0"
DEPTH 57'-0"

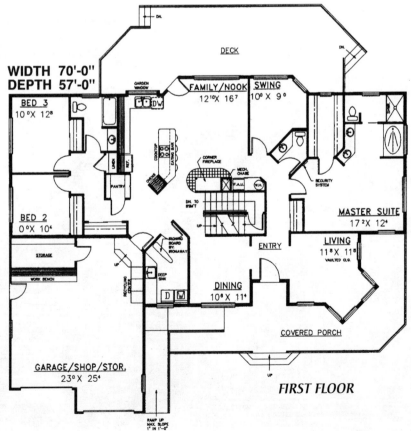

FIRST FLOOR

■ *Windows behind an expansive, covered porch present a warm and welcome feeling to all who enter*

■ *Outside ramp and extra wide interior doorways provides wheelchair accessibility throughout this convenient layout*

■ *Vaulted ceiling crowns the formal Living Room adding to its sense of volume and feeling of space*

■ *A large well-appointed Kitchen with a garden window and built-in pantry serves the formal Dining Room and the Family/Nook area with equal ease*

■ *A cook top island/eating bar with ovens on one end, serve to make informal eating convenient as well as providing even more counter space*

■ *A corner fireplace warms and provides a cozy, homey feel to the Kitchen and the Family/Nook areas*

■ *Extravagant Master Suite features a private, segmented Bath and an extra-large walk-in closet*

■ *On the first floor, two additional bedrooms share a full hall Bath*

■ *The second floor plan adds three more bedrooms and a full segmented Bath*

Brick-Pillared Front
Entrance Catches The Eye

No. 91338

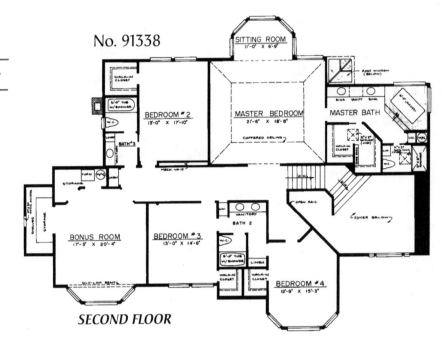

SECOND FLOOR

PLAN INFO:

First Flr.	*2,746 sq. ft.*
Second Flr.	*1,984 sq. ft.*
Bonus Rm.	*420 sq. ft.*
Sq. Footage	*4,730 sq. ft.*
Foundation	*Crawl space*
Bedrooms	*Four*
Baths	*Four*

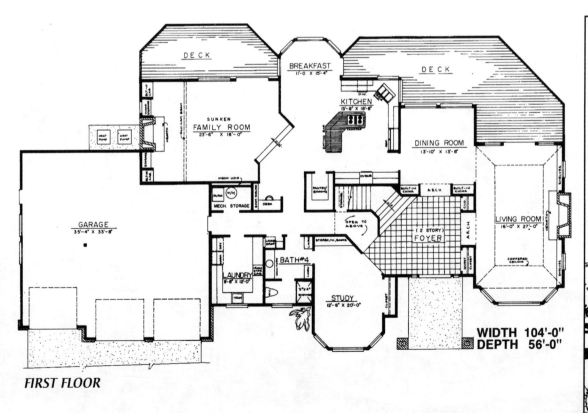

WIDTH 104'-0"
DEPTH 56'-0"

FIRST FLOOR

- An arched, two-story entrance leads to a formal Living Room that is crowned by a coffered ceiling, flooded by natural light through the great front window and enhanced by a large fireplace

- Elegant Dining Room has direct access to either the Kitchen or the formal Living Room

- An island cooktop with an eating bar, walk-in pantry, and a sunny Breakfast area makes this gourmet Kitchen a fantasy come true

- Spacious, sunken Family Room offers a large hearth fireplace, built-in cabinets and connecting outdoor deck to provide a great place for informal gatherings

- Master Bedroom suite features a coffered ceiling, adjacent Sitting area, and private Bath that includes a double walk-in closet, garden tub, double vanity and a separate shower

- Three additional bedrooms, each with a walk-in closet and adjacent full bath, will accommodate children of any age

- Great Bonus room will handle a variety of future needs

Split-Level Spanish Design

No. 90267

PLAN INFO:

First Flr.	*1,530 sq. ft.*
Second Flr.	*984 sq. ft.*
Lower Flr.	*951 sq. ft.*
Sq. Footage	*3,465 sq. ft.*
Foundation	*Basement*
Bedrooms	*Four*
Baths	*2(Full), 1(Half)*

SECOND FLOOR

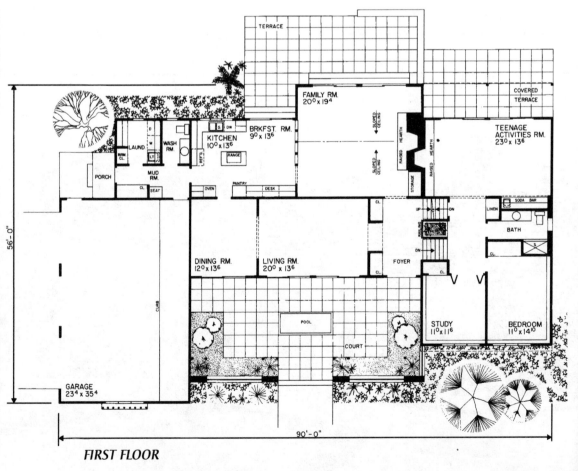

FIRST FLOOR

- *Very impressive Entry Court of this elegant Spanish style home is highlighted by a small pool and planting areas*

- *Open Foyer leads easily into Living Room, Family Room, and upper and lower levels of bedroom wing*

- *Living Room opens into formal Dining Room for gracious entertaining, both with sliding glass doors to the front courtyard*

- *Expansive Family Room offers a sloped ceiling, a raised hearth fireplace, sliding glass doors to an outdoor terrace and easy access to kitchen area*

- *Well-equipped and spacious, the Kitchen features a cooktop work island, a built-in pantry and planning desk, and an open Breakfast Room with sliding glass doors to terrace*

- *A room-sized walk-in closet and a private balcony make the Master Bedroom Suite a comfortable hideaway from a busy household*

- *Two additional bedrooms on the second level share a full hall Bath with a double vanity*

- *A unique Activities Room, on lower level, with sliding glass doors to a covered outdoor terrace affords another informal area for a large family with a variety of interests*

- *Another Bedroom and a Study on the lower level share another full Bath*

Victorian Touches Grace The Exterior Of This Exciting Home

No. 91724

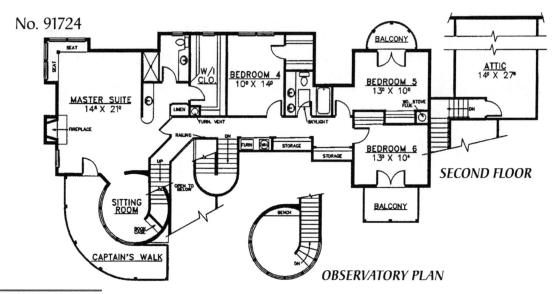

SECOND FLOOR

OBSERVATORY PLAN

PLAN INFO:

First Flr.	3,031 sq. ft.
Second Flr.	1,578 sq. ft.
Garage	514 sq. ft.
Sq. Footage	4,609 sq. ft.
Foundation	Crawl space
Bedrooms	Six
Baths	Four

WIDTH 101'-0"
DEPTH 56'-0"

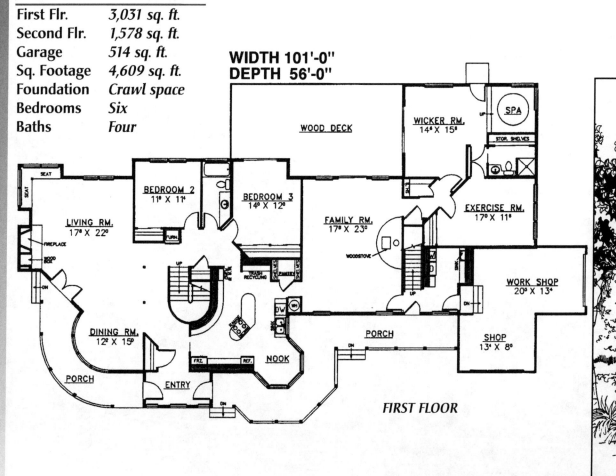

FIRST FLOOR

- ◼ *Richly embellished covered porches sweep across majority of front while turrets and gables adorn every turn*

- ◼ *Unique to this home, Kitchen and Entryway have vaulted ceilings*

- ◼ *Octagon-shaped eating Nook brightens any mealtime with windows at ground level, another row above, and ceiling stretching to window-lined turret overhead*

- ◼ *Huge Kitchen features range and oven located in work island, lots of counter space, and trash recycling center*

- ◼ *Circular Sitting room partially surrounded by captain's walk balcony leads up to observatory on higher level*

- ◼ *Two upstairs bedrooms feature private balconies while a third includes step-in closet*

- ◼ *Large Workshop supplies room for conversion to Garage if desired*

*T*hree *F*ireplaces *A*dd *C*oziness & *W*armth

PLAN INFO:

First Flr.	2,849 sq. ft.
Second Flr.	1,086 sq. ft.
Garage	721 sq. ft.
Sq. Footage	3,935 sq. ft.
Foundation	Slab
Bedrooms	Five
Baths	4(Full), 1(Half)

SECOND FLOOR

BEDROOM 3
11'-4"
X
12'-6"

DECK

BEDROOM 4
10'-10"
X
11'-0"

LIBRARY/
STUDY
18'-0"
X
16'-0"

BOOKS

H.

BEDROOM 2
12'-4"
X
12'-0"

H.

DOWN

C.

OPEN TO
ENTRY BELOW

No. 10670

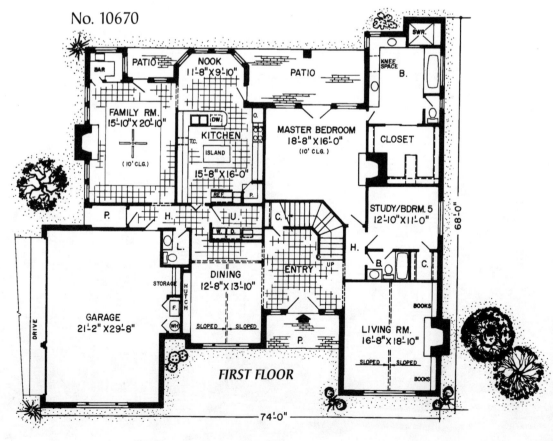

BAR

PATIO

NOOK
11'-8"X9'-10"

PATIO

KNEE
SPACE

SWR.

B.

FAMILY RM.
15'-10"X 20'-10"

(10' CLG.)

DW

KITCHEN
ISLAND

15'-8"X 16'-0"

REF

MASTER BEDROOM
18'-8"X16'-0"
(10' CLG.)

CLOSET

P.

H.

U.

C.

STUDY/BDRM. 5
12'-10"X11'-0"

68'-0"

L.

W.D.

STORAGE

HUTCH

F.

WH

DINING
12'-8"X 13'-10"

SLOPED   SLOPED

ENTRY

UP

H.

B.

C.

BOOKS

GARAGE
21'-2" X29'-8"

DRIVE

P.

LIVING RM.
16'-8"X18'-10"

SLOPED   SLOPED

BOOKS

FIRST FLOOR

74'-0"

- *Vaulted ceiling, gently curving staircase and high, arched windows in entry create airy celebration of light and space*

- *Formal Dining Room with built-in hutch and Living Room with appealing ceiling lines frame impressive Entry*

- *Large island Kitchen opens into a cheery Eating Nook*

- *Oversized pantry outside Kitchen lends extra room for day-to-day necessities*

- *Family Room includes fireplace, paddle fan, built-in, room-size wetbar, and direct access to backyard patio*

- *Superb Master Bedroom warmed by its own fireplace has French doors leading to personal patio*

- *Three additional bedrooms on second level with walk-in closets assure ample storage space*

- *Enjoy sunny afternoons on deck off Library on second floor*

Design Features Loads Of Wood & Glass

No. 93512

PLAN INFO:

First Flr.	2,030 sq. ft.
Second Flr.	1,409 sq. ft.
Basement	2,030 sq. ft.
Garage	782 sq. ft.
Sq. Footage	3,439 sq. ft.
Foundation	Bsmt, Slab
	Crawl space
Bedrooms	Four
Baths	2(Full), 1(Half)

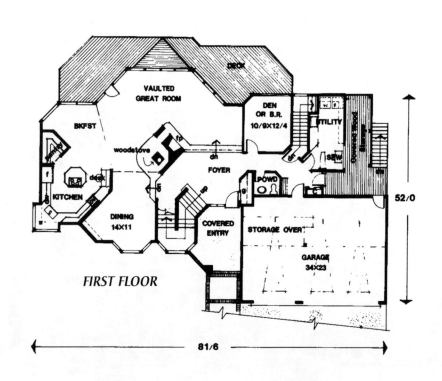

SECOND FLOOR

Vaulted Area

Attic

LIBRARY

rail

MASTER BEDROOM
16×18

M.B.

tub

seat
bay

shwr

w.i. clos

DECK

BEDROOM
12×13

dn

BATH

BEDROOM
17×10

storage

desk

garage below

FIRST FLOOR

VAULTED
GREAT ROOM

BKFST

woodstove

fp

DEN
OR B.R.
10/9X12/4

UTILITY

SEW

KITCHEN

desk

FOYER

dn

POWD

DINING
14X11

COVERED
ENTRY

STORAGE OVER

GARAGE
34×23

52/0

81/6

- *This unique and elegant home has a covered entry leading into an open Foyer, with a curved stairway, and set into a tower of windows, and steps up to the Dining and Great Rooms*

- *A curved wall of windows leading to an outdoor Deck and a vaulted ceiling add to the spacious feeling in the Great Room while the fireplace/wood stove area creates a cozy atmosphere*

- *Elegant formal Dining Room with expansive bay window and adjacent to the Kitchen and Great Room creates the perfect atmosphere for entertaining*

- *Natural light and wonderful views from the corner sink and Breakfast area are extras in this gourmet Kitchen with a cooktop island, walk-in pantry, built-in desk, and lots of storage and counter space*

- *Open Library area, on the second floor, overlooking the Great Room, creates a quiet corner to curl up and read and also provides access to upstairs bedrooms*

- *A lavish Master Bath, with an atrium tub, two vanities and a corner shower, highlights the Master Bedroom Suite that also includes a private deck and a walk-in closet*

- *Two additional bedrooms, one with a bay window and one with private deck, share a full Bath with a double vanity*

Traditional Splendor With Modern Accents

PLAN INFO:

First Flr.	2,376 sq. ft.
Second Flr.	1,048 sq. ft.
Basement	2,376 sq. ft.
Garage	3-car
Sq. Footage	3,424 sq. ft.
Foundation	Basement
Bedrooms	Six
Baths	4(Full), 1(Half)

*No materials list available

No. 91339

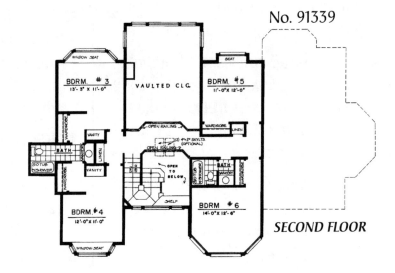

SECOND FLOOR

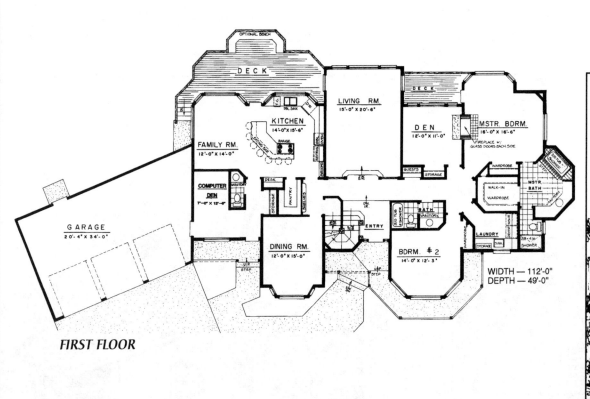

WIDTH — 112'-0"
DEPTH — 49'-0"

FIRST FLOOR

- Gourmet Kitchen with elegant eating bar comfortably seats seven people

- Enjoy family barbeques on backyard deck with optional bench and convenient access to Kitchen and Family Room

- Dining Room on other side of room-sized pantry in close proximity of Kitchen for ease in formal entertaining

- Overlook impressive Foyer on one side and vaulted Living Room from opposite side of skylit balcony

- Six bedrooms and 4-1/2 baths accommodates large families

- Bayed sitting area in Master Bedroom provides ideal quiet spot for avid readers

- Master Bath features plenty of storage space with huge walk-in closet and separate wardrobe

- Daylight basement to rear of home designed for two guest rooms, multi-purpose area and full bath

Colonial Classic Is Convenient & Spacious

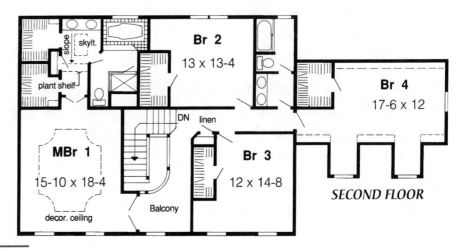

SECOND FLOOR

Br 2
13 x 13-4

Br 4
17-6 x 12

MBr 1
15-10 x 18-4
decor. ceiling

Br 3
12 x 14-8

Balcony

slope skylt. plant shelf

DN linen

PLAN INFO:

First Flr.	*1,508 sq. ft.*
Second Flr.	*1,722 sq. ft.*
Basement	*1,494 sq. ft.*
Garage	*599 sq. ft.*
Sq. Footage	*3,230 sq. ft.*
Foundation	*Basement*
Bedrooms	*Four*
Baths	*2(Full), 1(Half)*

An
EXCLUSIVE DESIGN
By Karl Kreeger

No. 20149

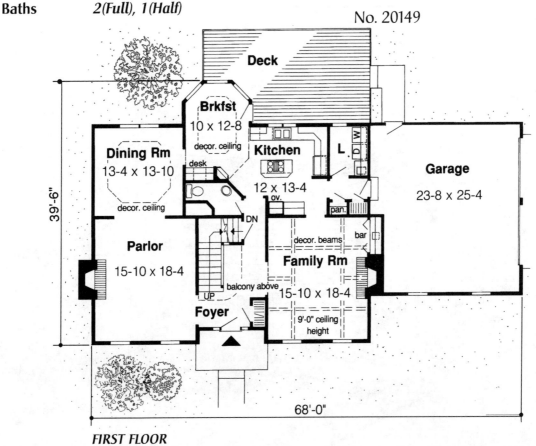

Deck

Brkfst
10 x 12-8
decor. ceiling

Dining Rm
13-4 x 13-10
decor. ceiling

desk

Kitchen
12 x 13-4
ov.

L.

D W

Garage
23-8 x 25-4

pan. bar

decor. beams

Parlor
15-10 x 18-4

DN

balcony above

UP

Family Rm
15-10 x 18-4
9'-0" ceiling height

Foyer

39'-6"

68'-0"

FIRST FLOOR

■ *Clapboard siding, twin chimneys, a central entry and shuttered, multi-paned windows present a Colonial face to the neighborhood*

■ *An open Foyer leads to a formal Parlor with a hearth fireplace and an expansive Family Room with decorative beams, built-in bar and large hearth fireplace*

■ *A range top island, double sink, built-in pantry and an abundance of counter and storage space makes the efficient design of the Kitchen even more convenient*

■ *Adding interest to the sunny Breakfast Room is another decorative ceiling treatment and access to the wood deck, further expanding living space in the warmer months*

■ *His-n-her walk-in closets, a decorative ceiling and skylights in the segmented Master Bath highlight the Master Suite*

■ *Three additional bedrooms, two with walk-in closets, share a full hall bath with a double vanity*

Everything You Need to Make

You pay only a fraction of the original cost

You've picked your dream home!

You can already see it standing on your lot... you can see yourselves in your new home... enjoying family, entertaining guests, celebrating holidays. All that remains ahead are the details. That's where we can help. Whether you plan to build-it-yourself, be your own contractor, or hand your plans over to an outside contractor, your Garlinghouse blueprints provide the perfect beginning for putting yourself in your dream home right away.

We even make it simple for you to make professional design modifications. We can also provide a materials list for greater economy.

My grandfather, L.F. Garlinghouse, started a tradition of quality when he founded this company in 1907. For over 85 years, homeowners and builders have relied on us for accurate, complete, professional blueprints. Our plans help you get results fast... and save money, too! These pages will give you all the information you need to order. So get started now... I know you'll love your new Garlinghouse home!

Sincerely,

HERE'S WHAT YOU GET!

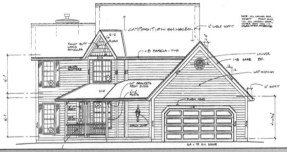

Exterior Elevations

Exact scale views of the front, rear and both sides of your home, showing exterior materials, details, and all necessary measurements.

Detailed Floor Plans

Showing the placement of all interior walls, the dimensions of rooms, doors, windows, stairways, and other details.

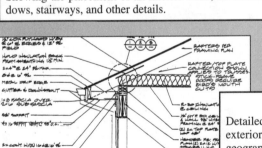

Typical Wall Sections

Detailed views of your exterior walls, as though sliced from top to bottom. These drawings clarify exterior wall construction insulation, flooring, and roofing details. Depending on your specific geography and climate, your home will be built with either 2x4 or 2x6 exterior walls. Most professional contractors can easily adapt plans for either requirement.

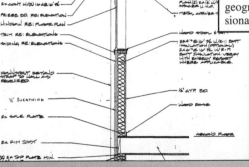

Kitchen and Bath Cabinet Details

These plans or, in some cases, elevations show the specific details and placement of the cabinets in your kitchen and bathrooms as applicable. Customizing these areas is simpler beginning with these details

Your Dream Come True!

for home designs by respected professionals.

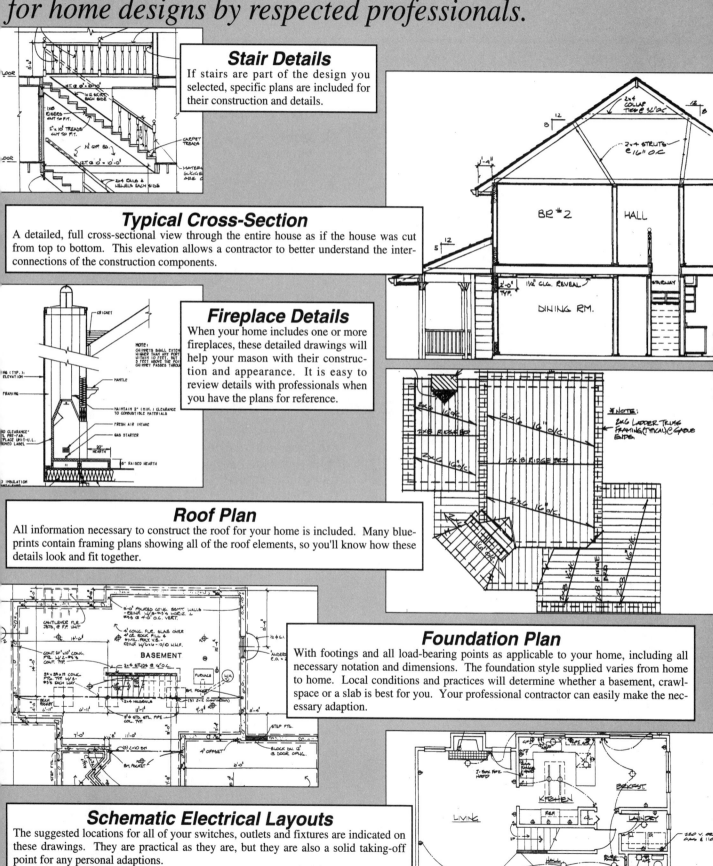

Stair Details
If stairs are part of the design you selected, specific plans are included for their construction and details.

Typical Cross-Section
A detailed, full cross-sectional view through the entire house as if the house was cut from top to bottom. This elevation allows a contractor to better understand the interconnections of the construction components.

Fireplace Details
When your home includes one or more fireplaces, these detailed drawings will help your mason with their construction and appearance. It is easy to review details with professionals when you have the plans for reference.

Roof Plan
All information necessary to construct the roof for your home is included. Many blueprints contain framing plans showing all of the roof elements, so you'll know how these details look and fit together.

Foundation Plan
With footings and all load-bearing points as applicable to your home, including all necessary notation and dimensions. The foundation style supplied varies from home to home. Local conditions and practices will determine whether a basement, crawlspace or a slab is best for you. Your professional contractor can easily make the necessary adaption.

Schematic Electrical Layouts
The suggested locations for all of your switches, outlets and fixtures are indicated on these drawings. They are practical as they are, but they are also a solid taking-off point for any personal adaptions.

Garlinghouse options and extras make the dream truly yours.

*R*eversed Plans Can Make Your Dream Home Just Right!

"That's our dream home... if only the garage were on the other side!"

You could have exactly the home you want by flipping it end-for-end. Check it out by holding your dream home page of this book up to a mirror. Then simply order your plans "reversed". We'll send you one full set of mirror-image plans (with the writing backwards) as a master guide for you and your builder.

The remaining sets of your order will come as shown in this book so the dimensions and specifications are easily read on the job site... but they will be specially stamped "REVERSED" so there is no construction confusion.

We can only send reversed plans with multiple-set orders. But, there is no extra charge for this service.

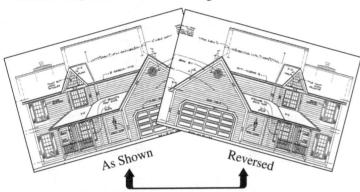

As Shown   Reversed

*M*odifying Your Garlinghouse Home Plan

Easy modifications to your dream home such as minor non-structural changes and simple material substitutions, can be made between you and your builder and marked directly on your blueprints. However, if you are considering making major changes to your design, we strongly recommend that you purchase our reproducible vellums and use the services of a professional designer or architect. Modifications are not available for plan numbers 90,000 and above. For additional information call us at 1-203-343-5977.

*O*ur Reproducible Vellums Make Modifications Easier

With a vellum copy of our plans, a design professional can alter the drawings just the way you want, then you can print as many copies of the modified plans as you need. And, since you have already started with our complete detailed plans, the cost of those expensive professional services will be significantly less. Refer to the price schedule for vellum costs. Call for vellum availability for plan numbers 90,000 and above.

Reproducible vellum copies of our home plans are only sold under the terms of a license agreement that you will receive with your order. Should you not agree to the terms, then the vellums may be returned unopened for a full refund.

*Y*ours FREE With Your Order

FREE

SPECIFICATIONS AND CONTRACT FORM provides the perfect way for you and your builder to agree on the exact materials to use in building and finishing your home *before* you start construction. A must for homeowner's peace of mind.

*R*emember To Order Your Materials List

It'll help you save money. Available at a modest additional charge, the Materials List gives the quantity, dimensions, and specifications for the major materials needed to build your home. You will get faster, more accurate bids from your contractors and building suppliers — and avoid paying for unused materials and waste. Materials Lists are available for all home plans except as otherwise indicated, but can only be ordered with a set of home plans. Due to differences in regional requirements and homeowner or builder preferences... electrical, plumbing and heating/air conditioning equipment specifications are not designed specifically for each plan. However, detailed *typical* prints of residential electrical, plumbing and construction guidelines can be provided. Please see next page for additional information.

*Q*uestions?

Call our customer service number at 1-203-343-5977.

How Many Sets Of Plans Will You Need?

The Standard 8-Set Construction Package
Our experience shows that you'll speed every step of construction and avoid costly building errors by ordering enough sets to go around. Each tradesperson wants a set — the general contractor and all subcontractors; foundation, electrical, plumbing, heating/air conditioning, drywall, finish carpenters, and cabinet shop. Don't forget your lending institution, building department and, of course, a set for yourself.

The Minimum 5-Set Construction Package
If you're comfortable with arduous follow-up, this package can save you a few dollars by giving you the option of passing down plan sets as work progresses. You might have enough copies to go around if work goes exactly as scheduled and no plans are lost or damaged. But for only $40 more, the 8-set package eliminates these worries.

The Single-Set Decision-Maker Package
We offer this set so you can study the blueprints to plan your dream home in detail. But remember... one set is never enough to build your home... and they're copyrighted.

New Plan Details For The Home Builder
Because local codes and requirements vary greatly, we recommend that you obtain drawings and bids from licensed contractors to do your mechanical plans. However, if you want to know more about techniques — and deal more confidently with subcontractors — we offer these remarkably useful detail sheets. Each is an excellent tool that will enhance your understanding of these technical subjects.

Residential Construction Details
Eight sheets that cover the essentials of stick-built residential home construction. Details foundation options - poured concrete basement, concrete

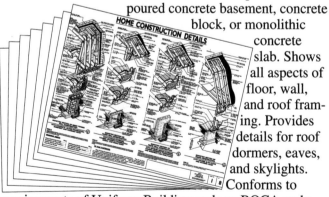

block, or monolithic concrete slab. Shows all aspects of floor, wall, and roof framing. Provides details for roof dormers, eaves, and skylights. Conforms to requirements of Uniform Building code or BOCA code. Includes a quick index. ***$14.95 per set***

Residential Plumbing Details
Nine sheets packed with information detailing pipe connection methods, fittings, and sizes. Shows sump-pump and water softener hookups, and septic system construction. Conforms to requirements of National Plumbing Code. Color coded with a glossary of terms and quick index. ***$14.95 per set***

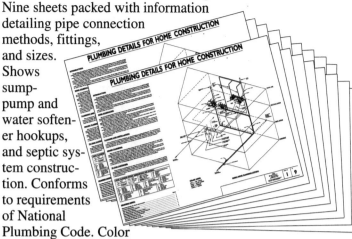

Residential Electrical Details
Nine sheets that cover all aspects of residential wiring, from simple switch wiring to the complexities of three-phase and service entrance connection. Explains service load calculations and distribution panel wiring. Shows you how to create a floorplan wiring diagram. Conforms to requirements of National Electrical Code. Color coded with a glossary of terms and a quick index. ***$14.95 per set***

Important Shipping Information
Your order is processed immediately. Allow 10 working days from our receipt of your order for normal UPS delivery. Save time with your credit card and our "800" number. UPS *must* have a street address or Rural Route Box number — never a post office box. Use a work address if no one is home during the day.

Orders being shipped to Alaska, Hawaii, APO, FPO or Post Office Boxes must go via First Class Mail. Please include the proper postage.

Only Certified bank checks and money orders are accepted and must be payable in U.S. currency. For speed, we ship international orders Air Parcel Post. Please refer to the chart for the correct shipping cost.

An important note:
All plans are drawn to conform to one or more of the industry's major national building standards. However, due to the variety of local building regulations, your plan may need to be modified to comply with local requirements — snow loads, energy loads, seismic zones, etc. Do check them fully and consult your local building officials.

A few states require that all building plans used be drawn by an architect registered in that state. While having your plans reviewed and stamped by such an architect may be prudent, laws requiring non-conforming plans like ours to be completely redrawn forces you to unnecessarily pay very large fees. If your state has such a law, we strongly recommend you contact your state representative to protest.

Domestic Shipping	1-2 Sets	3+ Sets
UPS Ground Service	$ 6.50	$ 8.50
First Class Mail	$ 8.00	$11.00
2-Day Express	$16.00	$20.00
Overnight Express	$26.00	$30.00
International Shipping	**1-2 Sets**	**3+ Sets**
Canada	$11.00	$15.50
All Other Nations	$40.00	$52.00

Canadian Orders and Shipping:

To our friends in Canada, we have a plan design affiliate in Kitchener, Ontario. This relationship will help you avoid the delays and charges associated with shipments from the United States. Moreover, our affiliate is familiar with the building requirements in your community and country.

We prefer payments in U.S. Currency. If you, however, are sending Canadian funds please add 30% to the prices of the plans and shipping fees.

Please Submit all Canadian plan orders to:
Garlinghouse Company
20 Cedar Street North, Kitchener, Ontario N2H 2W8
Canadian orders only: 1-800-561-4169/Fax #: 1-519-743-1282
Customer Service #: 1-519-743-4169

Before ordering **PLEASE READ** *all ordering information*

ORDER TOLL FREE
1-800-235-5700

Monday-Friday 8:00 a.m. to 5:00 p.m. Eastern Time
or FAX your Credit Card order to 1-203-343-5984
All foreign residents call 1-203-343-5977

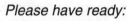

Please have ready:
1. *Your credit card number*
2. *The plan number*
3. *The order code number* ⟶

H4LX3

GARLINGHOUSE 1995 BLUEPRINT PRICE SCHEDULE:

TOTAL LIVING AREA	0000-1500 sq. ft.	1501-1800 sq. ft.	1801-2200 sq. ft.	2201-2600 sq. ft.	2601-3200 sq. ft.	3201-9999 sq. ft.
8 SETS OF SAME PLAN	$280	$290	$300	$315	$330	$350
5 SETS OF SAME PLAN	$240	$250	$260	$275	$290	$310
1 SINGLE SET OF PLANS	$180	$190	$200	$215	$230	$250
VELLUMS	$395	$410	$425	$445	$465	$495
MATERIALS LIST	$25	$25	$25	$30	$30	$35
Additional sets with original order $20						

GARLINGHOUSE

Blueprint Order Form

Order Code No. **H4LX3**

Prices Subject To Change Without Notice
Foreign Mail Orders: Certified bank checks in U.S. funds only.

Plan No. _____
❏ As Shown   ❏ Reversed *(mult. set pkgs. only)*

	Each	Amount
8 set pkg.		$
5 set pkg.		$
1 set pkg. (no reverses)		$
_____ (qty.) Add'l. sets @		$
Vellums		$
Material List		$
Residential Builder Plans		
_____ set(s) Construction	@ $14.95	$
_____ set(s) Plumbing	@ $14.95	$
_____ set(s) Electrical	@ $14.95	$
Shipping		$
Subtotal		$
Sales Tax (CT residents add 6% sales tax, KS residents add 5.9% sales tax)		$
Total Amount Enclosed		$

Send your check, money order or credit card information to:
(No C.O.D.'s Please)
Please Submit all United States & Other Nations plan orders to:
Garlinghouse Company
P.O. Box 1717
Middletown, CT 06457
•••••••••••
Please Submit all Canadian plan orders to:
Garlinghouse Company
20 Cedar Street North
Kitchener, Ontario N2H 2W8

Bill To: (address must be as it appears on credit card statement)

Name _____
Please Print

Address _____

City/State _____ Zip _____

Daytime Phone (_____) _____

Ship To (if different from Bill to):

Name _____

Address _____
UPS will not ship to P.O. Boxes

City/State _____ Zip _____

Credit Card Information

Charge To: ❏ Visa   ❏ Mastercard

Card # ⎿⎿⎿⎿⎿⎿⎿⎿⎿⎿⎿⎿⎿⎿⎿⎿⎿

Signature _____ Exp. _____ / _____

272